Joy Short:
A Life
in Southern Africa

GARDNER HALL

Mount Bethel Publishing
Port Murray, New Jersey

Foy Short: A Life in Southern Africa
© 2012 by Gardner Hall

Published by Mount Bethel Publishing, Post Office Box 123, Port Murray, New Jersey 07865. *www.MountBethelPublishing.com.*

ISBN: 978–0–9850059–0–0
Library of Congress Control Number: 2012901459

Cover Design: Kirby Davis
Typesetting: Jamey Hinds

Printed in the United States of America

Dedication

Dedicated to evangelists like Dennis Allan
who follow in Foy Short's footsteps by dedicating their lives to preaching
overseas and establishing independent congregations of the Lord.

Table of Contents

Acknowledgements

Ellen Baize, Foy Short's daughter, helped me more than anyone else with this project. She sent me reports and personal letters, gave hours of telephone interviews, made suggestions and corrections and has always been handy for advice. She is working on her own project, a biography of her grandfather, W.N. Short.

Foy and Margaret Short have also granted me complete telephone access and hours of interviews. Margaret has written several unpublished essays about their experiences, which have been helpful. She also went over the manuscript making needed corrections and very helpful suggestions. I am sure you can tell from this project how much I admire and appreciate the Shorts.

Sybil Dewhirst is Foy's sister who I have known and loved since my childhood in Athens, Alabama. When I was a child, she always had a smile for me and possessed a dignified yet very open and friendly personality that made her greatly admired. She has a sharper memory than Foy does of their childhood days and spent several hours with me on the telephone answering questions, especially about the childhood and teenage years she spent together with Foy. She's writing some personal memoirs for her family and has shared large portions of them with me.

Jim Short, Foy and Margaret's son, spent almost an hour on the phone with me, giving me stories from his childhood that his sister and parents didn't remember to tell me, for example, about the Short family trip to Barotseland. Then when I reminded Ellen, Margaret and Foy of this trip that Jim mentioned, they were able to give me more details. In the latter stages of the book, he sent me a number of emails offering wise advice and insight.

I met Foy and Margaret's youngest daughter, Kathryn (Kay) Smith, as I was almost finished with the first draft of the book. She helped me with a number of fascinating anecdotes and perceptions about what makes her parents tick.

Paddy Kendall-Ball probably loves Foy as much as anyone else in the world. He spent several hours with me, both in person and on the phone, giving lively stories about his experiences with Foy. He is now back in Zimbabwe, the land of his birth, building up his brethren and working to teach the gospel.

Several other people gave me shorter but helpful telephone interviews: Ken Green, Allen Brittell (gave information about his grandfather, Orville), Harrison Bankston, Gene Tope and Ray Votaw. Votaw's health wasn't good when I talked to him, but he was still able to give me a few stories and insights. He passed away in January of 2012.

Cherry Trimble, Sewell Hall, Ellen Baize, Jim Short and Margaret Short all helped with proofreading, especially Margaret.

I was blessed to meet Jamey Hinds when in South Florida. He mentioned to me in passing that he loved proof reading. When he saw a grin of anticipation on my face, he must have known he was in trouble. I immediately asked him if he could go over this manuscript. He agreed, not knowing what he was getting into! Then he offered not only to correct the manuscript but set the type. What a blessing!

Kirby Davis, a wonderful young disciple, has provided a beautiful design for the cover of this book. James Rattazzi, John Maddocks and David Rodriguez helped prepare pictures for publication. Gary Fisher and Charlie Brackett have given good advice about publishing.

Thanks especially to my wife, Beverly, who is so patient with me as I chase multiple interests.

—*Gardner Hall*

Introduction

The popular image of a missionary is that of a man camped out in the jungle, fighting off an occasional lion and preaching to the 'natives' in their own language. I know only one man whose experiences came even close to that — Foy Short."[1] Thus Sewell Hall introduced his friend, Foy Short.

Foy Short's easygoing demeanor, wry smile and dry sense of humor make it difficult to imagine him facing off with a cape buffalo, calming a building full of frenzied worshipers going through various types of "spirit" induced convulsions, or driving a group of eighteen oxen with a fifty-foot whip. Yet, these and hundreds of other singular experiences filled his seventy plus years of preaching and teaching the Bible in Southern Africa.

This will be a story about Foy Short's life and the way God used him in Southern Africa from his childhood in the 1920s to the political turmoil at the turn of the twenty-first century.

The Restoration Movement in Rhodesia/Zimbabwe*

Foy Short's story in Africa begins with John Sherriff, a stonemason from New Zealand who arrived in South Africa in 1896. Though originally linked with congregations associated with the Disciples of Christ, he "was influenced to change his convictions"[2] about instrumental music in worship and formed close ties with more conservative churches of Christ in the United States.

After a short stay in South Africa, Sherriff settled in Bulawayo, Southern Rhodesia,[1] where he practiced his trade as a stonemason. When he saw one

---

* A brief history of Zimbabwe (Rhodesia) can be found in an appendix at the end of the main story.

of his African employees reading the Bible by a campfire he determined to teach him and others.[3]

> John Sherriff… soon found the opportunity to commence a night school for some African boys, meeting twice a week from 7–9 PM in his own small room. English was his subject, the Bible was his textbook … By 1904 he had baptized two whites, six African women and sixty-seven African men and youths.[4]

Sherriff conducted church services in a small building in his stone yard. This structure became too small, so he moved to a larger hall. By 1906, when F. L. Hadfield and his family arrived from New Zealand, there were over 200 Christians. Sherriff turned the work over to Hadfield and moved with his wife, Emma, a short distance out of Bulawayo to start a school for mixed race Africans at Forest Vale Mission.[5]

Foy and his sister, Sybil Dewhirst, have fond memories of John Sherriff. They called him "Grandpa Sherriff." Foy described him as an English type gentleman with an English accent and a white beard and mustache.

Sherriff sent out his most advanced evangelists, whom he called "mustard seed,"[6] into other parts of Southern Africa. One was George Kosa from Johannesburg (who was originally from Swaziland). In 1907 Kosa returned to South Africa to preach to the workers in the gold mines. One of those he baptized returned to his homeland in Bechuanaland (now Botswana) where he preached to his own people. In 1949 Foy Short visited Bechuanaland to help resolve some problems. He found about 1,500 Christians there who were attempting to follow New Testament principles.[7] Another of Sherriff's "mustard seed," Peter Masiya (also spelled Misaya and Mesiya[8]), would be instrumental in helping Foy's father, Will Short, begin his work at Sinde in Northern Rhodesia (later Zambia). In 2006 Foy Short described Masiya's work in the early 1900s in an oral report to the Bellaire, Texas church of Christ.

When Peter Masiya returned to his home village, he announced
that he would be holding a meeting and preaching under a tree outside of the village that had a lot of good shade. He invited them to
hear him teach the word of God. The first Sunday … nobody came,
so he sang, read his Bible and prayed and returned to the village.
During the following week he talked to the people and invited them
again to come the next Sunday and nobody came. This went on for
a year. Every Sunday he would go out there, nobody would come,
he would read and pray and during the week he would invite them
again. Nobody went for a year. Finally his mother went and she was
baptized. After that others began to be baptized. By the time my
folks went up there [in 1923] there were a half dozen churches that
Peter Masiya had started. That was the beginning of the work there.
I don't think I would have had the tenacity to go out and preach every Sunday for a year. When the going gets tough, don't quit![9]

Another "mustard seed" was Jack Mzira, the Shona evangelist responsible
for establishing the congregations around Wuyu Wuyu east of Salisbury
(now Harare). In 1903 he became dissatisfied with what he was hearing in
a mission of the Church of England and began walking to seek something,
though he wasn't sure what. He walked first to Salisbury where he worked
for a while and then he began walking again. He arrived in Bulawayo and
found work in John Sherriff's stone yard. He studied the Bible with Sherriff
and obeyed the gospel. He returned to Mashonaland establishing churches.
John Sherriff said of Mzira, "He was one of the best preachers and elders of
his people that I know of."[10] Foy Short's father, W.N. Short, worked closely
with Peter Masiya and Jack Mzira.

Phases of "Mission Work"

Stanley E. Granberg divides the history of "mission" work of known
churches of Christ in Africa into three phases: (1) the mission station, (2)
the institutional era and (3) the mission team eras.[11] Foy Short would live
through all three eras, though he would emphasize a fourth approach that

he felt to be the biblical pattern, developing autonomous congregations. Foy Short spent his childhood in mission stations of the first era. Before World War II the government often gave missionaries large parcels of land (or leased or sold it to them at reduced prices) with the stipulation that they be developed and that natives in the area be taught basic literacy skills. Under this type of arrangement, John Sherriff, with the help of others from New Zealand and Australia, constructed the Forest Vale mission near Bulawayo.

Foy felt that the mission stations, which at first were little more than the evangelist's farm with a few extra buildings for teaching, did a good work in their initial stages. The natives could not be taught the Bible unless first taught basic literacy. Though Will Short, Dow Merritt, George Scott and other pioneer evangelists lived on what could be called primitive mission stations, they spent much of their time traveling through the villages, establishing and then training local congregations.

Foy's friend Eldred Echols, who was credited by Granberg with initiating the institutional era,[12] told of a revealing conversation he had with an old chief. The village leader contrasted the techniques of Foy's father, Will (W.N.), and other evangelists of the first era, who spent much time in the villages, with those of the second, who set up shop in their schools and institutions.

> I once sat with an old village chief who had known George Scott, Will Short and others of the pioneer missionaries. He complained that American churches no longer sent out missionaries of the caliber of those early preachers. In particular, it was a source of grief to him that they so seldom saw us, whereas those men regularly visited all the village churches and spent much time teaching and encouraging them. I pointed out that we had to spend a great deal of our time in daily classes, educating and preparing young people to become leaders, and so we were not free to travel as they had done. I went on to suggest that we were doing a better job for the future of

the church than the pioneers had done. The chief took immediate offense. "Young man," he admonished me sternly, "before you criticize your betters, you need to understand that those men had to farm or raise cattle to support their families, and they lived under harsher conditions than you have to, and yet they still had time to do a great deal more evangelistic work than you do. They were great preachers." And then he added peevishly, "I don't really know what you people are. School teachers, perhaps. Certainly not preachers."[13]

It didn't require a big step to transform the missions from simple farms with classroom buildings used by evangelists into regional centers that tended to control congregations in an area. Over a period of time, there also tended to be a greater emphasis on secular instruction that went beyond the basic literacy needed for reading the Bible. Foy remembers as a young man hearing concerns expressed by contemporaries of his parents about the direction the missions were headed, with more government regulations for the schools and an increasing emphasis on secular education. By 1947 when Foy returned to Southern Africa after several years in the States, this transformation of the primitive missions he knew as a child into denominational centers was well underway. His association with them gradually waned, especially after 1961 when his parents left the Namwianga Mission to move to Bulawayo.

"Missions" In Zimbabwe and Zambia

1. **Forest Vale** – Near Bulawayo. Started by John Sherriff. It was gradually enveloped by the city of Bulawayo after Sherriff's death in 1935.
2. **Dadaya** – About 120 miles southeast of Bulawayo, it became a center for the Disciples of Christ denomination. Garfield Todd, a New Zealander who directed the mission in the early 1940s, became Prime Minister of Rhodesia in 1946.[14]
3. **Sinde** — In Northern Rhodesia (now Zambia) about twenty miles from Livingstone and Victoria Falls. Started by Foy's father, W.N. (Will) Short, with the help of Peter Masiya in 1922. There is still a school there.

4. **Kabanga** — Also in Northern Rhodesia (now Zambia), about seventy miles northeast of Sinde and east of Kalomo. Started by Dow Merritt and Ray Lawyer in 1927 before the latter's untimely death that year. W.N Short then moved there and worked until his first trip back to the States in late 1928.

5. **Namwianga** — About four miles from Kalomo in Zambia. George Scott and W.L. Brown started building on land they bought here in 1932.[15] It has become a center of mission work for mainstream churches of Christ. In 2008 it had "a farm, a rural health center, a vocational center, two home-based orphan care facilities, a Church Development Center, and schools. The schools on the Namwianga site include a Basic (elementary) school, a Secondary school, and George Benson Christian College. The college trains secondary teachers in the areas of religious education, math, and English."[16]

6. **Nhowe** — W.L. Brown started a school here, about thirty miles east of Salisbury in 1941 and it has become an educational center for mainstream churches of Christ, "an outreach of the Oakland church of Christ in Southfield, Michigan."[17] There is also a hospital sponsored by the East Point church of Christ in Wichita, Kansas.[18]

7. **Wuyu Wuyu** — Mistakenly called Huyuyu by John Sherriff because he was hard of hearing[19] and referred to as Huyuyu en most articles in the *Word and Work* magazine. Started by John Sherriff in the late 1920s east of Salisbury (now Harare), fairly close (about fifteen miles) to what became Nhowe mission.[20] W.N. Short worked there in the early 1930s. There is a still a congregation on the site that Foy, his son-in-law and daughter, David and Ellen Baize, visit when in Zimbabwe.[21]

Summary of Tribal Terms

- **amaNdebele** — The name of the dominant tribe in Southwestern Zimbabwe. The British had difficulty pronouncing this word and referred to the tribe as the Matabele or occasionally as Natabele. Total population in Zimbabwe in 2001 was estimated to be 1,500,000.[22] Perhaps three million more live in South Africa.
- **amaNdebele** — An individual from the amaNdebele tribe.
- **isiNdebele** — Language of the amaNdebele (also referred to as Northern Ndebele and Sindebele[23])
- **Matabeleland** — Area in Southwestern Zimbabwe settled by the amaNdebele tribe. Bulawayo is the principle city.
- **Shona** — Largest tribe in Zimbabwe (about 75% of all Zimbabweans[24]) also divided into five main clans. "Most Shonas identify first with their own clans and then with the entire Shona people."[25] Harare (originally known as "Salisbury") is the principle city in Mashonaland.
- **Mashonaland** — Areas in Northern and Eastern Zimbabwe inhabited by those of the Shona tribe.
- **Tonga** — Tribe in Zambia and Northwestern Zimbabwe. The Tongas predominated in areas where W.N. Short and other pioneers established the first missions in Northern Rhodesia (now Zambia).

Therefore Foy Short learned their language, usually called chiTonga as a child.

Admiration and Concerns from a Personal Perspective

Reading letters and articles about Foy's father, W.N. Short, and other pioneer workers in Southern Africa fills spiritually minded readers with admiration for their sacrificial love and dedication to God. When considering whether or not to delve into this project, I started by reading through reports in old *Word and Work* magazines[26] and quickly identified with young Ray and Zelma Lawyer, the first Americans to work closely with the Shorts in Southern Africa. They filled their reports with expressions of love for the Africans and optimism about future plans to teach them. Then when I clicked on the November 1927 edition I read Don Carlos Janes' terse message, "A very sad word is cabled from Africa that Ray Lawyer died from an accident."[27] As I read those words in 2008, knowing nothing beforehand of what had happened, I felt the same type of shock that readers must have felt when first reading of the tragic accident more than eighty years ago. I'll admit that I shed tears as if he had just died. As I wept I thought, "How silly for a grown man to cry when reading this old history." Then when reading further accounts of Lawyer's death in his wife Zelma's book[28] and in Dow Merritt's book,[29] I found myself wiping my eyes again even though I'm not usually a crybaby! I had come to completely identify with the Lawyers and the little band of Americans working in Southern Africa. I had come to love them although they are all now dead!

Though I came to admire the pioneer workers in Southern Africa, I groaned inwardly as I read of the gradual introduction of practices that historically have led independent Christians away from non-sectarian focus on the Master towards harmful affairs with denominational machinery. One of the behind-the-scenes heroes in the story of pioneer evangelism in Southern Africa was Don Carlos Janes, who wrote a column in the *Word and Work* magazine designed to promote their support. In his articles, he rejoiced and wept with the missionaries and begged and pleaded with brethren to support them. You can sense his keen anguish when godly men and women in Africa such as W.N. Short lost their support during the depression. Only the Creator knows how much credit he should receive for the thousands converted through the efforts of evangelists he encouraged.

And yet, Don Carlos Janes left himself open to the accusation that he was a "one man missionary society." F.B. Srygley wrote, "No churches, so far as I know, have ever authorized Janes to take the position as missionary director for the churches ... No one appointed him to his present position but he assumed it by degrees."[30] Foy E. Wallace attacked Janes with characteristic gusto for being a "one man missionary society" and printed a copy of his last will and testament in the *Bible Banner* to support his accusations.[31] The fact that Janes was premillennial in his views, probably added fuel to the fire as far as Wallace was concerned.

How should primitivist Christians view obviously godly men such as Don Carlos Janes and Foy Short's predecessors who were courageous in their sacrifices, but whose projects were sometimes precursors of an unhealthy trust in denominational structures? I think admiration is still in order for their great sacrifices along with thanksgiving for God's mercy, even as we learn from their errors and strive to avoid them.

Establishing Independent, Autonomous Congregations

As will be seen in the main story, events on an ocean voyage to the States in late 1940 convinced Foy of the importance of distinguishing between the simplicity seen in first century churches that were taught by the apostles of Jesus Christ and the complications introduced by men in human religions. He always emphasized God's grace and mercy as taught to him by his parents. However, his Bible study and association with careful evangelists in North Alabama in the middle 1940s, especially Bennie Lee Fudge, also infused him with a desire to establish congregations in the mold of faithful first century churches. This implied making a distinction between that model and the human ones that tend to infiltrate God's people.

Jesus and Paul emphasized evangelism simply through personal teaching. Dedicated first century evangelists established independent congregations and worked closely with them. Local congregations were the only church organizations seen among first century disciples. Efforts to introduce other ecclesiastical organizations into the mix began in the centuries after Christ with the regional bishops and dioceses. Foy Short's efforts to evangelize Africans emphasized this back-to-basics (primitivist) model. He trained promising native evangelists so that they would in turn train others and establish independent congregations (cf. 2 Timothy 2:2). He trusted that Africans could learn self-sufficiency, and worked to establish independence rather than dependence among them.

Enemies of Autonomous, Independent Churches

Certainly worldliness, pride, lack of love and spiritual self-sufficiency are the greatest dangers to God's plan for his people. However, Foy Short was careful to avoid more subtle enemies to humble discipleship in Southern Africa.

1. Institutionalism — The word "institutionalism" is often loaded, but will be used here to describe the tendency to see the church of Christ as a network of congregations that has its institutions, schools and projects. Some try to give estimates of the number of members in "churches of Christ" ranging from 1,265,844[32] in the United States to three million worldwide.[33] However, the effort to give numbers often reveals a sectarian concept of what the church of Christ is. Biblically, the church is simply all the saved people in the world and only God knows their number for only he knows to whom he will extend his mercy.[34]

Disciples who are truly nonsectarian don't consider God's work to be done only by those they know. They are confident of the fact that wherever God is sought and his mercy extended, there are his people, often known only to him. Indeed, many known to be associated with various groups such as "mainstream churches of Christ" and others simply want to serve God and are relatively uncontaminated with the promotionalism and sectarianism that can be so distasteful to noninstitutional disciples. To consider the church of Christ to be composed solely of those influenced by "our preachers" and "our traditions" is blatantly sectarian.

Institutionalism, just like all forms of sectarianism, is a danger to primitivist service of Jesus Christ because over a period of time it tends to redirect the disciples' focus from a person, Jesus Christ, to the traditions and institutions of the network. The question in the minds of many becomes "What has the 'Church of Christ' always taught on this issue?" rather than, "What has Christ taught?" It fosters a dependence on the institutions supported by the network and erodes the nonsectarian principles that are found in the New Testament.

2. Dependence on American salaries — A second and even more subtle enemy of the establishment of autonomous congregations in third world countries is the unwise use of the American dollar in setting up support systems to provide salaries for native evangelists. It is subtle because there is Biblical precedent for congregations supporting evangelists as they work in other areas. However, some have pointed out that strictly speaking, the Biblical model, (for example, Philippi's support of Paul) is for churches to support evangelists they personally know and trust and with whom they can communicate, not those they can't know well personally and whose language they can't understand.

Several problems often arise when a system is set in place involving large amounts of support from American congregations to third world preachers they can never know well, usually on the basis of a recommendation of a traveling evangelist from America:
• An over-dependence on outside help with a resulting lack of growth.
• Misunderstandings between preachers and supporting churches when there are cultural and language barriers.
• Over-support.

- Fraud, greed and "public relations" manipulation. Besides the exploitation of obvious scoundrels who take advantage of American churches, even sincere men in underdeveloped countries can be tempted to get into the game of sending exaggerated reports, carefully posed photos of baptisms, bombardment with Email and other public relations tactics to keep the money flowing.

- The appearance of an unofficial hierarchy. At the top of the apparent system would be the American recommender. A preacher who has a number of men who depend upon his word for their daily bread and welfare can be quite powerful. Below the American recommender sometimes there is a native recommender. Under the American recommender and sometimes the native recommender would be those preachers who receive American dollars. Below those who receive American dollars would be other workers.

Instead of exposing sincere, humble evangelists in Zimbabwe to the sometimes overpowering temptation of American salaries, Foy Short encouraged them to earn a living "making tents" while encouraging the African brethren that knew them to help with their expenses and support as much as they could.

Veteran African evangelists who did not see the dangers of institutionalism clearly saw the danger of American salary systems for third world evangelists. Georgia Hobby wrote, "As far as I know, there are no Zambian preachers who are supported by churches in the U.S.A. or other foreign countries. It would be easy to have a large number of preachers hired by U.S.A. churches. But much of their effectiveness would be lost because their own people would not trust their motives."[35]

Avoiding dependence on American dollars for salaries and sending benevolence to needy Christians are two different issues. The first tends to be permanent and foster dependency. The second is usually temporary on the basis of need. Foy and Margaret Short worked diligently during the crisis of the 1980s and later years to send benevolence to saints during the time of famine and political unrest.

The results of Foy Short's efforts to encourage the establishment of independent, autonomous congregations in the area around Matabeleland speak for themselves. From a handful of weak congregations in the late 1940s whose leaders did not know how to combat religious error, there are now over one hundred known independent congregations in the area. Some of the congregations are very small and meet under trees but they are generally self-sufficient in the sense of not relying on foreign support or mission centers for their evangelism and edification. Though Foy Short was by no means God's only tool for the growth of these independent congregations, he was a key figure, and his efforts should serve as an example for others who are willing to do similar works.

A book that summarizes Foy Short's approach to evangelism is Roland Allen's classic, *Missionary Methods, St. Paul's or Ours*.[36] A more modern article from the evangelical point of view that deals with the problem of establishing dependency with American money is "Stop Sending Money, Breaking the Cycle of Missions Dependency," published in the March, 1999 edition of *Christianity Today*.[37]

Chapter 1

Roots and Childhood

B rother W.N. Short and wife of Harper, Kan., have decided to go to the mission field."[38] This brief notice in the *Word and Work* magazine may have seemed less than earth shattering to readers in 1920 and yet that decision by a newlywed couple would affect thousands of lives. It changed the course of their unborn children's lives. There would be no roaring twenties in America for them, no Babe Ruth, no secure small town lives, no secure neighborhood schools and friendly policemen. Instead they would learn to struggle to survive, battling malaria and other tropical diseases with their parents on remote outposts.

Though the decision of Will (William Newton or W.N.) Short and his wife, Delia (Nancy A'Delia) would mean hardship and occasionally even desperate times for their children, there is no indication that they ever regretted it. They and their children like Foy lived full lives of happy, meaningful service to God. But more important than the effect that their decision would make on their children, was its effect on thousands of Africans, who through their teaching and that of those who followed in their footsteps would learn the hope of a loving God.

Family Background

Foy's father was born in 1894 in Rome, Kansas. His grandfather, Jasper Newton Short came from Switzerland County, Indiana.[39] There, members of his family, of German extraction, left the Baptist church in the mid 1800s motivated by the preaching of John Beverly Vawter.[40]

Young Will was evidently an unwilling witness to much of the wrangling about instrumental music in the early 1900s and he later explained to Foy and other members of his family that this accounted for the fact that he was often reluctant to engage in any spirited exchange of different points of view with his brethren.

Foy's mother, Delia O'Neal, born in Johnstown, Missouri, was of Irish extraction. Her family was distantly related to the Dudley Ross Spears family also from Johnstown.[41] Spears was a respected preacher among noninstitutional disciples in the last half of the twentieth century and first part of the twenty-first.

Delia liked conversation and even occasional verbal jousting. When thinking of the combination of her reserved grandfather and more outgoing grandmother, Foy's daughter, Ellen Baize laughed and said, "You can imagine! Here is this Irish woman living with this taciturn man living in the middle of nowhere. The only person she has to talk to is him and he doesn't want any arguments. It speaks volumes for her! ... There was a period of nine months when she wouldn't have seen another person [she could talk to]!"

The O'Neal family moved to Cordell, Oklahoma in the early 1900s so that their children could have a "Christian education." J.N. Armstrong became president of Cordell Christian College in 1908[42] and exerted a great amount of influence on Delia and her husband-to-be, Will. Foy's sister, Sybil Dewhirst, said that Armstrong had "a wonderful influence on his students. He taught them to trust in the working of the Spirit and God's grace. Mother and Daddy imbibed that spirit."[43] Cordell Christian College would grow to be the largest school that was acceptable to known members of churches of Christ before it closed in 1918 because of the pacifist beliefs of many in its faculty and the resulting unpopularity in the surrounding community.[44] Cordell Christian College was a predecessor of Harding University.

Will's family moved to Cordell, Oklahoma when he was about fourteen years of age[45] for the same reason that Delia's family moved there, so their children could be educated by Christians. There, Will and Delia met, fell in love and because of Armstrong's influence, began to think of dedicating their lives to preaching overseas. However, their romance was interrupted when Will was drafted into the army.

Will Short's conscription into the army was a great challenge in his life. He did not feel that a Christian should kill. However, unlike some of his contemporaries at Cordell Christian College, he felt that if his government called, he should answer. So he entered the army while constantly begging his superiors for a non-combatant role. However, he made the mistake of displaying his excellent shooting skills and therefore his superiors were disinclined to remove him from combat duty. For a while he was in a type of limbo as far as his combat status was concerned and even required to wear a yellow armband so that he could be derided as a coward. However, his superiors stubbornly refused to transfer him. He overheard one telling another that when the bullets started flying, "Short will shoot the enemy." Meanwhile, he prayed for the strength to do otherwise. He was shipped to France and the very night he was to be rotated into the combat line, the armistice was declared and the war ended. Will Short felt that his prayers had been answered.[46]

While Will was in the army and after Cordell Christian College closed, Delia and her brother George, earned their degrees from Thorp Springs Christian College.[47] Then when Will returned from the army, he married Delia and the new couple settled in Harper, Kansas. Harold Foy Short was born January 17, 1921 in Harper, Kansas, near the Oklahoma border.

Africa's Call

Will and Delia Short originally planned to go to India to preach. However, news about conflicts among Indian preachers[48] made them change their minds. As they were thinking of where to go, they came in contact with

F.B. Shepherd who had been corresponding with John Sherriff in Southern Rhodesia. Shepherd told them about the need in Southern Africa and they began to make their plans to go, traveling among churches to seek support. Their primary supporters would be the brethren in Harper, Kansas.

Will, Delia and little Foy left for Africa in late 1921 before receiving all the money they needed. Such sacrifices were almost universal among early evangelists in Southern Africa. For example, Will's friend and fellow pioneer, A.B. (Alva) Reese, never received more than twenty five dollars a month during the first years of their stay in Africa, but Reese, who was a capable woodworker, supplemented the family income by raising their food and making furniture and wagons.[49]

John Sherriff is standing in the back holding Foy. Standing next to him (to his left) is his adopted daughter, Molly. Seated left to right: unknown elderly woman, Delia Short holding Sybil, Emma Sherriff, Theodora Sheriff and an unknown girl.

Over thirty years after arriving in Africa, Will lamented what he perceived to be a lack of that sacrificial spirit among young men contemplating overseas work at that time.

There was a time when a man who wanted to become a "missionary" was either a fool or one who sincerely felt that the Lord had called him to some land … He worked, talked, wrote articles, visited and worked again, until he had some means of going, and he did not rest until he got there for he felt that was what the Lord wanted him to do. And his wife went with him, even if she had to do without innerspring mattresses, and had no electric stove to cook on.

But today it seems different. When I was in my homeland I found a number of young people who were interested in going to some field provided the brethren send them but there was no desire to put out any effort. … The idea seemed to be … if they want me over there they can send me and my family with a good salary … and the time must not be over two or three years; we must not be thrust into the bush somewhere away from electric lights … But the main thing is that we must have the money … for it would not do to come back home a broken old man after a life spent in that land, and have no place to go and no one to care for me. No sir, the brethren know I am here and they can supply aplenty if they want me to go.[50]

After arriving in South Africa, the Will Short family took the train to Bulawayo, Southern Rhodesia where John Sherriff and his wife met them. Almost as soon as the young family arrived in Bulawayo, they had to begin their battles with a common African threat. Will wrote in his first diary entry from Africa, "Foy has malaria."[51] It is not difficult to imagine Delia's dismay upon seeing her infant child suffering the fevers and chills of the dreaded African disease shortly after their arrival. However, after a doctor's visit, Will reported a few days later, "Foy is better."[52]

The Shorts spent eighteen months working with John Sherriff on the Forest Vale Mission. Sherriff taught young Will Short the basics of working and surviving in Africa. Foy said that Sherriff's lessons and influence on his father were "invaluable." Foy's sister, Sybil, was born in Bulawayo during this period.

Sherriff encouraged Will to take his small family to Northern Rhodesia, now Zambia, to help one of his original African converts, Peter Masiya. Sherriff and Short made "one or two" exploratory trips to the region.[53] Finally, government papers were approved for a mission at Sinde, about twenty miles from Livingstone and the Victoria Falls in Northern Rhodesia.

Starting Sinde Mission

Will Short went alone to Sinde to prepare the way for his family, arriving on March 20, 1923. He wrote briefly in his diary, "I hated to leave and Delia did not want to see me go, but it was necessary."[54] All evangelists who must leave their families can identify with those words. Upon his arrival, he found that Peter Masiya and African disciples converted by him had already cut poles for the construction of a house and prepared "a lovely vegetable garden all ready for use."[55] Will wrote, "I wish Delia and the babies were up here now!"[56]

After trying to make the place at least barely habitable he sent word back to Bulawayo for his family to come to Sinde. They — along with Molly Sherriff and two "colored" (mixed race) girls raised by the Sherriffs named Ella and Rhoda Bent — arrived at Senkobo Siding on July 4, 1923. Sybil recalled her parent's story about their arrival.

> I was a few months old when Mother took Foy and me by train from Bulawayo to join Daddy at Sinde Mission. Daddy met us at Senkobo Siding with a borrowed sledge equipped with a basket for hauling grain, pulled by yoked oxen. He had lined the basket with quilts and pillows where Foy and I rode in comfort with the luggage while he and Mother walked alongside the sledge.
>
> We traveled slowly on higher ground beside the old washed out roadbed that had eroded into deep ruts where sand was deep enough in places to bury the runners of a sledge. The lead-boy suddenly realized the sledge was too close to the rut and frantically tried to pull the oxen away from the edge while the driver and Daddy struggled in vain to hold the sledge upright. Mother watched in horror as the sledge tipped slowly on its side, spilling Foy, me and the luggage onto the sand. No one was hurt and the sledge was righted and reloaded and we reached the mission before dark.[57]

Sinde Mission wasn't an ideal place for Europeans to live. Eldred Echols described conditions in the late 1940s:

> The area was unhealthy, especially for whites. It was low-lying and hot, and malaria was rife. The medical officer of the district, Dr. McGregor, wanted the mission closed because of the prevalence of disease, but it stayed open and the mission personal continued to be taken into the government hospital in Livingstone for treatment.[58]

Will Short described some of his difficulties in his first report to *Word and Work* magazine:

> We are nearly twenty miles from the post office and trading point, and eight miles from a siding on the railroad. No way yet for us to get bout [sic] anywhere, other than walking, (except that I have a bicycle). When we want anything from the town, it is either sent out on the train to the siding, and then carried out by natives, or the natives go the twenty miles to town and carry it from there. I hope to have it different, however, before long, if I can manage financially.
>
> I did not have the house finished when wife and babies came out, but by degrees am getting it completed. Am trying to keep the expenses down as much as possible, by doing the work myself, (with native help), yet there is quite a bit of expense one way and another in getting up a house, school-house, etc. But these things must go up.[59]

Sybil said of the temporary pole house her father built, "We lived in that while Daddy burned brick to make a brick house that took many months."[60] Though weighed down with the need for backbreaking work just to provide food and shelter, Will was elated with the prospects for spreading the gospel around Sinde.

Two young men [named Mubela and Nlonda according to his diary] were baptized in the name of Christ, Sunday Sept. 2nd. May they prove faithful unto the Master who bought them. Others are interested, and are being taught more. Over one hundred out to meetings on Sundays. This is very encouraging to us, compared to the few who were at meetings in Bulawayo. This makes nine baptisms since I came the first of April.[61]

Will soon made friends with his African neighbors. When a troublesome lion began to kill livestock in the village, he set up an ambush to kill it. He wrote in his diary on October 1, 1923, "Staid [sic] up in the tree last night, but no lion came around. I got some sleep up on the platform, but was awake some, though I was depending on Peter D. to call me if he saw the lion."[62]

Childhood

Foy's childhood memories of Sinde Mission and Kabanga Mission are dim, but his sister, Sybil, has several from stories their parents told from those early years. One thing that stands out in her mind is her mother's efforts to protect her children from mosquito borne malaria. "Every evening when the sun went down, she gave us our baths and then she bandaged our arms, legs and feet to prevent mosquito bites during supper and family devotions. Once in bed under mosquito nets, bandages were removed and rolled up ready for the next evening. People in the States sent old sheets to tear up for bandages."[63]

Foy Short (left) as a toddler with Alex Claassen.

In spite of Delia Short's efforts, malaria affected every member of her family, especially her husband. They all took a daily dose of quinine, the only medication known to control the effects of the disease at that time. Sybil tells how their parents gave it and other medicines to their own babies and other small children.

> They mashed the pill in a spoon, put a little sugar and water with it and while one of them held the baby's head and arms firmly, the other held its nose and poured the liquid into its mouth. The baby swallowed it because it had to swallow in order to breath. Giving them medicine was often a matter of life or death. I saw them give babies medicine like that and Mother said that was how they gave us quinine as babies. As soon as we were old enough they taught us to put the pill on the back of our tongue and gulp a lot of water to get it down quickly.[64]

Foy remembered an occasion where his father became gravely ill with malaria at Sinde and was helped by an African evangelist, Kambole Matapamatenga whom his father loved deeply. Peter Masiya had converted Kambole.[65]

> One time when my dad had malaria, we had no transport. He needed to get my dad twenty miles to Livingstone to a hospital. They couldn't get enough carriers to carry the litter. Kambole took the turn of two men and carried one end of the litter all twenty-five miles to Livingstone. He wasn't very big but he must have been very strong.[66]

Foy gained a useful tool during his childhood years among the Tongas of Northern Rhodesia, their language. Sybil said, "Foy could speak chiTonga quite fluently and sometimes translated for mother." Foy wrote in an undated radio transcript probably from the late 1950s, "We children spent a part of our time playing with the little black children, and learned to speak their language. We learned to make little clay oxen and cows and men for toys, just like the native children were so expert in doing. We even tried to like some of their favorite foods."[67] He then described trying unsuccessfully to learn to enjoy eating flying ants and locusts. Though he left the language when he was almost nine years old, he still remembered enough when he moved back into the area in the late 1940s to be able to communicate with the tribesmen.

A few details about the Short's early days in Sinde Mission come from Ella Clark Quinch, the young mixed race girl who along with her sister, Rhoda Bent, accompanied the Shorts from Forrest Vale Mission to Sinde. Ella, who along with her sister was raised by John Sherriff and his wife,[68] spent about two years as an early teen with the Shorts at Sinde and came to have a deep love for them. Many years later, her daughter, Adele Margerison became very close to Foy and his wife, Margaret. Adele told Margaret several stories her mother told her about the Shorts. For example,

> One Sunday at service Granny Short was not in a good mood and took no notice of what Sybil was up to and didn't stop her playing around or making a noise. She said Grandaddy Short stopped in the middle of his sermon, walked down and took Sybil out and spanked her, then brought her back and sat her next to Gran Short and then went back to his preaching.[69]

Challenges for Foy's Parents

Part of Will's work at Sinde mission involved hiring and supervising African teachers. He had to farm so that his family could eat while he worked constantly on construction projects to improve the primitive facilities. When he found the time, usually during the dry season, he made forays into surrounding villages to preach. He wrote F.B. Shepherd in late 1924,

> I am in bed again for a few days. I have been feeling very well for awhile, and by not trying to do any work to amount to much, I am able to keep going. Saturday, I suppose I lifted too much. Then Sunday, took a six-mile hike preaching at a village about three miles from here. Well, that finished me and I have been in bed since . . .
>
> The house is coming along very fine, only for lack of funds I am loosing up on it a bit until we get some money to buy more material. I am letting a number of boys go. We are in about as bad

circumstances this year financially as we were last year. Have a little garden, a few chickens and are getting a little milk, very little, but some for the babies.[70]

Ray Lawyer arrived to help the Shorts on March 6, 1925. Will wrote in his diary, "I was exceedingly glad to see him!"[71] Delia, who loved conversation, was probably even happier to have someone else to talk to. Lawyer's wife, Zelma, arrived shortly afterwards. The Lawyers were friends of the Shorts at Cordell Christian College and their arrival must have been a tremendous boost.

Lawyer wrote about a trip he and Will Short took into villages in the area.
We have just returned from a hundred and fifty mile journey among the natives. The weather had been extremely hot and dry. … We visited a number of villages where we were told a white missionary had never been. We enjoyed the work except that at times our feet got pretty sore. Our riding mule slipped away and ran home so we had to walk for about seventy-five miles. Bro. Short limped along for the last few days but didn't say much about it. … There were only a few confessions but we had a good hearing at most of the villages. We are well pleased with the way we were received. Seed was sown for future harvest.[72]

Will Short wrote of another 200 mile trip a few months later:
Just last week Brother Lawyer and myself returned from a two-weeks trip among the villages. We had a profitable trip, and one that we hope will bring honor and glory to God, and save many souls. Three stepped forward to show their faith in the Lord Jesus. We made over 200 miles, with the boys carrying our luggage. It is a great life to be out among people who have never heard of the Gospel plan of salvation, and who are eager to learn — learn anything. Out in the open, with our families at the Mission by themselves! We were out of communication with them for over a week.

But we had a Comforter, the Lord himself, who cares for us all.

We saw the tracks of all kinds of deer, hyena, zebra, and lion — and crocodile! All these kept something exciting for us to talk about, as we tramped along one day after another. We had one mule for riding while the other carried a load. But the one mule gave us much rest, except where we had to leave it behind on account of the tsetse fly.[73]

The Dow Merritt family arrived in August of 1926 to help the Shorts and Lawyers. The George Scott family arrived in 1927. Since there were now four families, they made plans to start a new mission to be called Kabanga about 70 miles northeast of Sinde. The original plans were for the Shorts to work with the George Scott family at Sinde, while the Merritts and Lawyers worked to establish the Kabanga Mission. The latter two families were building their homes while living in grass lean-tos on the new mission in late 1927, when Ray Lawyer was tragically killed in a freak accident. He stumbled and fell on a spear that he was carrying on a hunt. Relays of Africans carried him on a stretcher as quickly as possible to the rail line where he was transferred to Livingstone. However, in spite of the best efforts of Merritt, a medic during World War 1, Lawyer passed away a few days after his injury. He left a godly widow and a little band of shocked but still determined missionaries. Zelma Lawyer returned to the States in 1928 and taught many years at Abilene Christian College. She was especially close to Foy's sisters, Sybil, Beth and Margaret, when they were at Abilene. She wrote a fictionalized account of her African experiences in 1943.[74] Sybil maintained contact with Jean, the Lawyer's daughter who lived in Portland, Oregon in 2009.

Though nothing in any published work hints of any friction among the families, Will Short's diaries reveal that there were strains. He wrote in December of 1927,

Bro. Merritt came down for a talk. He said we could not work together but we do not see it that way. We are willing to overlook their mistakes and keep our hearts right. We pray God to help us and give us wisdom. Merritts had sorely misjudged us and already prejudged. We feel they see things in a different light now.

Such tension could be expected among families who had to work closely together in extremely remote areas. This one evidently resolved itself after a conversation between the affected parties.

Kabanga Mission, 1928

Ray Lawyer's death made Will Short decide to postpone a trip to the United States to move his family to Kabanga to help Dow Merritt. He didn't want Merritt to be left holding the bag regarding Lawyer's obligations to finish the house there and pay the workers. Kabanga was an even more remote mission than Sinde, "two and half days" on an oxcart from the nearest train stop. The Shorts worked there until their trip back to the United States in late 1928. Don Carlos Janes reported in January of 1928, "The Shorts are occupying the house Bro. Lawyer started at

John Sherriff and porters with supplies ready to leave on a long trek.

Kabanga, but without floors, doors or windows, and with unfinished roof. They keep the light burning at night and have the gun handy for intruding wild animals."[75] Short later wrote Janes that he was "snowed under here trying to get all this work done."[76]

Occasional boxes of goods sent from brethren in the U.S. brightened the lives of the families. Will Short wrote in his diary in January of 1928,

>Boxes came from home. Children just jumped and squealed with delight. Foy's blackboard was run over with the wagon, but did not

render the board unfit for use. Foy can write a little in it now. And his tractor is quite a joy to him. Sybil was so happy she didn't know what to do. Her sleeping doll is so nice. She is afraid she will break it as she broke the other small one. She said, "Momma put my dollie up. I do not want to break it." … Beth also received a sleeping doll and both girls a little trunk of doll clothes each. Delia received some pans, dresses, etc. I received a [illegible], a flashlight and a few small articles. All very useful and we are thankful for all. God is very merciful to us and gives us blessings far beyond what we are worthy of, what we ask and even what we think.[77]

At Kabanga as well as all rural missions, the Shorts had to keep an eye out for dangerous animals. Sybil recalled,

I was nearly six when Mother was busy sewing and said I could make a cake. I was standing at the kitchen door beating the eggs with a fork when a movement on the top step caught my eye at the same time I heard the yard worker crying, *"Tijana!"* (run) I saw a large snake crawling onto the verandah and dropped the bowl with a crash and ran screaming to Mother. I managed to say "SNAKE!" and she hurried to the door and saw that the African had killed the snake with his hoe.[78]

Short reported in 1928 that he had made a 280-mile trip to preach in villages. He walked 180 of those miles and was able to surprise his good friend, George Scott, at Sinde mission where he posted some letters.[79] He added, "I am getting anxious to get back home, but I have a long way to go yet. There are over a hundred miles (just guessing) to be traveled before I get back and by going about among the native villages it will take a good deal of time."[80]

Though always optimistic in his official reports about such expeditions, Will's diary revealed a little more of his inner feelings when he set out on them.

Finished putting things together this morning and then started at noon. … Walked fast. Reached Kabanga Valley in 2½. I had a small buck just as I was nearing camp. Much water in the flats. I hated to leave home but this work has to be done and I am the only one that can get away. And I believe I am the only one able to do the village work. Delia was a bit blue about my leaving, but did not show it overmuch.[81]

A letter from the elders at Harper, Kansas to the *Word and Work* described Will Short's weakened condition after the trip.

He was home but one day when he was obliged to go to bed with fever which continued for two weeks. Then, when they decided he must go to the hospital, he was obliged to ride lying on his back in a donkey cart all night over rough roads until they could reach the motor road; then he rode all day and another night by motor car and trains before reaching the hospital. The fever has left him lame, we hope only temporarily. He is again back at Kabanga Mission and engaged in teaching and preaching the gospel at that place, and hopes to be able to walk and preach again soon …[82]

Dow Merritt said that Short took a number of similar trips and that "on half these jaunts he took his eight year old son, Foy, with him." When he took Foy they rode an old gray mule. "When he went alone he used the old, worn out mission bicycle."[83] Merritt described Will Short's preparations. "Besides the roll of bedding, the box of food, and two large canvas water bags, there was also carried a box of cooking utensils, a smaller box containing medicine and dressings, a suitcase and a heavy rifle." He added that often five men were needed to carry the equipment plus one interpreter.[84] Don Carlos Janes reported in April of 1929, "Sister Scott reports 138 baptisms at Sinde and outstations by Bros. Short, Scott and helpers in 1928. … The day school at Sinde last year had an enrollment of around 100; 3537 treatments were given the sick. There are about 60 acres under cultivation."[85] The report gives an idea of what the three missionary families were accomplishing in the late 1920s. Finally in late 1928, enough money was collected for Will Short to bring his family to the United States to rest and talk about their work among American churches.

Trip to America 1928-1930

Will Short wrote a detailed report of his trip from Africa to the United States to *Word and Work*.[86] Zelma Lawyer accompanied the family on their trip home. After visiting brother Sherriff in Wuyu Wuyu and brother Hadfield in Bulawayo, the family traveled to Cape Town where they boarded the *Gloucester Castle* of the Union Castle Line for the voyage to England. The ship stopped at St. Helena, the remote island in the South Atlantic where Napoleon had been exiled. Foy remembered the long stairs called "Jacob's ladder" that led up to the house where Napoleon lived. The ship next stopped at Ascension Island where the natives brought some turtles to the ship that weighed nearly 600 pounds that were destined for the table of the King of England. The travelers saw the Graf Zeppelin flying overhead before finally docking in England twenty-four days after leaving Cape Town.

After arriving in England on October 17, 1928 and spending four days there, the Short family departed for America on a 17,000-ton ship, *Tuscania*, that encountered a strong gale in the North Atlantic. The "ship shook and trembled from head to stern, then stopped in mid-ocean unable to go forward further without danger of tearing itself to pieces. This was another time to put ourselves in the hand of God."[87] Foy remembered the storm.

After arriving in the States, Will Short traveled around the country, giving reports to churches and working to print some songbooks in the chiTonga language. The trip was a blur of churches and travel to young Foy. After a little over a year of visits and travel, Will took his family to the West Coast to set sail for Africa from the other side of the continent. He wrote in May of 1930, "All the way through the west was a profitable trip. We saw many brethren, and encouraged the mission cause very much, we believe. Had fine visits at Vancouver and at Victoria, brethren came to the boat to visit with us. We did not have the time that we needed, but Africa is calling and we must hasten on."[88] Don Carlos Janes wrote in July, "Brother Short was in Sydney May 11 intending to sail for Africa on the 16th."[89]

One of the great blessings that Will Short obtained during his visit to the states was a 1930 Chevrolet that he brought back to Africa on the ship. The car lasted him for many years even after it had holes in the floorboard. He wrote in 1938:

> I would like to say a word about our motorcar, and give honor where honor is due. After eight years of faithful service, it is still going. Sixty thousand miles over these roads is what I think [is] very good going.Our spring trip to Bulawayo is the only time that it has given us any real trouble, and that was one connecting rod burned out because the oil pump failed. The body is very badly broken up but we hope it will last a little longer, until we can manage another.[90]

Wuyu Wuyu

When the Shorts arrived in Rhodesia in 1930 after their trip to the States, they decided to move to a new mission started by John Sherriff east of Salisbury in the heart of Mashonaland. Jack Mzira had evangelized the area and Sherriff decided to put a mission there. When obtaining the property, Sherriff mistakenly understood the natives to be saying Huyuyu and that's the way the place is spelled in the *Word and Work*. However, someone later found out that since Sherriff was hard of hearing he misunderstood what the Africans were telling him and that the actual name of the place was Wuyu Wuyu.

Wuyu Wuyu would be home for the Will Short family until support from the States almost dried up completely during the great depression. The *Word and Work* is filled with pleas during the early 1930s for financial help for the foreign evangelists, but it usually wasn't forthcoming during the economic crisis. W.L. Brown wrote, "Brother Short is receiving only about $65 per month."[91] At one time during the depression the family received only twenty dollars a month from supporting churches.[92] Brethren in Northern Rhodesia sent the following radiogram to Don Carlos Janes, "Livingstone, Rhodesia Feb. 24, Deficit 500 dollars; Merchants refuse credit; No meal; Must close if no funds. Property endangered; Locusts; Crisis."[93] Though Will Short did little complaining, John Sherriff did it for him. He wrote after visiting the Shorts,

> To try and increase their income and pay off debts, he was trying to sell his rifle, and had left their car in Salisbury to be sold, and was visiting farms and villages on Foy's cycle, preaching . . . Brethren, I know times are hard, and money scarce, but I hope and pray Bro. and Sister Short won't be compelled to sell that car.[94]

In spite of the economic difficulties, Will Short's reports were always optimistic.

> Since the first of the year 19 have been baptized in Salisbury and 13 at the outstations with 6 more at Salisbury school to be baptized soon. We had one baptism out here. The work in Northern Rhodesia is doing nicely as reports go. Would like so much to go up there this year. We really need to get away with the children for a change. Two years here now and they are feeling it. But we will have to await the Lord's directions in the matter.
>
> Our children are doing very well in their correspondence school work. Foy is trying for a scholarship the last of this year if he can. Brother Sherriff said he would throw his hat over Table Mountain if he passed. But whether he passes or not is something for him to work for, out here by himself as he is.[95]

Short mentioned Foy's education. He and his sisters studied a government correspondence course. However, such instruction terminated at the end of the seventh grade, at which time those in remote areas were expected to send their children to boarding school in Salisbury.

Foy and Sybil both remember the problems their parents had with aggressive baboons at Wuyu Wuyu. There were granite escarpments behind their home that were full of them. They were often in the garden and the Africans often had to chase them away. The family also had dogs, including a Great Dane called Budge that was one of the family favorites. Sybil recalled,

> One day a worker came running to tell Daddy that baboons were in the garden and he couldn't chase them out. Daddy shut the dogs in the workshop, fastening both the top and bottom halves of the Dutch door. Then he went to the garden intending to shoot into the air and scare the baboons away, but a large male decided to argue and Daddy shot but only wounded the baboon and it went up into the nearby hill. Daddy followed cautiously, knowing how dangerous a wounded baboon could be. When he saw the baboon it was crouching under a bush, about to spring. The baboon sprang as he raised his gun and fired and at the same instant something "whooshed" past him, knocking him to one side, as Budge hurled himself at the baboon. The baboon was already hurtling forward when the bullet struck him and he and Budge met in mid-air and the baboon's great teeth ripped Budge's jugular vein.

> One of the workers had left the top of the Dutch door open and Budge had jumped over the bottom half of the door to race after his master. Daddy was sure it would have been his own jugular vein had it not been for Budge. There was nothing he could do for the dog. Foy dug a grave and we gave Budge a tearful funeral; then Foy cut and sanded a piece of wood and burned on it the inscription: "Here Lies Budge, Killed By a Baboon, December 11."

Donkeys!

There were always challenges on the farm with the donkeys. Once when Will was having trouble with them, Delia told him, "You know daddy, there may be just one donkey too many out there."

Donkeys also provided amusement for the children. Foy made a donkey cart that Sybil recalled when writing a poem for Margaret and him on their fiftieth wedding anniversary.

> He built a cart when he was ten,
> With two old wheels and boarded sides.
> He hitched the donkeys, offered rides,
> And his three sisters clambered in. [96]

On a later occasion Foy got into some trouble when trying to help his sisters and some visiting children learn to ride donkeys. His sister Sybil wrote in her personal memoirs,

> One weekend the Van der Merwes were visiting and we children wanted to ride donkeys. Foy had the largest donkey and led the group. Ella and I were next, each on a donkey, followed by Beth on a smaller donkey… We rode in single file down the sloping driveway then turned and came back up the drive. Farther up the hill the main herd of donkeys was grazing and one of them brayed. When Foy's donkey heard that, he decided to buck Foy off and join the other donkeys … Our donkeys had been going very sedately … and all was well until they saw and heard Foy's donkey, then they began to run, spilling girls in all directions …
>
> As Daddy gathered us up to assess the damage, girls were crying … Mother checked us over, sympathizing with the hurts and Ella's mother was almost hysterical, crying, "I knew I shouldn't have let her ride." Ella's hand was only bruised and Beth revived with a small knot on her head but we never forgot that donkey ride.[97]

Foy wrote the following as an adult after colliding with a donkey on the road:

> Donkeys! They are in great demand in the communal (tribal) areas. They are used for plowing, for general transport and for taking the family shopping or to church services. It is quite a sight to see a five-donkey team galloping down the road with the family lurching

behind in a two-wheeled cart. Donkeys seem to survive drought even better than goats, but they don't have the traffic sense that goats have on the highways. Throughout the communal areas, animals feed along the sides of the highways and roam across them at will. You can usually count on goats getting off the road when cars approach, but *not* donkeys. They either stand right where they are in the middle of the road, or else amble unconcerned across, or up the middle, hence are the cause of many accidents.[98]

Family Leisure Time and Yearly Gatherings

Sybil recalled quieter times in the evenings at her home in Wuyu Wuyu. "When we were sick, Daddy would always read to us. He sat in the door where it was light and read *First Steps for Little Feet* and other children's books. We always had Bible reading every morning and every night."

Around 1933 the Shorts came across an old Edison cabinet type record player that had eleven records with one song or piece of music per side. There was some classical music, humorous songs and cowboy songs. They especially enjoyed the hymns including *Rock of Ages*, *The Old Rugged Cross* and *Under His Wings*. One of the "crazy" songs was titled *Stop Your Tickling, Jock*. Sybil said, "If anyone was in a bad mood, someone put that record on and we would all start laughing." The Edison had a diamond point needle that did not wear out.

The small band of missionaries was very close, especially the first families in the region: the Shorts, Merritts, Reeses, Sherriffs, Lawyers and Scotts. A brief summary of the background of these families and others will be placed in an appendix in the end of the book. Once a year they had a reunion, often around the holiday season. It became a tradition to have the reunion alternating years in Northern Rhodesia and then the next year in Southern Rhodesia.

Foy's sister, Sybil, recalled observing the adults from a child's perspective,

When Mother told us to go to bed, Foy and I got ready for bed then crept into the hallway to sit on the floor by the door to the living room so we could hear the grownups talking. I particularly remember how I enjoyed hearing them talk about Bible subjects and discuss pros and cons on some things. Mother liked to play devil's advocate and Margaret Reese helped her, which made for some lively discussions. Sometimes they argued but I never got the feeling anyone was angry and sometimes they went into peals of laughter. I don't know how long Foy and I sat there, but I never forgot the warm feeling that came out of that room.[99]

Worship services always make an impression on young children. Sybil has pictures in her mind of meeting many times with Africans for services under big shade trees. She recalled the church at Wuyu Wuyu in the 1930s.

Until the church building was finished, or if we were meeting in a village, we met under a shade tree and the white people were given chairs or stools to sit on, the native women sat on their own grass mats and most men carried their own little stools. At the mission, Sunday worship began as soon after eleven as the people arrived and sometimes we got home after 2:00 or 3:00 o'clock. Native mothers nursed infants and toddlers and brought food for older children.

The main African preacher was Jack Mzira. His village was about three miles from the mission and his family, including his one-hundred-year-old mother, walked to and from meeting every Sunday. We girls liked for him to speak because he didn't talk too long! The other speaker was Tom Mugadza, he didn't know when to stop and we could see Sunday dinner being at 3:00 o'clock or later. I am not speaking for Foy, who was older and by then could understand and speak the language.[100]

Boarding School

When Foy and his sisters finished the seventh grade correspondence courses, Will and Delia followed local tradition and sent them to boarding school in Salisbury. Foy's work for the test at the end of his correspondence courses paid off as he won a scholarship to cover the boarding and school fees at the Prince Edward School. His name is still on a large board in the school auditorium listing the names of all scholarship winners in the history of the school.[101]

L to R: Sybil, Foy and Beth ready to leave for school in Salisbury after vacation

Foy studied at the Prince Edward School for five years and earned the equivalent of an Associate of Arts degree. When he attended Abilene Christian College later, he would only need to study two years to obtain his bachelor's degree.

Foy played on the school's rugby team. His school magazine, an impressive publication, described his rugby skills in 1938. "H.F. Short: A determined front rank man, who was substituted only because he did not fit the size of the rank. One of the most fearless tacklers in the team, and a great opportunist in the loose [*sic*]."[102]

Foy's headmaster (principal) wrote a glowing recommendation for Foy upon his graduation. After listing a number of awards that Foy won while at the school, he wrote,

> He is of strong physique and has played for our 1st Rugby XV. He took part in practically all school games, cricket, tennis, boxing and swimming. He gained the Certificates and Gold Medallion of the Royal Life Saving Society. In the Cadets, he was a good shot. His other interests include Debating Society, Book-binding and Printing.

He has a sterling character for honesty, right behaviour and high principles. In personality he is quiet but frank and pleasing; he is well liked here and has promise of strength of character. I am certain he will do well, for he is conscientious, reliable and competent.[103]

Sybil remembered that "very autocratic teachers" ruled the roost at the boarding schools. "We had nicknames for all of them." She also recalled that bells regulated everything. "We got up by bells, ate by bells and did our homework by bells." The school session began in January and the older children were only able to come home from Salisbury for the midterm, at the end of the term (three weeks twice a year) and a six-week Christmas break.

One problem that the Shorts had to face was the fact that there was no known group of Christians in Salisbury at the time that worshiped God in English and believed exactly like they did. However, Will visited a very small congregation of twelve to fifteen people known to have connections with "the Brethren." After talking at length with the members, he felt them to be scriptural in most of their work and teaching and decided that his children could attend there when unable to return home.

Will wrote in 1960 about this period in their lives.

> When our own children were small, and until they had to go away to boarding school, wife and I tried to teach Bible principles so they could stand for the Lord when they had to leave us.
>
> Then the time came that they had to go, first to the boarding school, and then out to live their own lives. We have seen very little

Foy's rugby team at Prince Edward School. He's on the second row on the far right with the blond hair.

of our children since then. But today, Sept. 11, we heard our eldest
son preach the gospel here at Queens Park East, and he rose to
heights of power in extolling our Saviour and his church.[104]

Macheke

As the depression deepened and support from American congregations
dried up, Will Short decided that it would be impossible to continue living at Wuyu Wuyu mission and feed his family at the same time. However,
he was able to obtain a farm twenty-five miles away at Macheke, which
he called Faroe.[105] He worked to evangelize his neighbors in the new area
while maintaining contact with African brethren at Wuyu Wuyu. Though
he must have been disappointed at having to dedicate more time to farming, Will remained upbeat in his report to *Word and Work*.

We have now moved off the Reserve. We could not meet the requirements of the Government to hold the mission lease, so it was
cancelled. But the Government gave us a farm about 25 miles from
the mission, which we can purchase. It contains about 3,000 acres,
at $1.00 per acre, payments to be spread over 20 years with no in-
terest. We are moving our buildings and material to this place. Thus
we will be buying our place instead of leasing always.

The church building, however, is not to be moved. It remains
where it is to be used by the congregation there. A large congregation meets every week, and native leaders are able to go ahead with
the meetings. We are to keep this as a preaching center and I will
go in to help them as often as possible. In the meantime I will help
teach at other places. New opportunities are opened up with our
move, and we hope to use them as often as possible. We will also
work with the white people of the farms. About 25 were present for
our first meeting of white people.

A very fine meeting was held at the mission during Christmas
holidays. Two and three native teachers speaking at each service.
591 people were present at our service on Christmas day.[106]

Foy's father sent fewer reports to *Word and Work* after moving to Macheke, but checked in occasionally, especially to report on his efforts to teach European farmers in the area. Sybil pointed out that her father picked the smallest farm and refused to cultivate tobacco, because he said he wouldn't raise anything he didn't believe people should use. He raised corn, peanuts and grain.

After Foy's baptism when he was ten years old he began to help his father with preaching and work on the farm at Macheke. He learned the Shona language from his boyhood friends well enough to translate for his father on preaching expeditions, primarily during school holidays. Of the three African languages he learned, chiTonga, Shona and isiNdebele, he probably felt most comfortable with Shona, at least during the time he spoke it extensively.

Foy's daughter, Kay, recalled that when traveling through London in about 2005, Foy heard some people sitting in front of him speaking Shona. He went up and introduced himself to them in the Shona language. They were very surprised but happy to see this pleasant elderly man of European ancestry speaking to them in their native tongue. Margaret laughed and said that after talking for a while with Foy in Shona, the young Zimbabweans told her that Foy could speak the language better than they could.[107]

Oxen

Paddy Kendall-Ball described Foy as "very strong" physically[108] and much of his strength must have developed through the hard farm chores as a teenager. Foy said, "My job was to drive the oxen and draft work with wagon or plow." He learned to drive teams of up to 18 oxen to haul up to five tons of corn and produce for local farmers to the railroad station. It wasn't an easy task. He said, "On years when there had been a lot of rain on the roads they would become stuck." The oxen were also used for plowing with a three disk plow to plow three furrows at a time. Foy said,

I learned a lot about people by dealing with the oxen. There were oxen that were quite willing to work and would work hard. There were others that if you so much as touched them with the whip they wouldn't pull. They'd stop. There were some that would just lie down when they felt the yoke on their neck. I learned that you had to be careful not to scold people.

He told of one particular ox that gave him problems until one of his companions remembered an old African trick.

There was one ox that I was trying to train, but every time you put a yoke on his neck he would lie down. I tried everything I knew. One thing they often did was twist their tails, and that would make them get up but it didn't with this one. They'd get a bucket of water and put their nose in it. Sometimes that would make them get up, but this one just shook his head and threw it off. We were at our wit's end when one of the Africans remembered that we had plowed up a snake just a little before. We got that snake and he held that next to the ox's nose and he jumped up! From then on, all we had to do was drag that snake along the animal's nose and he would keep going and pull for all he was worth.

Foy's sister Sybil recalled Foy and his oxen as they hauled mealies (corn).

When Foy hauled mealies for the farmers he had 16 or 18 oxen yoked to the big wagon and was gone several days at a time with his African assistants. When it was time for him to be coming down the road on the way to the railroad at Macheke, we girls listened for his whip cracking and his voice in the distance shouting to the oxen. Then we ran to meet him and rode on the wagon back to the house.

On one of his trips his wagon with its load of mealies got stuck in a river and the oxen couldn't pull the heavy load out. It looked like rain was coming and they needed to get out of the river and keep the mealies dry. Foy and his helpers carried the 200 lb. bags of

mealies, on their shoulders or backs, from the wagon to the bank;
then the oxen pulled the wagon out and they reloaded the mealies.
It was a long hard job but they got it done and a tarp over the bags
before the rain came.[109]

Foy's work with oxen went so well that after finishing school in December
1938 he began a transport business using an ox wagon to haul farm produce from neighboring farms to the train siding in Macheke, and then
bring back supplies from Macheke to the farms. In that way he raised money to help pay his way back to the States for college.[110]

When Foy returned to the States in 1940 to attend college he visited a number of congregations. Don Carlos Janes reported, "Foy Short, nineteen, who
returned from Africa alone, made some instructive addresses in Louisville
as he passed to the West. He also demonstrated the giant whips with which
as many as sixteen oxen are driven at once..."[111] Foy said in 2008, "I still
have that whip!"

Snakes and Other Critters

Still other "critters" challenged Foy and his family as they tried to eke out a
living from the hard land.

> Our houses over there were thatched with long grass that would
> grow eight to ten feet tall. They'd cut that and use it to thatch the
> roof. There was one house that had old grass on it that needed to be
> replaced. I was up there [on the roof] stripping that old grass off. I
> started looking and there was a *boomslang* (a tree snake and quite
> poisonous) coiled up under that grass. When I saw that, I just start-
> ed sliding down the roof to get off of it. I flew off and jumped away.

Eldred Echols said that Foy's father Will "had a cool hand with snakes." He
told of an occasion when Will was preaching in the living room of a home
in Namwianga when "a yellow Cape cobra slithered from the kitchen and

made his way across the center of the room." Without interrupting his sermon, Will …

> moved quietly over to the snake and put his foot across his neck.
> Then taking the snake's tail in his hand with its head still pinned to
> the floor, he scooted it across to the screen door. He threw open the
> screen door and took his foot off its neck at the same moment, and
> then "cracked the whip" with the snake, popping its head off. He
> then went on with his lesson, quite unperturbed by the interruption.[112]

Foy mentioned locusts.

> Every so often there would be a large swarm of locusts that would
> come along and it would take a couple of days for the swarm to get
> past. Usually it didn't do any damage as long as they were flying.
> But when they settled in the evening, they would be as much as six
> inches deep. The next morning when they flew off, there wouldn't
> be a green leaf anywhere. The grass was all gone. There was no feed
> for the cattle.

Fortunately, the Shorts had to deal with a locust invasion only once at
Macheke. Others suffered more.

And then there were the occasional dealings with lions. Sybil wrote in her
memoirs:

> One evening Francois deWet came to the house telling us that a
> lion had taken a calf from his cattle kraal the night before; he lay
> in wait for it the next evening and shot but only wounded it and
> the lion had gone into the bush and he came to get Daddy and Foy.
> They got two farmer neighbors and a tracker to go with them to
> look for the lion.
>
> When the men came back they were laughing because when
> they found the lion lying in a shade obviously dying, they had a
> discussion about who should shoot! Francois had wounded it so

they said he should kill it but he said Mr. Short was the oldest so he should have the honor of the kill. They decided to line up and all five of them shoot at the same time![113]

Older Teen

Foy became adept as a mechanic while a teenager. He scrounged parts from an old four cylinder Ford engine and used his father's forge and anvil to build a workable steam engine to turn a crank for a corn-milling machine. His science teacher visited the farm and Will showed him what his son had made. His teacher was highly impressed. In his later life, according to Ellen, he rebuilt his Volkswagen's engine two times even though the local Volkswagen mechanic told him that it would not be possible for that job to be done except by someone with specialized training. After Foy did that supposedly impossible task, the mechanic tried to hire him for the local Volkswagen dealership in Gwelo.

After the corn hauling season ended one year, Foy and a friend from a neighboring farm fixed up the ox wagon like an old Conestoga wagon and took his family and the neighboring family on a camping expedition to an area about 15 miles away from their home. Sybil said, "The adults slept under the tree on camp cots, the girls slept in the covered wagons and the boys slept underneath it. We had the time of our lives for about five days."[114]

When Foy finished boarding school at Salisbury with the equivalent of a two-year college degree, he hoped to obtain a job as a game ranger. Meanwhile, he worked on the farm for two years. The more he worked, however, the more he realized that he needed to further his education in the United States and so he began to make plans to leave Rhodesia temporarily. Though his father wanted him to attend Harding College, Foy made no commitment and simply decided to check out the possibilities when arriving in the States. Will Short wrote in early 1940,

Things of this earth are passing away as 1939 has passed. May we be strengthened to strive for things immortal. ...

We are hoping the older children, at least, will be able to get home for a little while to attend some Bible school. They have finished their schooling here, and we want them to have a little time in Bible school before going into the real mission work, although they are helping a great deal now.[115]

Sybil mentioned plans for both Foy and her to go to the States when writing an informative report for her father that appeared in the August, 1940 issue of *Word and Work*. Before referring to the upcoming trip to the States, she talked about other interesting aspects of the work.

I have been appointed to write this letter this month and I hope I will be able to make it interesting.

Brother Brown and family are still with us and we are enjoying their stay very much. On Sunday mornings, Sister Brown takes a Bible Class with the native women, and Foy, my brother, has one with the men, while I take the white children. Then we have the regular morning meeting. Three white people and a large number of natives have given themselves to the Lord during the last two months.

Last Sunday was during a free weekend for school children and there were thirty-two of us at a neighbor's home for the day. We had two classes for children. Beth, my sister, taught those under nine and I taught those over nine and under sixteen, while Brother Brown had those over that age. Then we had two services besides that, one in the morning and one in the afternoon.

I passed the Cambridge School Certificate Examination last December with five credits out of six subjects which I took. Our papers were sent to England to be graded and they were returned only a few weeks ago. The six subjects which I took were Mathematics, English (grammar and literature), Afrikaans (oral and written), Latin, Art, and Science (Physics with Chemistry). I won credits in all but science and received special credits in English, Literature and Afrikaans Oral.

I am now helping mother with the teaching. She teaches
Margaret Ann, my little sister, and Betty Brown, while I teach Allen
and David Brown. We are using the Correspondence School from
Salisbury.

Foy and I are looking forward very much to a few years in a
Bible College soon, so that we will be more fitted for the Lord's
work which we want to do. If possible we would like to be there in
time to start in some school this year, for by that time Foy will have
been out of school here for two years and I will have been out for
one year. Also the sooner we start the sooner we shall be able to return to Africa. Our prayers for you always, pray for the work of the
Lord here. Thanking you again.[116]

Just before Foy left for the States, Will wrote:
We wanted the children to get away to U.S.A. in Sept., but that boat
was cancelled. Now it is not certain just when they will go, but we
want them to go as soon as possible. In the meantime, Foy and
Sybil are helping us here. Often Foy cycles 25 miles to a congregation, has meetings and Bible class for 4 hours, then gets home by
dark.[117]

Foy, however, was able to leave Southern Africa in December, 1940 just before World War II would have made his travel impossible. His experiences
in the States would mold him further into the effective evangelist that he
became.

Chapter 2

Stateside

Foy's trip to the United States in 1940 marked a turning point in his life for several reasons. Obviously, it was his first time to launch out on his own from the sheltered life in the Rhodesian back country into a world that would be dominated five more years by the Second World War. Spiritually, the ocean voyage would challenge his faith in ways that he could have never imagined before.

Thomas Hartle reported on Foy's visit in Cape Town, South Africa on his way to the States,

> We are glad to report that we have had with us from the first of November Brother Foy Short of Salisbury, Southern Rhodesia, passing on his way through to the U.S.A. to college to study for a period of two years. He sailed on the 9th of November. Also passing through on their way to the U.S.A. were Brother and Sister S.D. Garrett and family and Sister Sybil Short. They arrived here in Cape Town on Dec. 6, 1940. The association with these brethren and visitors was not soon to be forgotten. Brother Foy Short gave an address on the outline of the mission work. We indeed admired him as a young man for the purpose and desire he was setting out to do.[118]

When Foy boarded the *S.S. President Polk* on November 9, 1940[119] for the three-week voyage to New York he realized that thirty-two Mormon missionaries who had just finished their two-year tour of duty in South Africa would be accompanying him. He said, "Within a couple of hours I found myself cornered! For the next three weeks until we got to New York, they had a daily session with me. They were determined to convert me to Mormonism."[120] Poor Foy had never had any experience talking with those of other religious persuasions. He had certainly never encountered any Mormons at Macheke or Wuyu Wuyu. His father had never taught him much about the doctrines of various denominations and sects and he felt powerless before the Latter-Day-Saint onslaught. As soon as he arrived in New York he wrote his father, "I'll have to have to find some answers or else I'll have to become a Mormon."[121]

Though the ocean trip involved lifeboat drills and concerns about German U-boats, Foy's primary memory was his helplessness in the face of his Mormon interrogators. He determined never to be so defenseless again and to make an intensive study of Christ's system of faith as contrasted with human systems. He would emphasize that difference in his teaching for the rest of his life.

Foy's sister, Sybil, was able to depart Cape Town on the ship, *The City of New York*, less than a month after Foy's departure, traveling with the S.D. Garrett family. She recalled that when they left Salisbury the temperature was 105 degrees. When they landed in Boston on January 8, 1941, the temperature was ten degrees below zero! She also remembered vividly the lifeboat drills and blackouts. Though the United States was technically neutral in December of 1940, its ships such as *The City of New York* were still in danger on the high seas. Foy and Sybil's sister, Beth, was able to come on the same ship six months later. On its following run from Cape Town to New York it was sunk on March 29, 1942 by famed U-boat captain, Georg Lassen.[122] Sybil recalled, "Our neighbors at Wuyu Wuyu were Methodist missionaries and they had a son on that trip. He was rescued from a lifeboat."

When Foy arrived in New York, he was met by Homer Reeves who took him to the subway for transportation around town. Foy quickly learned that New York was no Rhodesia. When he arrived at the gate to the trains, he followed his English upbringing by letting all the ladies go first. Reeves walked on before realizing that Foy wasn't with him. He went back to the gate where Foy was letting the ladies through and told him that in New York you don't do that!

Foy traveled across the States, visiting congregations, family members in Oklahoma and checking into the possibility of attending several colleges. He visited Harding College in Searcy, Arkansas since it was the successor to his parents' school, Cordell Christian College. However, he received better financial grants from Abilene Christian College and began to make plans to attend there along with his sister Sybil. He recalled that at the end of his visit to Harding several older students took him aside and advised him not to go to Abilene because of its anti-premillennial stance. However, neither Foy nor his father believed in premillennialism, though his father did not think that differences over the theory should affect fellowship. Foy later turned down a scholarship offer from the Don Carlos Janes foundation because Janes' name was linked so prominently to that theory.

Will and Delia Short's mentor at Cordell Christian College, J.N. Armstrong, was also the founder of Harding College. Armstrong was "deeply disappointed" that Harding did not match Abilene's offer of financial aid for Foy and Sybil.[123] Delia Short had written Mrs. Armstrong that she couldn't imagine "their going to any other school [than Harding] as long as you and Brother Armstrong and families are at Harding."[124] Armstrong lamented, "We have the distinction of having more missionaries in the foreign field than any other school, and we are now losing their children [to other colleges]."[125] However, it was to Abilene that Foy, Sybil and Beth would go and it was there that they would make the special friendships that would stay with them the rest of their lives.

Abilene Christian College

A.B. Barret established what became Abilene Christian College as a preparatory school in 1906. After becoming a fully accredited college in 1919 its enrollment increased to around 600 students by 1925.[126] New land was purchased for a campus northeast of Abilene and the college was able to survive there, though threatened with bankruptcy during the Great Depression. When Foy Short arrived in 1941, Don Morris was president and the school was about to enter the World War II era.

Foy and Sybil went to Walter Adams, the dean of students, for placement in classes. After checking the transcripts from their Rhodesian schools, he offered to start both as juniors, though Sybil decided she would start as a second semester sophomore.[127] However, she later took summer classes so that she could graduate early and get back to a boyfriend in Rhodesia. Therefore she and Foy graduated together in 1943.

Abilene had a group of highly respected Bible professors in the early 1940s including R.C. Bell, Homer Hailey, Charles Roberson and Paul Southern. However, no one influenced Foy during his days at Abilene more than a fellow student, Benjamin Lee (Bennie Lee) Fudge did. Foy said, "Bennie Lee was the closest thing to a brother that I ever had."[128] Foy's own brother, Bill, was born after he left Rhodesia, and therefore he never had as much adult to adult personal contact with him as he did with Fudge.

Fudge, from Limestone County in North Alabama, was older than most of his fellow students in Abilene. He had been raised in extreme poverty and forced to become the primary breadwinner for his family at fourteen years of age when his father became disabled. He and his younger brothers alternated between going to school and sharecropping to support the family.[129] Fudge was known for carrying his Bible into the fields to read whenever the mules were resting. Finally, he was able to graduate from High School when he was twenty-one years old. After he worked a few years to earn some more money, he attended David Lipscomb College in Nashville, which was then a Junior College. After finishing his studies at Lipscomb and graduating as class valedictorian,[130] Fudge transferred to Abilene where he would meet Foy and Sybil.

Soon after meeting Sybil, Bennie Lee asked her for a date. After [the date] he told a friend, "If Miss Short were not determined to go to Africa, I'd marry her." After the same date she told one of her companions, "I wouldn't marry him if he were the last man on earth."[131] They married the day after they graduated from Abilene and thus Foy's best friend became his brother-in-law.

Fudge moved back to North Alabama with Sybil where he preached, started Athens Bible School and ran the C.E.I. bookstore in Athens until his tragic death from pneumonia in 1972. Though small of stature, he was always a whirlwind of productive spiritual activity. He once wrote Foy, "I certainly wish there were forty of me."[132] Sewell Hall credits him for being one of God's primary tools for the explosive growth among churches of Christ in Limestone County from the 1940s through the mid 1960s. Ellen Baize, Fudge's niece by marriage, recalls that her uncle's dream at Abilene "was to go back to Alabama and see a church on every corner in Limestone County." She then laughed and said, "He succeeded!"[133]

Benjamin Lee Fudge was greatly influenced by what historians Bobby Valentine and John Mark Hicks have called the "Nashville Bible School Tradition"[134] that came primarily from the influence of David Lipscomb and James Harding. Their approach to the scriptures emphasized God's grace, separation from the world, trust in God's providence and strict construction in the interpretation of the scriptures. Some who today claim the Lipscomb-Harding heritage as their own do not emphasize that latter characteristic. Historian Richard Hughes believes that Barton W. Stone's teachings had a strong influence on Lipscomb and Harding.[135] Lipscomb and Harding's grace-plus-convictions approach heavily influenced churches in North Alabama in the early part of the twentieth century. When Chris Cotten read Valentine and Hick's description of the "Nashville Bible School Tradition" he realized that he knew it well from visiting preachers he heard in his childhood in Nashville in the 1980s and 1990s, but that the preachers who reflected it were primarily from Alabama. He thought it was the

"Alabama tradition."[136] Bennie Lee Fudge would pass on these values to his protégé, Foy Short, although Foy had probably already received a good dose from his parents who in turn had received them from J.N. Armstrong, a student of Lipscomb's.

Foy doesn't remember the first time he saw Bennie Lee Fudge, though he thinks it would have been in the mission study club. They soon became fast friends. Bennie Lee called Foy (Harold Foy, H.F.) "Horse Face" and Foy called his friend (Benjamin Lee, B.L.) "Bird Legs."[137] They occasionally used these and other similar monikers in their personal correspondence through the years.

Foy at Abilene Christian College

Abilene's grants for the children of missionaries did not cover all expenses, so Foy worked five hours a day in the cafeteria as a server and cleaner to complete his payment. Foy's wife, Margaret, said, "He washed [the floors] so well they made him manager of the bookstore."[138]

A glance through the 1943 Abilene yearbook, *The Prickley Pear*, shows that Foy was popular and respected at the school. He was president of the student council, leader of the evangelistic forum and a member of several other student organizations including the missions study club that was led by his buddy, Bennie Lee Fudge. Foy led the group his junior year. He recalled that his fellow students constantly teased him about his accent, which probably added to his popularity. "They called me a 'limey,' " he said. "Then when I got back to Africa they called me a 'yank.' " *The Abilene Reporter News* mentions Foy in a number of articles about social activities at the college. For example, picnickers at a Sub-T-16 Social Club event "gathered around the campfire to hear stories by Foy Short."[139]

Besides Fudge, Foy met several other students at Abilene who would be his friends in the future. He influenced one, Eldred Echols, to go to Africa. Echols spent the rest of his life there and wrote two books about his experiences. Others like Doyle Banta and Charles Chumley worked with him at North Alabama Bible School a few years later. Foy recalled that Banta preached every Sunday about forty miles north of Big Springs, Texas. Sometimes Foy would accompany him. Foy was Banta's best man at his wedding.[140]

L to R: Foy, Sybil and Bennie Lee Fudge

Foy remembered that his friend, Ralph Graham, was not only extremely conservative, but also very militant. He had a car with a loudspeaker and on occasions parked it in front of the Methodist or Baptist church with several other preacher boys. They would then turn the amplifier up to preach to the Methodists or Baptists inside. The beleaguered churchgoers called the police on several occasions to get relief from the over zealous college boys.

Foy called his classmate Mack Kercheville, "a very fine man." Kercheville was a pioneer in preaching among Spanish speaking people.

Foy had an especially interesting anecdote about his fellow student, Ira North, who would later be known not so much for his emphasis on doctrinal purity, but rather as "Fiery Ira" the promoter. "I remember the day we graduated and were saying goodbye to each other, he met me on the steps of the auditorium. Because some of the hard preachers thought I was a bit soft, he said, 'Foy, you just remember to stick to what the book says. Don't you leave what the book says.' "

Teachers

Foy said that R.C. Bell "had a tremendous influence on me. He was a very spiritually minded man." He added, "Back in those days there was a thing about hard preaching or soft preaching. Unless you called names when preaching about denominationalism, you were a soft preacher. R.C. Bell was considered a soft preacher because he emphasized the spiritual side more than the doctrinal side of Christian living." R.C. Bell was a regular contributor to Foy's support in Rhodesia until his own salary was cut in August of 1950 and he was unable to continue.[141]

Homer Hailey was another favorite. Foy said that he emphasized both the practical and doctrinal aspects of the scriptures in his teaching. "He was so clear and made things so understandable." Foy took two classes that dealt specifically with common religious errors. Hailey taught one and Paul Southern the other. Foy wanted to make sure that he never found himself defenseless again as he was on the long ocean voyage with the Mormons. Foy remembered J.G. Thomas as being "quite active and quite a leader in the class." He remembered one thing in particular about Charles Roberson. "In the first class he said, "The three R's of learning are repetition, repetition, repetition. From then on, every day he would come into class and ask, 'What are the three R's of learning?'"

Howard Schug encouraged Foy and others who were interested in foreign evangelism. He and Don Morris supervised a collection of student essays on the topic that was published in 1941 under the title, "The Harvest Field."[142] Foy wrote a chapter on Korea and of course, Africa, and co-wrote one on Cuba. His teacher Howard Schug and J.W. Treat focused their emphasis on evangelistic efforts in Latin America.

Abilene had a blind music teacher, Leonard Burford, who made a big impression on Foy when he taught him song leading. Foy said, "He had a pattern for each time, 4/4, 6/8, etc. I don't know how he knew, but if you didn't have the pattern right, he knew."

Foy graduated in 1943, ranking second academically among transfer students to Abilene Christian College. His buddy, Bennie Lee Fudge, ranked first.[143]

North Alabama

When Foy graduated from Abilene he thought about going directly back to Africa but Bennie Lee Fudge talked him into going to North Alabama. Foy said, "He knew all the churches there and could introduce me to them. If I could work among them for a while and get them acquainted with me, I would have a better chance of getting their support [for the work in Africa]. I had in mind to stay there about 5 or 6 years before going back."

Foy had already been to Athens the summer between his Junior and Senior year at Abilene to work for the summer with Jack Rollings at the Market Street congregation. After his first sermon there, brother Bullington, one of the elders (Foy thinks it was J.C Bullington), invited him home for lunch. While relaxing on the front porch with Foy he asked him, "Foy, do you mind if I give you some advice?" Foy responded, "No." The elder said, "For a sermon to be immortal, it doesn't have to be eternal."[144]

Foy's responsibilities at Market Street during the summer of 1942 were to preach, teach the young people's Bible class and do door-to-door evangelistic work. The *Limestone Democrat* reported on July 1, 1943,

> Bro. Foy Short of Southern Rhodesia, Africa, will begin an open-air meeting Sunday night at the Squire Brooks place on the New Cut Road. This meeting and the Carey meeting are the first of a number of such meetings we expect to conduct in new places over the county this year... Irven Lee, A.J. Rollings, M.A. Creel and Foy Short are

working each morning this week with the Grant Street church in Decatur in a Daily Bible school for children.[145]

The *Alabama Courier* and *Limestone Democrat* have a number of such notices in the Church News section about various meetings and projects conducted by Foy and other preachers in Athens and Decatur during the mid 1940s.

The first congregation Foy worked with after graduation was the Memorial Drive congregation in Decatur, Alabama. The congregation had about forty members with the Cagles and McCorkles being some of the stronger families in the congregation. Foy's work involved visiting wayward Christians and door knocking to find new contacts for the gospel.

Athens Bible School

Foy helped his friend Benjamin Lee Fudge with his dream of starting a school with Christian teachers in Athens. The North Alabama Bible School, which eventually became Athens Bible School first met on September 6, 1943, offering classes for students in grades 7-12.[146] Foy was on the first faculty along with Bennie Lee Fudge, Charles Chumley, A.J. (Jack) Rollings, Irven Lee, George Williams, Wayne Mickey and George Hook. Foy taught Algebra, Geography and Bible and was the official bookkeeper since he was a business major at Abilene. He and the other faculty members worked without pay from the school, supporting themselves in various other ways.

Foy had special memories of several of his fellow teachers. He said of Irven Lee, "He was a wonderful man. Though very soft spoken, his lessons were as firm and solid as they could be."[147] That description of Lee, could also describe Foy who shared his temperament and style in numerous ways. Foy mentioned Lee along with A.J. (Jack) Rollings as Alabama preachers (besides Fudge) who had an especially good influence on him.[148] Foy called A.J. Rollings "one of the most passionate men I've known." Then with characteristic understatement he added, "He had a memory for poetry." Hundreds of Athens Bible School alumni who studied American and English Literature under Rollings from the 1940s into the 1980s could attest to that fact!

.

After Foy returned to Rhodesia, his closest friend, Bennie Lee Fudge kept him up to date on news from Athens. For example, Fudge told him in 1948 about the elders of the new Sunset congregation (later Eastside): Carl Richter, Earl Chandler, E.A. Cox and brother Jarrett, the school janitor. He opined that they were the best eldership in Limestone County with the possible exception of the Market Street elders.[149]

Meeting Margaret Hall

Foy's time in Alabama not only established long-term contacts with brethren who could help him for the rest of his life in Africa, but there he found his lifelong companion, Margaret. He had been somewhat interested in a young lady at Abilene but she had no interest in moving to Africa, so according to Foy's daughter, Ellen Baize, "that was that!"[150] However, Margaret would be another story.

Margaret's family came from Eastern Madison County, Alabama. The spiritual strength in the family came from her mother's side of the family. Margaret's maternal grandfather, Joseph David Jones was known as "Walking Bible Jones" in North Alabama and Tennessee.[151] It was said that he memorized the whole Bible![152] His father, Daniel Jones, was a Baptist preacher, but allowed Joe to visit other churches. One day Joe came in and said that he wanted to be baptized into the church of Christ. His father said, "If you do that, pack your bags and move out." However, Joe's mother, Permelia, came to her son's defense and told her husband, "You've said all your life that one church is as good as another. He might as well go to the church of Christ as anywhere else." Later Daniel and Permelia became Christians according to biblical teaching and Daniel preached among churches of Christ in North Alabama and Southern Tennessee. Both

Daniel and his son Joseph worked with Charles Holder. A grainy picture of the two can be found in Holder's biography.[153]

Margaret's mother, Sarah Morris (she was called Morris more than Sarah), was born in Chattanooga, Tennessee. Shortly afterwards, her family moved to Limestone County, Alabama where she lived until her mother died when she was nine. Then she shuttled between different sets of relatives in Madison and Limestone Counties until she became an adult. [154]

She met Shelby Jordan Hall who wasn't a Christian. Ellen Baize said of Hall, "He said he wanted to become a Christian but not before they married because people would say he became a Christian just to marry her."[155] However, after he married Morris he never obeyed the gospel. Therefore Margaret's spiritual influence in her childhood came almost completely from her mother.

Morris spent her adult life in Gurley, Alabama and became such a leader in her home congregation on Hurricane Creek that the congregation became known as the "Morris church." Her granddaughter, Ellen Baize said, "The men didn't know anything about singing. They would announce the song and she would start it from the pew. ... She kept everything going. When she died it folded." Margaret pointed out that in spite of her mother's leadership abilities, she was very careful not to violate the Biblical principle of subjec-

Margaret in the 1940s

tion. She said, "My mother was indeed the driving force in the little congregation, but only because it was forced on her. You wouldn't find anyone more anxious not to usurp authority than she."[156]

Margaret inherited her mother's decisive, achievement-oriented temperament. She graduated early from High School at fifteen years of age and
wanted to attend Freed-Hardeman College but her parents thought she
was too young to travel so far away from home, so she went to a business
college in Huntsville. However, she couldn't get a job because she was
too young. Finally she turned sixteen and got a job with Central Service
Association, which did billing for the various cooperatives and municipali-
ties throughout the Tennessee Valley. She traveled in Southern Tennessee
and Northern Alabama in her work.

Margaret first met Foy when she visited relatives in Athens, attended the
Market Street congregation and heard him preach. He has no memory of
seeing her on that occasion. Afterwards, they had other brief encounters
at social engagements that Foy didn't remember. However, in August of
1944, her landlady, a Mrs. Taylor who was a Christian, said, "I think you'd
enjoy meeting this young preacher down the street." She and Foy therefore
met formally and four months later in December of 1944 they married!
Margaret said, "He proposed not by saying 'Will you marry me?' but rather,
'Will you go to Africa with me?' "[157]

Margaret's mother, Morris, was thrilled at her daughter's choice of a husband. When asked if he ever had problems with his mother-in-law, Foy
said, "No, she treated me better than her own daughters." Ellen Baize said
of her maternal grandmother, "She always wanted a son who was a preacher, but was thrilled that she was going to have a son-in-law who not only
was a preacher but a missionary."[158]

Margaret's decisive temperament was in many ways the opposite of Foy's
easy-going nature and yet opposites like them often attract and make
good couples. Each sees in the other qualities that they themselves need.
Margaret's forthrightness balanced Foy's relaxed style. Foy appreciated his
wife's determination. Only a strong and resolute woman like her could

survive the culture shock of leaving the United States to live in Africa for decades and eventually flourish there. Once when Ellen went to her father to complain about her mother's directness, Foy told her, "You need to be more like your mother."[159] He wrote in 1996, "Margaret is busy packing our suitcases for the Zimbabwe trip — and dragging me protesting all the way, into the fuss and flurry. I'm so glad I married her! She sees that I'm ready to catch planes, etc."[160]

Foy and Margaret's youngest daughter, Kay, mentioned taking her father to a doctor's appointment in Nashville in September 2010. They were early for the appointment, so she decided to take him to Centennial Lake where they watched the ducks and geese swim around the lake. As they watched, she began to tell her father how much she admired his remarkable life and accomplishments and how many people he had touched by his "absolute dedication to his Lord and Savior."

He immediately said, "I couldn't have done it without your mother."[161]

Final Years in Alabama

After Foy married Margaret, he continued to work with the church on Memorial Drive in Decatur but also began to make plans to return to Africa. Finally, Foy resigned from the congregation and from Athens Bible School in the middle of 1946 so that he and Margaret could depart in July 1946. However, after resigning, there were delays, first with passports and then a shipping strike and it became obvious that they weren't going to be able to leave for Africa as soon as they hoped. Then, the Grant Street church supported Foy to work in the Eastern and Southern parts of Decatur where there were many mill workers and wayward disciples. They were able to start a congregation in south Decatur that later became the Somerville Road church of Christ. He started another in east Decatur that was called Eastside. He also preached in various parts of Morgan County where there were no full-time preachers. He reported to the church in Ferris, Texas about a tent meeting in Danville, Alabama.

Last year the audience had numbered about 50 and much opposition had been shown. To our surprise, the audience the first night numbered more than a hundred. ... One night our 150 chairs were insufficient to seat the audience. It was originally planned to run the meeting for ten days. But at the request of the people from the community we went ... for a total of 18 days. There were six who obeyed their Lord in baptism.[162]

Foy's parent's visited North Alabama in May 1947. The *Alabama Courier* printed a picture of them and "their little son, Billy" with the following caption,

Mr. and Mrs. Short are the parents of Foy Short, minister of the Beach St. church of Christ in Decatur and Mrs. Bennie Lee Fudge of Rogersville. Two other daughters, Mrs. Henry P. Ewing and Miss Margaret Ann Short are in Abilene, Texas. This is the Short's first trip home since 1930. They originally went to Africa from Kansas in 1921. They are now visiting their children in this section for a few weeks.[163]

Foy and Margaret's oldest son, Harold, was born while they lived in Decatur. Ellen said that Harold was like a perfect child to her parents. While she and her younger brother Jim were always "rowdy," Harold seemed to always be mature beyond his years. He started preaching in Rhodesia when he was sixteen but soon would face spiritual challenges that would test his young faith. However, such family crises were still far in the future in 1947 when Foy and Margaret finally were able to get their passports and travel arrangements in order. The African frontier was calling them and it was time to go.

Chapter 3

Back to Africa

Foy and Margaret traveled back to Rhodesia with J.C. Reed and his wife, Miriam. Foy had convinced Reed go to Africa when he was at Abilene Christian College. The Reeds had an eighteen month-old toddler, two twins that were six months old and another baby on the way. Harold was twenty-two months old. Though air travel was still more expensive than an ocean voyage in 1947, the Reeds' supporting church offered to pay the difference so that the Shorts could fly with them and help with the babies.

The Shorts left Decatur on a Greyhound bus for New York City where they waited a few days in a hotel for their flight and for the Reeds. The two families were supposed to leave New York on the morning of July 7th, but since there was a storm in the Atlantic they weren't able to actually leave until later in the afternoon. The storm also required them to travel to the Azores Islands through Gander, Newfoundland, instead of going directly as originally planned. They ate most of their meals at the airports along the way; breakfast at Gander, afternoon tea in the Azores and finally supper in Lisbon, Portugal. There, the two families had to wait five hours while the carburetor on one of the plane's engines was repaired. All through the flights and long waits in various airports, Foy, Margaret and the Reeds had to feed and console four babies.

Finally the plane, a four engine Lockheed Constellation named "Golden Fleece" by Pan American[164] left Lisbon and stopped in Dakar, Senegal before arriving at Accra, Ghana about 3 PM on Wednesday. The plane was supposed to take off for Leopoldville, Congo (now Kinshasha, Zaire), but since there were no facilities for night landing in Leopoldville, the decision was made to wait in Accra at a BOAC (British Overseas Airways Corporation, now British Airways) rest house until the early morning of the tenth. Margaret said, "Those of us with small children were given rooms with beds. The rest had to sleep on couches. We left about 3 AM and got to Leopoldville for breakfast."

On the flight from Leopoldville to Johannesburg, South Africa the pilot dropped down from his cruising altitude of 17,000 feet to 5000 feet to circle Victoria Falls. Margaret described the airplane ride as "rough."[165] She said that most of the people on the plane, including Foy, were airsick when it descended for the passengers to view the falls. She and J.C. Reed were among the lucky few who were able to enjoy the view without nausea.

When the families arrived in South Africa, they found out that they would be unable to get tickets on the weekly train to the Rhodesias for three weeks. They didn't have money to stay at the hotel for that length of time, so they contacted the American Consul who was able to pull strings to get them tickets for the train to Rhodesia in one week.

Johannesburg was going through an unusually cold snap when the two American families were there. Margaret said, "Foy had told me that Africa was hot and I wouldn't need any heavy clothes. … I had a coat that I didn't want to get rid of and fortunately had it with me. We had to go buy Harold a heavy coat. … Miriam stayed with her children J.C., Foy and I took Harold and did a lot of sight seeing."

Finally the Shorts and Reeds were able to load their luggage and babies on the train for their trip north into the Rhodesias. After traveling 500 miles the travelers had a one-day layover in Bulawayo where they were able to spend time with brethren. Verna Hadfield told an amusing story about several young girls in the congregation at Colenbrander Avenue in Bulawayo who had only recently been allowed to wear lipstick. When the group decided to go to the train station to greet the Shorts and Reeds, the girls were told that they should leave off the lipstick for the day so as not to offend what would certainly be old-fashioned missionaries. However, when Margaret stepped off the train stylishly dressed and with makeup, Verna reported that the girls were delighted.[166]

After the brief visit with the brethren in Bulawayo, the Shorts boarded another train for their final destination of Namwianga Mission, near Kalomo in Northern Rhodesia. They arrived there at three o'clock in the afternoon the next day.

Foy dutifully reported his travel expenses to the church in Ferris, Texas including bus fare from Decatur to New York, $37.30, train fare from Johannesburg to Kalomo, $56.05 and hotel expenses in New York, $36.94, and Johannesburg, $53.50.[167] The airfare for the family from New York to Johannesburg was $1885.50. Of that amount, Foy and Margaret had to pay $898 apiece for themselves while baby Harold traveled for a mere ten percent of that, $89.50.[168]

Namwianga Mission, Northern Rhodesia

George Scott and W.L. Brown started the Namwianga Mission in 1932. It was about four miles from the town of Kalomo, in Northern Rhodesia.[169] Foy's father built the chapel and several other buildings in the 1950s. In 1947 Alvin Hobby was the principal of the school at Namwianga but wanted to visit the States, so Foy agreed to take his place as principal for six months.

Margaret had prepared herself to deal with primitive living conditions in Africa, and was immediately put to the test. She, Foy and the Reeds were assigned the oldest house in the complex that had been built by Scott and Brown. The Reeds lived in the front part of the house and she and Foy lived in the back, which she described as a kind of "lean to." She said, "The living room had a screen and wasn't enclosed. That's why I kept on saying to Foy,

'How do I know a lion won't jump through?'" She said,

> The only door that locked was the one between the living area
> and two very small bedrooms and a third even smaller one we
> used for bathing and dressing. Any time Foy was away overnight,
> Harold and I would go into that sleeping area before dark and lock
> the door. I had plenty of reading material and stories and nursery
> rhymes to read to Harold. I took in plenty of drinking water and
> anything else we might need through the night. The only time I re-
> member feeling nervous was one night when we had a very severe
> thunder storm and it looked and sounded like the lightning was
> striking all around us.[170]

Foy laughed at the idea of a lion, but several years after she and Foy left, some lions did get into the compound and killed some cattle.[171] When thinking back on his wife's response to living conditions in Namwianga, Foy said, "She was very brave about it."

Shortly after their arrival in Northern Rhodesia, Foy and Margaret went with some of the Americans to villages some distance from Namwianga. The first day of the trip Foy shot a dulker (a small antelope) and the whole group had dulker meat that night for supper. After observing her over a short period, several of the experienced workers told Margaret that she adjusted to African life more quickly than anyone else they knew.[172]

Margaret remembered being careful about snakes, "I would go out at night and take torches and look for snakes and make sure they weren't on the steps or in the toilet." She had been warned to do this as some of the others had actually encountered snakes in kitchens and outdoor toilets. During the six-month stay at the mission, she had no snake scares. However, the week after she and Foy moved out and turned their apartment over to the Hobbys, they encountered a snake on the steps of the house. The champion snake killer among the American evangelists was Gladys Brittell who was "reported to have killed, during her years at Sinde [Mission], some 65 snakes in the neighborhood of the wood pile and the outdoor privy … with a .22 rifle that had no sight."[173]

Bringing water into the house was not easy. Margaret said,
> We got there in the middle of July in the dry season. They had had a drought the year before so water was very scarce. All the other houses had big water tanks that collected rainwater. The house we had had one too but it leaked since no one had used it for a long time so we had no water for drinking. We had to go down to the river and get muddy water. … What we used for drinking was boiled, and then we would let it sit a while.

Foy and Margaret enjoyed the company of their companions at Namwianga Mission. Besides the Reeds, they worked with the J.C. Shewmaker family, the A.B. Reese family, Myrtle Rowe and Sybil Rickman. They often saw other American workers from other missions in Northern Rhodesia: the Brittells from Sinde Mission and Boyd Reese and Eldred Echols from Kabanga. Margaret worked in the mornings as a secretary for the school, while a babysitter watched Harold. Then she took care of Harold in the afternoons. Occasionally she and Foy would go to Kalomo. They didn't have a car so they would put little Harold on the seat of their bicycle and walk along beside it down the road to the little town. Margaret said, "There were some stretches of the road where the sand was not too deep for all three of us to ride, with me on the carrier behind Foy and Harold on the cross bar in front of him."[174] She recalled that the primary businesses in the town were a butcher shop and a department store that was managed by an Indian.

Foy's responsibilities involved teaching and making sure that the other teachers and classes were in order. The first period at the school was always a Bible class, followed by more secular courses. Foy taught math and woodworking. He also made numerous forays into surrounding villages on his bicycle with Eldred Echols to preach. He wrote D.H. Moyers of the Ferris,

Texas church that he, J.C. Reed and Eldred Echols had just returned from a trip to a village where white men had never preached before and baptized 22 people.[175]

He wrote his parents who were visiting Texas a more detailed account of his activities at Namwianga. Regarding an interesting class on evangelism with several young Tonga men he said,

> In the class are Johnson Cigali, John Chongo, Pear Aason, Ephraim, Paul Mweetwa. You may know all or at least some of these. … They ask all kinds of questions, and are very interested in what we are studying. They said the other day that every Christian in Northern Rhodesia ought to be forced to take a course in personal evangelism. I just hope that they will remember some of the things we study together, and will practice them themselves, and will teach others what they themselves have learned.[176]

He mentioned a number of villages that he and Echols visited. "Eldred and I have traveled over 340 miles on our bicycles since the middle of August on preaching trips. So far we have visited Sokis twice, Munakanyemba twice, Sindowe once, and Simapuuka once, Kalefula twice, Mulamaba once and Pukuma once."[177] He gave a weather report. "It is now raining! The first rain since last season. And last season was near drought, so you can imagine how badly rain is needed here."[178]

Foy's childhood ability to speak chiTonga returned to him while at Namwianga. Margaret said, "I think he has a natural knack for learning other languages. I was amazed at how quickly he picked it up again, since he was so young when he left."

Foy laughed when recalling an incident that occurred shortly after he arrived at Namwianga. Some boys were talking among themselves in chiTonga, wondering when the Superintendent of schools for Northern Rhodesia would be coming back from his leave in England. Foy then spoke to them in chiTonga and told them when he was coming back. The boys were absolutely shocked that this new principal could understand and speak their dialect. They got the word out quickly that you couldn't make fun of teachers or talk about sensitive issues around Foy in their native tongue.

Expeditions Into the Zambezi River Valley

While Foy was at Namwianga, he and Eldred Echols made several long overland trips east into isolated areas of the Zambezi River escarpment where no preaching had ever been done by any Western religious group and where many inhabitants had never seen white men. These trips were like several that his father and other pioneers in Zambia took in the 1920s and 1930s. Foy pointed out that there were no roads into the area, not even for wagons, but simply footpaths. They had maps for some areas, but more often than not relied on the directions of the Africans to find villages where they could introduce the natives to Jesus Christ. Often the Americans and their Tonga companions had to chop trees to clear the way. They occasionally only traveled about a mile a day in areas with thick vegetation, but in the savannah country they could cover twelve to fifteen miles a day and occasionally even more.

On Foy and Echol's first trip, they took two Tonga boys and two oxen that dragged a sled made from two forks of a tree.[179] They visited a number of villages where white men had never been seen including one called Pukuma (or Pukuma's village), where they would see some impressive spiritual success when returning several months later. On their first trip, however, the inhabitants of the village were so afraid of them that they fled when Foy and Echols approached. Foy and his companion camped out close to the village to see if they could win the confidence of the villagers. A few eventually ventured forth to watch the two evangelists and finally most of the inhabitants came out to observe them warily from a distance. They were too nervous, however, to receive teaching so the two young men left and eventually returned to Namwianga.

In writing about this trip Eldred Echols wrote a page and half about a misunderstanding between him and Foy about a missing water bag. He thought that Foy had drunk from it, and "berated" him for it, only to find out that one of the Tonga boys had put it in a different place. He felt that the encounter caused their friendship to be "never again as warm and un-guarded as it had been."[180] When asked about the confrontation sixty years later, Foy laughed and said, "I was amused at his summary of things. He felt much more disturbed about it than I was. It never bothered me. Maybe at that time it did, but I soon got over that."

After moving to Bulawayo, Foy chided his best friend Bennie Lee Fudge for not getting along as well with Echols as Foy thought he should, "You and he always manage to cross each other up."[181] Then he said, "Eldred and I got along fine when we were up north together." Foy's letter to Fudge shows that any coolness in the friendship perceived by Echols was not felt by Foy a year later in 1949. He always talked with great respect and fondness for his old friend, Eldred Echols.

Foy and Echol's fact-finding trip to the East encouraged others from the missions to plan a return expedition to the area to try to teach the natives there. This second more ambitious journey to the escarpment and down into the Zambezi River Valley made such an impression on the group, that all who published works about their lives in Southern Africa; Echols, J.C. Shewmaker and Alvin Hobby wrote at length about it. J.C. Reed wrote an article in the *Gospel Advocate*[182] about the trip that included Foy and Eldred Echol's names as co-authors.

The group decided that they would try to take a two-ton Ford Model T truck powered by a charcoal gas producer that Orville Brittell had modi-fied.[183] They loaded it with many of their supplies and an opaque projector powered by a carbide flame with drawings that could be used to present the gospel message. Thus equipped, the expedition set out into the areas previ-ously explored by Foy and Eldred Echols.

Eldred Echols wrote more than eleven pages about the adventures of the second expedition through various villages, but the highlight of the trip was the breakthrough in Pukuma, the village that he and Foy had visited several months earlier. When he, Foy and their companions showed up in Pukuma the second time, they were welcomed as friends. The initial fears of the villagers were replaced with openness.

The evangelists tried to tell the elders about God in a dialect of the chi-Tonga language, using a Tonga brother named Mjuku as their primary interpreter.[184] One of the elders said, "We also believe in a God who created the world, but we don't know how to worship him, or even if he wants us to worship him." The natives said that they sacrificed to their ancestors hoping that they could intercede to this God on their behalf. The evangelists asked the villagers if they didn't think it reasonable that God would tell his people how to prepare themselves to meet him. One of them said, "It does seem reasonable, but we have no knowledge that it is so." The evangelists showed them a Bible and said, "This book is God's word to his people. ... The elder looked at the Bible a moment and then asked. 'Did God himself hand you this?' "

The evangelists reasoned with the villagers about God and his book for several days in the face of some resistance, especially from the women of the village who were led by an elderly woman named Binamoono. Finally on the third day, after a gospel presentation under the starry skies, the chief elder, whose name was Pukuma,[185] dramatically gave his reasons for believing that God had spoken through the book that Short and Echols had brought them. When he finished he said, "I stand." According to Echols, "A shocked tremor went through the groups. Then another man stood, then another and another until finally a large group were standing to profess their faith in Christ."

When recalling the second excursion to Pukuma's village, Foy talked about material used to teach the illiterate natives with the opaque projector. He said,

We … had to have an interpreter to interpret the captions under each slide. Those people all had a strong belief in a great creator God, who created all things. They believed that he created all things and rules in the affairs of men through the spirits of their departed ancestors. We never had to argue about the existence of a God, the creator of all things until the advanced education of our civilization got over there with all the universities.

He also reminisced, "The old, old, old men told of their fathers having had a visit from David Livingstone, when he made his trip through there. None of them, however, had ever seen a white man."[186]

A few months later Foy and Echols returned a third time to Pukuma but were disappointed to find many of the new Christians drunk when they arrived. However, Foy patiently remarked that many Corinthians were at first drunkards.[187] When the villagers sobered up, Foy taught them that they must leave their drinking and be faithful to partake of the Lord's Supper each Sunday. They seemed to respond well to his message and fourteen more were baptized. They helped Echols and him to find other villages in the area where they could preach.

When searching old files in 2010, Ellen Baize found a seven-page type written report by her father about this third expedition into the Zambezi River Valley. In it, Foy mentioned that he and Echol's primary goal was to visit a town called Mulola where the gospel had never been preached. Natives from Pukuma and Siawaza told them that Mulola was "six huts wide and two miles long."[188] Foy wrote about the challenges he and Echols had in trying to maneuver their oxen and supplies down into the Zambezi River Valley, following old trails that often disappeared into the vegetation that was increasingly thick in the lower elevations closer to the river. Though unable to reach Mulola in their allotted time, Foy rejoiced that twenty-one were baptized in all and the new churches in Pukuma and Siawaza were strengthened. Googling "Mulola, Zambia" confirms that there is a place by that name on the Zambezi River[189], though Foy and his companion were unable to reach it.

Eldred Echols reported that when evangelists visited Pukuma years later, there was still a congregation there composed primarily of the women who had originally opposed the Bible message.[190] Googling "Pukuma" turns up information that it is located at 3605 feet in altitude above sea level and that in 2004 it had a population of 1363 and an airstrip.[191]

After moving to Bulawayo, Foy conceded that he might be unable to do this type of work in unexplored regions again. He said that it held "a great appeal" to him. "The simple trustfulness of the primitive African when he realizes you are trying to help him is very appealing."[192] When initially frustrated with his work in Bulawayo, he even wrote his best friend, Bennie Lee Fudge, "I wish I could forget the white work and concentrate on this type of work [among tribal Africans] altogether."[193] Though he would do much village work in the future, most of it would be in towns and rural communities of Matabeleland around Bulawayo, where there had already been at least some exposure to Western culture.

Foy did make at least two other trips into the previously unexplored areas of the Zambezi River Valley. One was with C.H. Bankston, Henry Ewing and Alan Hadfield. On another in about 1959 he went only as far as the Kolomo River with his brother Bill Short, son Harold, Harrison Bankston and Johnny Pretorius.

On the latter trip, Harrison Bankston, who was about fifteen years old, recalled coming to a gorge overlooking the Kalomo River and seeing two crocodiles on a sand bar on the river. Bill Short, the only one who had a rifle, shot one of the crocodiles, which immediately slipped wounded into the water. Foy and the boys found a way to clamber down the embankment to the river and lasso the wounded croc. While trying to drag it out of the water and up the steep side of the embankment, they accidentally knocked

Bill's new rifle off of the rock where he had laid it and with horror they watched it fall into the river below. The next thing they knew, Harrison jumped into the river and successfully recovered the gun, even though he knew that the mate of the croc they killed and perhaps others were still there! Harrison recalled in October 2010, "I didn't tell Dad and Mom about that."[194]

Radio Program from Mozambique

While still at Namwianga mission, Foy and Eldred Echols began to make arrangements to broadcast a shortwave radio program from Lorenço Marques in Mozambique (then Portuguese East Africa) featuring Reuel Lemmons as the speaker. The Central church in Cleburne, Texas sponsored the program.[195] Foy said that the program "had a lot to do with getting work going in South Africa." He said in his six-page summary of his work, "Most of the responses for the correspondence course that was offered were from South Africa."[196] There were few congregations in South Africa in the late 1940s. The church in Johannesburg used instrumental music in worship while the small church in Cape Town had split over its use.

Foy and Margaret handled the encouraging amount of correspondence and feedback that came from the program during the first two years of its operation. He reported in August of 1948 that after a few months he had received 48 requests for Bible material.[197] Foy traveled by train to Durban in 1949 to baptize a contact from the program. Finally, after visiting the Shorts and others in Bulawayo, several families from the States were able to move to South Africa in the early 1950s and follow up on contacts there. By the end of 1950 over five hundred letters had been received in response to the broadcast, about a hundred of them from the area around Johannesburg.[198]

The broadcast led to a constant flow of letters between Foy and Reuel Lemmons, discussing how much singing should be included in the programs, what besides the correspondence course to offer listeners who wrote in, for example, inexpensive New Testaments, tracts, copies of sermons, etc. Foy often sent typed excerpts of letters from listeners to Lemmons. The two even discussed concerns over Lemmons' accent, though Foy felt that most of the concern wasn't from Africans but rather "those out here from the U.S.A."[199] In the same letter he recalled that when visiting Cleburne before leaving for Rhodesia, "I heard you make some announcements … at church services and … I certainly didn't notice any peculiarity in your accent." Lemmons modestly and graciously offered to let someone else do the speaking on the program. "If my 'Texas accent' distracts from the program, then I am just as anxious as anyone else to change speakers and get the most effective man possible."[200] However, Foy thought that the Texas inflection wasn't that big of an issue and that people he talked to about the program "were quite extravagant in their praise of the sermon material and construction."[201]

Foy and his friend, Bennie Lee Fudge, also corresponded extensively about the radio program since Fudge was constantly promoting contributions for it among churches in North Alabama. Some would promise to help, but then be late with their payments, which brought complaints from the church that was sponsoring it.

In discussing the content of the broadcast Foy told Fudge,

> We want to avoid anything … that might give the impression that we are trying to import an American religion into this country. If the people ever get that idea, we are finished. The theme must be strictly and emphatically a plea for a restoration of New Testament Christianity. We want to avoid giving the impression that we are another denomination trying to proselyte followers. Our theme must be simply, "Back to the Bible." For that reason, we do not want to sign off with any such statement as "You have just been listening to a religious programme sponsored by the Ferris Church of Christ." We do not want to invite people to join our group, we want to invite them to come to the Bible and take their stand on it alone.[202]

Grappling With Doctrinal Problems

After Foy left Namwianga, his friend J.C. Reed who stayed there became very discouraged with several situations in Northern Rhodesia (Zambia). He wrote in 1949 about what he felt to be a de facto missionary society there, the "General Meeting of the Churches of Christ Missions Registered."[203] He gave a several specific objections to the organization:

1. It secures the permits for all workers coming into the country, thus controlling the entry of workers.
2. It owns all the church property in N.R.
3. Through its placement of missionaries and native teachers it, in actual practice, controls the churches.
4. It pays native teachers for preaching during vacation months. (This should be done by the church.)
5. It is such a mess that some of the missionaries make no effort to keep the schoolwork and the church work distinct.
6. The situation is further aggravated by the fact that the women vote in the general meeting and have the power by fact of being more numerous than men to control the church through this means.[204]

He added, "This is the worst mess that I have ever been mixed up in." Interestingly enough, Foy defended the "General Meeting of the Churches of Christ Missions" against Reed's charges in a series of letters to Bennie Lee Fudge. In essence he said that the organization was necessary to get workers into the country and fulfill legal requirements in other areas.[205] He asked Fudge, "Is the Athens Bible School a missionary society?"[206] Fudge, however, wasn't convinced by Foy's arguments saying, "I'm still bothered about the organization set up in Northern Rhodesia. It may be all right, but it sure looks like a step in the wrong direction to me."[207] He then pointed out what he perceived to be weaknesses in Foy's reasoning. However, he said, "In spite of my misgivings I am not about to fly the coop and start a racket about the Northern Rhodesia work. I know that there is plenty I don't understand." As for Foy's comparison of the National Association in Northern Rhodesia/Zambia with Athens Bible School, Fudge said, "I see absolutely no comparison. That organization by its very name 'Churches of Christ Missions' is doing the work of the church. Athens Bible School is not."[208] The issue dominated correspondence between Foy and Fudge in the latter part of 1949 and came up time and again for several more years. Foy generally defended the "Churches of Christ Missions" organization while Fudge expressed strong doubt about it.

Years later, when thinking of this exchange, Foy thought that though some of Reed's concerns were legitimate, others were probably overblown. Also, it should be pointed out that Fudge's concerns had nothing to do with the "sponsoring church plan" because he and Foy both thought that such an arrangement was acceptable in the early 1950s. Fudge was simply concerned that that the title, "General Meeting of the Churches of Christ Missions," indicated something akin to a missionary society.

There were also concerns through the 1930s and 1940s that brethren in Southern Africa were too soft in their opposition to premillennialism, the theory that Jesus will return to earth to reign a thousand literal years. The premillennial publication *Word and Work* had promoted the work in Southern Africa from the very beginning and several early preachers there, S.D. Garrett in particular, promoted the concept. Though most preachers in the region in the latter 1940s did not believe the theory, J.C. Reed felt that many were too tolerant of it. He was particularly concerned about the arrival of Arthur T. Phillips, an avowed premillennialist, and the warm welcome he was given by most of his fellow workers at Namwianga. By the time Phillips arrived in Namwianga, Foy had already gone to Bulawayo and therefore wasn't involved directly in the controversy about him, but expressed to Bennie Lee Fudge that he felt his friend Reed had overreacted and used unwise tactics in trying to get his fellow evangelists in Namwianga to take a harder line against Phillips. When J.C. Reed returned to the States in 1951 because of discouragement with trends at Namwianga Mission he wrote an article in the *Gospel Guardian* documenting his concerns.[209]

On another front, Bennie Lee Fudge wrote Foy about Alvin Hobby's visit to Nashville "under B.D. Morehead's wing."[210] Hobby was the principal of the Namwianga School whom Foy had temporarily replaced. Morehead had been accused of sympathizing with premillennialists.[211] Fudge said in his letter, "Brother Goodpasture was terribly wrought up over it, and I had to do some tall talking in Hobby's defense." However, Fudge felt that Hobby was learning that it would be difficult to work with premillennialists. "Hobby sent an article to the *Word and Work*, appealing to the premillennialists to cease their teaching on the question and Bro. Bolls refused to publish it, on the ground that to do so would be to agree to cease teaching the Bible. He gave Alvin quite a rebuke, which I think has helped him quite a lot."

Foy wrote back to Fudge about conversations he had with his friend, J.C. Shewmaker. He told Shewmaker that if a man "believed the theory but kept it to himself and made no effort to teach it, I certainly would have no right to refuse to allow him to eat the Lord's supper with us."[212] However if someone promoted the theory, Foy could not "support, endorse or encourage" that person.

Though the controversy about premillennialism waned in Southern Africa, it would be replaced in the1960s by disagreements about institutionalism.

Moving to Bulawayo

A few months after Foy and his family arrived at Namwianga mission, F.L. Hadfield from the English-speaking Colenbrander Avenue congregation in Bulawayo, Southern Rhodesia, contacted him and several others about the possibility of moving there to work with the church. Hadfield, who helped start the congregation, was the most influential leader in the late 1940s. Though Hadfield and others in Bulawayo staunchly defended the right of the congregation to use instrumental music in their assemblies for worship, they did not go along with the modernist tendencies in the Christian Church. In fact, they rejected a "Disciples" preacher from South Africa because he denied the virgin birth. Margaret said, "They were much more conservative than that!"

Foy said,
> The congregation had worked out a compromise with the Bailey family from the "Old Paths" churches in England and Jimmy Claassen who was also opposed to an instrument. They did not use it in the Sunday morning "breaking of bread" service and the others did not attend the evening services where they did use it.[213]

Margaret recalled that when she, Foy and several others traveled to Bulawayo to consider working with the congregation, they stayed in the guesthouse of the White Star Poultry farm that was managed by Leonard Bailey who was also the co-owner. The brethren finally asked Foy to work with them, agreeing to dispense with the organ completely for a six-month trial period.

Foy's father had always been concerned about the lack of work done among the English speaking population of Rhodesia and had encouraged Foy to consider dedicating himself primarily to that type of work when he returned from the States. The invitation of the Colenbrander congregation opened the doors for him to pursue that plan.

Foy and Margaret made their plans to leave Namwianga to move with Harold to Bulawayo in January of 1948, just after the Hobbys returned from the States. The only possessions that they had were their clothes, a second hand sewing machine that had originally belonged to Margaret's mother and a mimeograph machine. With youthful optimism they set out for Bulawayo and a new life there.

Foy estimated that Bulawayo had about 30,000 whites in 1948, mainly of British descent, who lived around the town center. There were larger numbers of mixed race and Ndebele Africans in adjoining areas. Many English servicemen who had been stationed in the area during the Second World War fell in love with it and chose to make their homes there after the war. It was used as a training ground for RAF pilots who were easy prey for German fighter aircraft when learning to fly over England. Housing was therefore in short supply and very expensive.

While waiting to find their own housing, Foy, Margaret and Harold moved in with the Jimmy Claassen family who had a large two-story house. Claassen was the man after whom Foy and Margaret named their second son Jim, and Gladys, his wife, was the daughter of F.L. Hadfield.[214] The Shorts lived in one room and ate their meals with their hosts. Margaret and Gladys Claassen shared the costs and also the planning of meals.

When Foy first arrived in Africa he received $200 a month from his supporting church in Ferris, Texas. The brethren there thought that surely he would need more, but Foy felt that $200 per month would suffice. However, after arriving in Bulawayo with its booming economy, Foy realized he would need more and the congregation at Ferris upped his salary to $250 a month.[215] According to Margaret, Foy was always reluctant to ask for more salary than that which would be necessary to live close to the poverty line. None of the young couples at Colenbrander Avenue were well off, but they wondered why the American brethren didn't send the Shorts more.[216] Foy told Margaret that many people sacrificed to send them and that they should be willing to sacrifice too and Margaret was willing to do just that. Margaret helped supplement the family income a little, "enough for voice lessons," by keeping books for a small furniture factory. Later with Foy's help she kept books for a slightly larger factory. She believed that their supporting congregation would have sent more if Foy had asked for it, but he was reluctant to do so.

The congregation that met on Colenbrander Avenue, with about 25 members, had been influenced by English customs. For example, services were organized and conducted by one man called the presider who called on others for participation. There were chain prayers and the women covered their heads during prayer.

At the end of the six-month trial period, the Shorts were invited to stay on permanently, with one of the older men telling them, "The young people prefer you to the instrument."[217] The young people in the congregation were mainly children and grandchildren of the Christian families who had come from New Zealand. There were several young married couples. Most of the singles were in their late teens and early twenties. There were also some younger children from that area who attended Sunday school.[218]

Nine months after arriving in Bulawayo, Foy and Margaret were finally able to rent a house in the new suburb of Queens Park East. A note from Jimmy Claassen's doctor stating that he was a nervous kind of person and needed to have children out of his house, helped cut through some of the paper-work.

To provide more housing as cheaply and quickly as possible, the houses were built with what was called pisa construction. The walls were built of mud packed into frames and then painted. They were jokingly called mud huts! However, they served their purpose and Foy and Margaret said the house looked pretty good to them. Their house was on the second row of houses to be built.[219] They had to do without many conveniences, especially in the beginning. She said, "Our toilet was not usable at first, as the sewer trenches were still being dug. So, there were small temporary buildings wired to pegs in the ground and with buckets that were picked up every day by the city's sanitation department."[220]
She added,

> During that time somebody sent us some used clothing. We used the clothing to buy several chairs, a dining table and several small tables. Some of this furniture looked quite good and we brought one of the larger chairs and some of the small tables back to the States with us for the children to keep. African men would take the

articles of clothing and then go door to door to sell them. They preferred to have used clothing to money as there was a big demand for the clothing in the townships and they made more money selling them.

She added, "We didn't have a refrigerator during the first years we were out there. Unwrapped meat and bread were delivered by bicycle."

The Shorts' primary mode of transportation after moving to Bulawayo (besides their two feet) was a 1925 motorcycle that Orville Brittell improvised for them. Margaret said, "The pillion seat was quite high in the back. I would ride on the back and Foy and Harold would ride on the tank." The road from the Claassens' house into town was strip road. When cars met, they each moved over to the side keeping one set of wheels on a strip of pavement. Motorcycles did not have to move off the strip of pavements onto the gravel, but bicycles did. Foy and Margaret's motorcycle only had a bicycle light, so at night they had to move off the strip as cars could not sense that the approaching vehicle was a motorcycle. All of the maneuvering on and off the paved strip on the motorcycle was quite frightening to Margaret.[221]

Margaret recalled how their transportation improved after moving to Queens Park:

> Soon after we moved to Queens Park, Leonard Bailey gave us a baby Ford open tourer with a canvass top, which I replaced at once with my Singer [sewing machine]! This little car gave us good service and Foy used it for visiting churches in rural areas over very poor roads. In October of 1949 the pound was devalued, so the rate of exchange was then two dollars to the pound instead of four. This increase in salary enabled us to make a down-payment on a small English Austin pickup, with a canopy, which made it possible to carry passengers in the back. By that time, a number of families had moved from Queens Park as houses became available in more

affluent suburbs. We began to drive to several areas to pick up Sunday school children who had moved, so we got the pickup for this just when we needed it. Bro. Claassen did some of this with his large Chevrolet. Later on, others also helped.

Brethren help push the "baby Ford" out of the sand.

The devaluation also allowed the Shorts to manage a down payment on a small refrigerator. Margaret said,

October is very hot there — it is called suicide month — so what a welcome addition that was. It was supposed to be delivered one Saturday morning but they weren't able to do so until Monday. I had so anticipated it that I felt I could hardly get along without one for another two days, even though it had been two years and three months since I had had one![222]

Teaching Children in Queens Park

Soon after Foy and Margaret moved into their new two-bedroom home in Queens Park in September of 1948, while he was preaching at Colenbrander Avenue, he and Margaret decided to start teaching neighborhood children and teens in their home on Sundays. The Colenbrander Avenue congregation agreed that this would be a worthwhile project. Several members from that congregation brought the few children that had been studying there to the children's Bible study at Queens Park and also helped with the teaching. Foy felt that he was greatly helped in his teaching of the children by the fact that there was no "competition" from other churches of any kind in the immediate area. Of this work he said,

When we started having Sunday school in our house, I went around to every house in that suburb inviting people and again and again I was commended. The people said, "Our church isn't doing anything out here. And we want our children to go to Sunday school." So it was really a golden opportunity that dropped in our lap.

Margaret recalled,

We had classes in the kitchen, living room and both bedrooms and finally our next-door neighbor offered us the use of one room …
For seating in the classes, Foy assembled picnic-type tables, held together with large bolts, so they could be assembled when needed and then taken down and stacked against the back wall of the house. There were no sidewalks and even the side streets were not paved at first, so when it rained, a lot of red mud was tracked into the house. Fortunately, they were cement floors and we had a yard worker who came in and washed them.

I will be forever grateful to Auntie Gladys Claassen for giving us lunch every Sunday through all the years we were having services there. We could just take the tables down, go to lunch and have clean floors when we came back![223]

Ellen Baize found a circular letter in an old file that her father wrote after five sessions of the "Sunday School" to distribute to homes in Queen's Park. The letter, dated March 10, 1949 advised parents that 17 children attended the first Sunday School session, 25 the second, 48 the third, 45 the fourth and 56 the fifth Sunday. Eventually the Shorts enrolled 120 children in their Sunday Bible classes. Foy advised the parents that there were four classes for children from preschool through fourteen years of age and reassured them that the teachers were experienced and furnished with good material. As to which denomination sponsored the Sunday School, Foy wrote, "We the teachers are doing our best to be strictly UN-DENOMINATIONAL. We plan and try to teach nothing but the un-denominational Bible story of God and His dealings with man-kind, and of Jesus and His loving work of redemption."[224]

One of the homes Foy visited was that of a nine-year old Paddy Kendall-Ball. Kendall-Ball was born in South Africa and his family moved to Bulawayo in 1947 by way of Northern Rhodesia/Zambia. His parents worked in various stores in towns and mining areas in Southern Africa. Kendall-Ball said, "One day a man with thinning hair knocked on the door. 'My name's Foy Short and we're starting Bible classes for children here in Queens Park on Sundays.'" Paddy's father, though not a religious man, encouraged his four oldest children to attend the Bible classes in the Short's home. Rona Claassen taught Kendall-Ball his first Bible class. He became a Christian at fourteen years of age and after a brief "falling away" as a teenager to pursue sports, he became a protégé of Foy's, studying intensively with him as a young man and eventually dedicating himself to preaching the gospel.

Beginning Work Among the amaNdebele

When Foy arrived in Bulawayo there were only about four congregations composed of African brethren around Bulawayo that had been taught

Foy using a translator to preach in a small village.

by men from the Christian Church from New Zealand. He said, "Soon after we got there, I conducted a three week Bible study course for the African preachers who came in from the countryside. … They knew nothing about Bible authority: what it was, how to establish it, how to follow it. That was the main thing I stressed." Foy wrote in August 1949,

Today is the second day of a 10 days special training course for native leaders of the church in this area. We have ten men in the class. … We have four one hour courses each day in each of the following: The New Testament Church, Denominational Doctrines,

Problems of the African Evangelist, Preparation of Sermons. These fellows are as keen as mustard. They keep the questions coming as fast as I can answer them. … It is a joy to teach such enthusiastic seekers after truth.[225]

Newman Gumbo is a respected evangelist who has been preaching for many years in Zimbabwe. His mother was a Christian that lived in the Rangemore area, just out of Bulawayo. Gumbo told Ellen Baize that their early teachers from the Christian church set up a system where if you were a man, you were required to give one shilling each week; if you were a woman, you were to give sixpence; and children were to give a tickey (three pennies). If you did not have the money, it was written down and an account kept of how much you owed God. Foy, of course, taught them that giving must be as they prospered and from the heart. Gumbo recalled that his mother and the others were very happy when they realized that God did not make this rule. They no longer had this burden of owing God money, but could give freely.[226]

Foy found that the Ndebele preachers wanted to learn about differences between the Biblical pattern and the teaching of different religious denominations that were in their villages. After his helplessness in facing Mormon missionaries as a young man on the ship to America, Foy sympathized completely with their plight, and dedicated large portions of his teaching sessions to contrasting the Bible approach to serving God with that of the popular religious denominations. Foy described a typical study session with his Ndebele brethren. "Normally there were tons of questions. If there was a lull in the questions I would start discussing a particular denomination and the doctrines that characterized that denomination." Foy felt that emphasizing the difference between the work and worship of Bible churches as opposed to that of popular religious denominations was one of the keys to the steady growth of churches in Matabeleland.

Foy's teaching efforts among the amaNdebele involved two approaches:
(1) going into their villages and teaching the churches one on one, and
(2) occasionally during the off season when the brethren weren't plowing
or working extensively in the fields, inviting them for a two or three week
session of extensive studies in Bulawayo. Shortly after Foy began his sessions with the African teachers, one of them said, "Now we can go out and
fight the enemies of the gospel. Now we have the weapons to fight them
with what the Bible says."

During the late 1940s and 1950s, several times a month Foy made trips of
between two and four days into the country, sleeping on the ground outside of the villages. Sometimes the whole family went with him. Foy said
that during that time it was completely safe to do so, something that would
unfortunately change in later years. Margaret remembered a long trip to a
congregation near the Botswana border in the early 1950s. She said, "The
flies were so bad, I had to keep everything covered up. We made beds on
the ground."

Foy reported to the brethren in Ferris, Texas about a trip to a community
about 110 miles west of Bulawayo. The first night of the meeting he issued
a challenge in reply to a charge by opposing preachers in the area that the
African brethren were preaching something "which no white man would
embrace." Foy wrote,

That charge had a profound effect on the natives. They have a
boundless confidence in the intelligence and wisdom of the white
man and so they embraced that if no white man would embrace the
teaching, then surely it must be because there was no truth in it.

Of course my appearance on the scene as a white member was
a partial answer to the charge. Then I offered a reward of 5 pounds
to any person who would show us the scripture that named the
London Missionary Society (leading denomination in the area)
or the Catholics or the Methodists. The next day that neck of the

wood fairly hummed. I met one man in the village the next day who said that he had searched his New Testament and found that my words were true. Native members told me that discussions and arguments had raged in every village and at every gathering in the area the next day. The result was that the second night we had over 500 present for service. The London Missionary Society preacher … dismissed his service and brought his entire flock to attend our services. At that service I repeated my offer and mentioned the fact that so far there had been no claimants for the reward. I also emphasized the fact that we must go by the Bible alone in religious matters …[227]

After services the second night of the meeting twenty-one people requested baptism. Though they had difficulty at first finding enough water in the dry season, Foy found a farmer four miles away with a small pond, who reluctantly granted permission to use it for baptisms. The final number of those baptized was 40.

Foy described some of the unique features of these large evening evangelistic meetings in the villages of the amaNdebele in 1950,

The singing at these night services is a curious affair to newcomers to this country. Barring an occasional flickering little kerosene storm lantern, there is usually no kind of lighting system apart from the smoky wood fire. Consequently the majority of the audience is in darkness. And even if sufficient lights were available, so few have songbooks that 90 per cent of the audience would be unable to sing from books. To overcome these difficulties the song leader cuts off quickly at the end of each line, and shouts out as fast as he can the words of the following line, then immediately begins singing with the congregation. This takes a great deal of breath and quick thinking, but some of them are so proficient at it that scarcely a beat is lost throughout the entire song. Of course, unless you are an expert linguist, it is rarely possible to distinguish the words shouted out by the song leader, he says them so fast.[228]

The initial successes among the amaNdebele in the late 1940s and early 1950s would be precursors of ever increasing spiritual opportunities in Matabeleland.

The Work at the Colenbrander Avenue Church

The Colanbrander congregation met in the prosperous northern section of Bulawayo. Foy began his work by knocking on doors of the homes in the area, trying to stir up interest in the gospel among the inhabitants, but he soon found out that affluence and hunger and thirst for righteousness aren't often companions. He didn't have much success with his door knocking efforts.

Foy and Margaret also knew that the differences about instrumental music might not be easily resolved, but they worked diligently to establish good personal ties with the group. Margaret said, "We got together socially one night a week and had frequent Saturday trips to the Matobo Hills for picnics and climbing. Some of those granite hills were quite sloping and easy to climb, even with Harold. Others were more challenging and one in particular was extremely challenging!"[229] She was amazed that F.L. Hadfield, who she called "Grandpa Hadfield" and "a remarkable man," could climb the hills with the young people. Regarding Hadfield she said, "We had great respect for him in spite of doctrinal disagreements." He once told Margaret, "Every time I see you with your baby I think of Radiant Motherhood."

From the very beginning, Foy and Margaret practiced singing with members of the congregation. They were helped by the fact that both were musically talented. Margaret said, "We were determined to show people how good singing could be without an instrument."[230] Gladys Claassen, who had experience conducting school choirs, helped them with the singing practice and the Shorts came to have a deep love for her. She provided invaluable service to them for many years not only at Colenbrander Avenue but also later at Queens Park, even though they never were able to convince her that instrumental music in worship was unauthorized. Margaret said, "We would sit around at the Claassen's dining table at night and learn all the songs in the hymnbook, *Great Songs of the Church Number Two* except one or two that nobody particularly liked." She mentioned learning the rather difficult hymn, "*O Lord our Lord, How Excellent is thy Name.*" The congregation also continued to use a British songbook, which Margaret said, "had some lovely songs not in the other book."

In spite of increasingly close personal ties and improved acappela singing in the congregation, the older people still weren't happy about not using their organ and made efforts to defend its use. Foy had to sit through Bible classes where instrumental music in worship was defended with arguments such as "Grandpa" Hadfield's that only the parts of the Old Testament that were sealed with blood at Mount Sinai were taken away by Christ's death. Therefore, according to Hadfield, all its other precepts, including the use of instruments, were still in force unless specifically mentioned as being abrogated in the New.[231] Foy tried to respond diplomatically that this line of reasoning if applied consistently would force us to prohibit raising mules, wearing clothes made of several types of material and command us to stone those who profaned God's name, because such laws weren't "sealed with blood" on Mt. Sinai, nor specifically rescinded in the New Testament. Later Foy had an informal debate with Hadfield on the issue and Foy felt that Hadfield lost his composure while he kept his, resulting in more sympathy for his position.[232]

On another occasion, a brother asserted that those who opposed instrumental music in worship were "narrow minded and bigoted and had the same kind of spirituality as the Pharisees."[233] Foy decided to respond gently to such attacks both in his private and public teaching. His quiet approach had a great effect on many of the younger Christians. After writing about the Christian who had insulted him and others who believed in acapella singing in worship he wrote, "Fortunately the young people of the congregation show a different attitude with the exception of one or two. It is with them that I think I am accomplishing something."

The disagreements about instrumental music at Colenbrander Avenue were discouraging to Foy and Margaret during the first year of their work. They thought about going to Johannesburg and following up contacts from the radio program there. However, Foy's parents and the Jimmy Claassen family encouraged them to stay.

Foy wrote about this challenging time.

> We ... were told by missionaries in other parts of the Rhodesias as well as some visiting preachers from the States that we were wasting our time in Bulawayo. We were about ready to follow their advice and go to South Africa when one day while singing in the car — Harold was about three and was joining in the singing by then. We sang, "If I have longed for shelter in thy fold when thou hast given me some fort to hold, dear Lord, forgive." We decided then that we had been given a fort to hold.[234]

After singing about the necessity to hold the fort, Foy and Margaret determined not to give up the work in Bulawayo. Margaret said, "After deciding that we needed to stay, we began to evaluate more clearly what had been accomplished such as the progress with the young people at Colenbrander and the work among the African brethren. We soon began to see further progress."[235]

Near the end of 1949, three families from the States came to Bulawayo and stayed several months while waiting for permission to go to South Africa. The Colenbrander congregation had to do an extensive amount of paperwork to obtain permission for them to stay several months in Southern Rhodesia. The American families were uncomfortable with the British worship customs and began to press Foy to oppose them. Two of the families were particularly forceful in their objections. Though Foy agreed with the American brethren on some issues, especially that there should be no instrumental music in worship, he sympathized with the Europeans and New Zealanders of the congregation on others, for example, the need for women to be covered when praying. Foy and Margaret felt uncomfortable with the aggressiveness that their American friends displayed in confronting their brethren.

After some exchanges with the American visitors, Foy wrote Bennie Lee Fudge asking his opinion of 1 Corinthians 11:1-16 to see if the two agreed that women should be covered when praying.[236] They did. He also expressed concern to Fudge about differences with some of his American visitors about moderate drinking of alcoholic beverages, smoking and frequent attendance of "picture shows."

Two of the Americans wrote an article titled, "Seventeen Things that are Wrong with the Bulawayo Church." Without consulting Foy, they sent it off to be published in the States.[237] Before the article could be given wide circulation, it came to the attention of the church that supported Foy. An elder there strongly defended Foy, saying in effect, "Brother Short has kept us completely informed about the situation in Bulawayo. The things that he tolerates are not unscriptural but matters of culture. We know exactly what is going on and have every confidence that what brother Short is doing what is right. And I will thank you if you will keep your nose out of our business."[238] Margaret said of the Americans, "They were stirring up a lot of ill feeling... They never did understand the people there or the work we were doing, what we had accomplished and were still accomplishing, and were very critical." There was a discussion one night in the Shorts' house in Queens Park that upset Foy and Margaret. She said,

> One man was so rude to brother Hadfield that we could hardly
> sleep after they all left. We were just so upset that they had been so
> rude to this elderly man … We were very upset and disappointed

that the visitors had created so much unpleasantness and ill will. This was the last straw for the older folks and they began to agitate to have the instrument back, or else they would start worshipping with the Baptists down the street. This situation really left us with no option but to leave and start another congregation. As stated before, we knew that a separation would likely be necessary eventually, but would have liked a little more time and certainly would have preferred to leave under more pleasant circumstances.[239]

A month after his American friends clashed with brother Hadfield, Foy read a lengthy statement to the congregation in which he "explained thoroughly and kindly" their reasons for starting another congregation.[240] The next Sunday Foy, Margaret, the Bailey and Claassen families and several of the young couples and single members met for worship in the Short's home in Queens Park.

Foy and Margaret maintained cordial relations with brother Hadfield and the brethren at Colenbrander Avenue. She said,

Though I had always been happy in the company of our Rhodesian friends, I sometimes said to Foy, "Wouldn't it be nice to have some fellow Americans come out for a while?" After the experience of having some come, I realized I had a lot more in common with the Rhodesians than those particular ones at least and never had any such thoughts again! I was truly at home there![241]

Beginning Worship Services in Queens Park

The Shorts and their companions had several immediate obstacles to overcome when starting the new congregation. Few of the residents in the community had heard anything about serving God without belonging to a denomination and wondered if some peculiar new American sect was being established in their midst. Also, the idea of having services anywhere except a church building or cathedral was strange to most of them.

However, the contacts made through the children and teens opened doors more quickly than would have been possible otherwise. By this time a number of young people were old enough to be baptized into

One of the first services in the new building at Queens Park.

Christ and through them, the Shorts were able to convert some of their parents.[242] Foy said, "Among those baptized in those first few years were such gems as Paddy Kendall-Ball and Carol (Roberts) Bankston, two that will be known by many church members over here, Christine Drinkwater Roberts, Barbara Tilbury, Jackie and Robert Watts, Fred and Leonard Cluley, Glenn, David and Jean Kidwell and Paddy's siblings, Eileen and Ken. Some family members were baptized a few years later, e.g. Reg and Ann Kidwell."[243]

Foy wrote in April of 1953,

> The work is growing here now by leaps and bounds. I am so happy I can scarce contain myself. Last Sunday morning with that fine crowd of about 40 present, the biggest number we've had at services since starting the work in Queens Park, Margaret sat with tears in her eyes almost throughout the entire service, and I could scarcely speak part of the time. But the tears were tears of joy and gratitude. … We feel that we are over the "hump" now.[244]

Paddy Kendall-Ball talked about Foy and Margaret's influence upon the young at Queens Park:

> They worked wonderfully with the young people. He wasn't buddy-buddy with them, but just gave them a lot of attention. In return they received tremendous respect from the young people. Their

home was opened constantly. You could go to their house at any time and talk to them or have lunch or supper with them. Every Friday night they had young people in their house. That's where a lot of the young people bonded together… He played baseball, British bulldog and all sorts of stuff with us. They were young enough in those days.

Margaret had a very important role in building up the work at Queens Park. Her daughter, Kay, recalled that Carol Bankston told her mother that without the love she received from her, she might never have become a Christian. Carol was extremely shy as a young girl, but Margaret made a point of including her in activities and making her feel special. That special attention made a difference in young Carol's life at a time when her shyness was about to cause her to stop attending Sunday morning Bible classes.[245]

In 1951 Margaret's doctor swapped houses with the Shorts because he had been offered an office on the corner next door to their house. So, the Shorts moved into their new, three-bedroom house with a slightly larger living room for services.

Emphasis on Singing, Training the Young

Foy, Margaret and the others continued to emphasize singing in the new congregation, using the same book they had been using for practice from the beginning in Bulawayo, *Great Songs of the Church Number Two*. Ellen Short Baize recalled, "We had singing class before service on Sunday evening. They would emphasize simple things like, 'Watch the song leader and start with him… If you're saying we can't have instrumental music, you need to have good singing.'"[246] Margaret said, "We had special practices with the young folks to teach them four-part singing. One thing we always emphasized was using correct phrasing instead of just pausing because it was the end of a bar, thus understanding better what we sang."[247] She added, "Several of the new converts had good voices and some knowledge of music. For instance, members of Kidwell family were musical and Mrs.

Kidwell had a lovely soprano voice." The group invited the parents from the neighborhood to services to see how well the children were learning. One Scottish lady said, "I couldn't believe that singing. I thought surely there was an organ."

Henry and Beth Ewing arrived later in about 1953 and helped Foy and Margaret's efforts to train the congregation to sing well and preach in the community. Beth was Foy's sister. According to Paddy Kendall-Ball, Ewing had an open, engaging way of encouraging the new young Christians that was a great blessing to the growing group. Ewing taught the young people to sing the *Hallelujah Chorus,* adding to the already impressive repertoire that Foy, Margaret and others had been developing from the beginning.[248] The singing tradition at Queens Park continued into the 1970s. Sewell Hall said that when he visited in the late 1970s, "The Queens Park auditorium had a big ring and it made fifty people singing sound like 500."

Paddy Kendall-Ball called Queens Park in the 1950s "A breeding ground for young Christians." Melville Sheasby was one of the young men from Queens Park who later grew up to preach the gospel. He said, "The congregation was a very friendly one and the men most involved in leading it were a close-knit group. We had many thrilling spiritual experiences..." Sheasby wrote in his blog about experiences with the Queens Park Church.[249]

Services were still conducted in the style of English Old Paths churches. There would be a presiding brother who would sit behind the Lord's table and announce those who would read, serve at the Lord's table, lead singing, etc. After the lesson the presider would make the announcements.

When asked to give his impression of Foy during his years at Queens Park, Kendall-Ball recalled his comportment during a debate in the building conducted with a leader from a religious sect.

Foy had a distinct way of holding his Bible. It was soft covered.
The left side rolled back in his left hand to reveal the text in front
of him. I remember him standing up there... I thought, "This guy
is a bulldog." He didn't get angry, he didn't get uptight he just very
calmly said, "This is what the scripture teaches." As he read the
text, I thought, "This is force! This is like a bulldog! He's got hold of
something and he's not going to let it go!" That was my impression.

Jim Short recalled that Africans had several nicknames for his father. One
was "Mr. BCV" (Book, Chapter and Verse) for his insistence on Bible authority. He said, "Another name that they have told me they use for him is
"Harde Kop" which is an Afrikaans expression for 'Hard head.' Their mean-
ing, though, is not someone who is simply stubborn or unwilling to listen
to reason, but ... holding on relentlessly to truth."[250]

The men at Queens Park conducted men's training classes. They taught
song leading and how to conduct the Lord's Supper, Bible reading and
preaching. Those who participated in the preaching class had to prepare
five-minute talks, and then after delivering them take advice from those
who listened about how to improve their delivery. Later the men would be
asked to speak extemporaneously on different topics or Bible verses. Paddy
Kendall-Ball said, "For a while they had one of the young men preaching
every Sunday night for ten or fifteen minutes. Then, one of the older guys
would preach ... For us young fellows, that was a real training ground."

Foy encouraged brethren from Queens Park to join his efforts to help the
growing Ndebele churches. Every Sunday several mature men would take
younger men with them to visit their African brethren in rural churches
around the area. Paddy Kendall Ball recalled his first visit to a rural congregation in Stanmore with Henry Ewing. He said in 2008, "The congregation
is still there." When returning about twenty-five years later to the congregation in Stanmore an older disciple came up to him after he finished his ser-

mon and said, "I remember you from when you preached your first sermon here … You preached on faith from Hebrews 11."

Kendall-Ball recalled visiting one congregation with five brethren from Queens Park.

> They wanted all of us to preach. We preached about 20 minutes. The older men preached longer. When one of the older men thought you'd preached enough, they would just start singing wherever you were in your sermon. That was the sign that it was time to stop. … Going to the African brethren was a wonderful experience for us.

Children

The Shorts added three children to their family while in Bulawayo. Ellen was born on August 10, 1949. Foy proudly wrote the church in Ferris, Texas, "I must tell you about our new little daughter. She was born about 8:25 A.M. on August 10. She weighed 8 lbs. 5 oz at birth."[251] Foy and Margaret named her Ellen Marie. When it was time to go to the hospital for the birth, the Shorts little Ford wouldn't start! Foy laughed and said, "Margaret couldn't drive so I had to be in the car." Margaret said, "I wasn't an experienced enough driver to know just when to try to get it into gear again after it picked up speed!"[252] Margaret said that the medical service in Bulawayo was excellent for the birth of her children. She gave birth in a special maternity hospital, the Lady Rodwell Maternity Hospital, where all the nurses were also midwives.

Ellen was always close to her father. She thrived as a child in Bulawayo and Gwelo and feels that she received an excellent education in the public schools, which she described as teaching according to "the English tradition" and "very rigorous!" In her high school years she studied English literature including Shakespeare's plays, poetry and several novels. Tests included essay questions that required quotations from the literature. In her Latin class, she had to translate from different works. It was necessary

to choose between
French and Afrikaans
as a foreign language
and she chose to study
French for four years.

Ellen went to Florida
College in 1965. Later,
when visiting the
Franklin Road con-
gregation in Nashville,
Tennessee she met
David Baize who was
doing graduate work

Foy Short family early 1960s. **Seated:** Margaret, Foy and Kathryn.
Standing L to R: Ellen, Harold and Jimmy.

at Vanderbilt. She married him and they lived in Nashville and Tullahoma,
Tennessee before settling in Hampton, Virginia. Ellen and David made occasional visits to Zimbabwe in the 1990's and 2000's, building up congregations that Foy worked with in his younger days.

Jim (James Lester) was born in Bulawayo in 1951. Ellen described her
brother as "the outgoing talkative one. He was always the one who could
get into trouble, but then melt their [his parents'] hearts with his sanguine
cheerfulness." She laughed when saying, "When they would spank us they
would come in and talk to us about it, saying that they really hated it, but
had to do it. He'd be the one who'd say, 'I'm so glad you spanked me. I don't
want to grow up bad.'"

Jim was very close to his sister Ellen while growing up and their close-
ness continues until now. She calls him "a very loving and caring person."
Ellen said that she seemed to always have an intuition when he was going through a difficult time in his life and would call him at just the right
time. After preaching some years in Rhodesia, Jim now lives in Southern
California.

Kathryn (Kay) was born on August 5, 1957 in Bulawayo. She visited the States when she was thirteen years old and stayed with David and Ellen Baize when they were newlyweds. She returned to the States at age 16 to go to college at Southern Illinois University in Carbondale, Illinois. She met her husband, Roger Lee Smith, at the old Joseph Avenue congregation in Nashville. He now owns an insurance agency in the Nashville area. Her parents bought a house three houses down from Kathryn's in White House, Tennessee, so Kathryn was able to keep an eye on them as they advanced well into their 80's. Foy and Margaret then moved into an apartment in Kathryn's home in 2010.

Rhodes Centennial Exhibition, 100th Anniversary of Cecil John Rhodes' Birth

Margaret loved classical music and the arts, yet she was willing to adapt to African life where she thought opportunities for cultural experiences would be limited. However, she was pleasantly surprised to find a highly developed musical and artistic tradition in Rhodesia. A highlight of those early years for her was the Rhodes Centennial Exhibition in 1953, a three-month celebration of the 100th anniversary of Cecil John Rhodes' birth. It featured world-class concerts, opera productions and invitations to various receptions.

Margaret was thrilled to receive invitations to two receptions at Government House. The first was for the Queen Mother and Princess Margaret. She supposed that she and Foy received this honor because the planners had announced that they intended to include all sectors of the community in the royal reception and they were among the few Americans then living in Bulawayo. All their friends and "friends of friends" were excited for them. Through a mutual friend, a lady Margaret had never met offered to lend her a fur stole to wear. Margaret gratefully accepted it for the royal reception in July, which was the middle of winter. The black velvet stole that Margaret made was warm enough for the second reception in August. She also made a long black and gold dress which she wore for both receptions. Because of the large number invited, instead of having the usual receiving line, everyone was asked to form two groups, with an aisle between for the Queen Mother and Princess Margaret to walk through and greet them. Margaret and Foy were on the front of one group and Margaret said, "We could have reached out and touched them."

The second formal invitation was to be presented to Mr. Ball, President Eisenhower's personal envoy to the Rhodes Centennial. They were also introduced to Sir John and Lady Kennedy. Sir John was the Governor General of Southern Rhodesia. However, what moved Margaret the most was something that happened the night before the meeting when she and Foy went to see an operatic production of *Aida*. Before the concert, the orchestra played the national anthem of the United States in honor of Mr. Ball's presence. In her six years in Africa, she had only been able to hear the national anthem once, faintly over a shortwave radio. When hearing it played unexpectedly that night, tears flowed freely. Only those who have spent years living abroad can understand that response.

Camps

As a part of their efforts to teach young people, Foy and Margaret decided to start weeklong camps for them in July (winter in Southern Africa) so that they would have extensive time to study and work with them. Their first camp was in 1950 at Maleme dam in the Matobo Hills. Paddy Kendall-Ball remembered that the camp was held at the foot of a mountain with a natural spring. He said, "We could hear baboons in the trees behind us."

The Shorts took seventeen boys with them on their first camp. They slept in tents and Margaret cooked for them on an open fire with rocks on the ground. Foy taught Bible classes during the morning. After lunch there were two more classes until about 3 p.m. Then, the group turned to recreation, which involved games like softball, hiking and occasionally climbing nearby hills called *kopjes*. The last day of camp Foy gave the boys at test covering all the material they had studied and was encouraged that only one made a grade of less than seventy.[253]

That first year of camp a drizzly cold rain that the Africans called *guti,* accompanied the camp activities. Margaret felt that she was coming down with the flu and thought that she might have to return to Bulawayo, but the thought of Foy's having to do everything motivated her to stay and cook in the drizzle. She felt fine by the end of the week. Ellen, who was only a year old and already walking, had to stay in the cab of the truck at the open window watching while her mother cooked over the fire in the *guti.*

The next year of camp, 1951, the Shorts invited girls as well as boys and had about thirty campers, more than they were expecting. That year they camped at the foot of a granite *kopje*, which had a rock overhang that provided shelter for Margaret when she cooked.[254] Margaret said, "I was seven months pregnant with Jim, but I still did the cooking over a fire for everybody. Somebody came up and helped us that year… They thought they were going to have to take me to the hospital at any time but I was fine. I was even able to climb some of the *kopjes.*"

Soon Ellen became old enough to participate in camp activities. She recalled sleeping under the stars, early wake-ups, and an inspection before breakfast "to make sure we'd washed behind our ears, our nails were clean, that type of thing." A highlight of the camp day would always be the evening campfire that would start with a devotional. After the devotional there would be skits, singing, scary stories and other typical camp activities around the campfire.

The official "ghost stories" were told around the campfire, but Paddy Kendall-Ball and other mischievous teens delighted in scaring younger campers after lights out and the adults were asleep. He said, "We put a light up in the trees that we could switch on and off. Then we'd start telling ghost stories. We would take them out and turn the light on and say, there's the light there! Someone would get up in the tree and go, 'wubbbbblluuuuu.' They would be terrified."

He said,

> We didn't do much mischief with Foy and Margaret. But one year when C.H. Bankston was in charge. We gave him a hard time.
>
> Robert Watts and I rang the bell the middle of the night and woke everyone up. Then we went into the girls' area and grabbed their beds and threw them down. We were really naughty boys.
>
> C.H. didn't know who did it. No one told who did it, but everyone knew that it was Robert and me. He said, "If you don't tell me who's responsible, no one is going to Shumba Shaba Mountain." It was the major thing everyone looked forward to. Finally Robert and I admitted it. He said, "You're not going."

Then he laughed and said, "I was seventeen and teaching one of the [Bible] classes."

Ken Elder, an evangelist in Northern Rhodesia (Zambia), helped Foy at the camp in the latter 1950s. Paddy Kendall-Ball described him as "a very tough and robust sort of a guy, an ex marine." Elder drove the boys down to a reservoir near the camp to do night fishing. Kendall-Ball said, "One night we were fishing and heard this moaning noise behind us, 'uunnnhhh.' We said, 'What's that?'" Elder said nervously, "nothing." But immediately he put the boys in the car and drove them back to camp. Kendall-Ball said, "We think it was a leopard."

Paddy said, "There was a lot of screaming in the girls' tent one night at Leticia Rock. Some of us bigger fellows, Robert and I, got in there and killed the snake. I've got a picture of that. It was an ordinary house snake. It was harmless."

After Foy and Margaret moved to Gwelo, Melville Sheasby[255] introduced the group to a camp at Leticia Ranch that was owned by a man named Ossie Connolly who was wealthy and owned a steel plant. Eventually he built huts and other buildings for campers. Paddy Kendall-Ball recalled that a huge man of African descent worked for Mr. Connolly. "He was about six feet four inches tall and took a half of one of the big 55-gallon drums to make mealie meal." The boys at the camp admired the African's size and strength as well as the scars he had all over his body. Sam, one of Mr. Connolly's older sons told the boys that the African man had killed a leopard with his bare hands and that the scars were from the battle with the leopard.

Though stories of camp usually involve fun and hijinks, the real mission was to have time to teach the Bible, pray and provide good influences for impressionable teens. Paddy Kendall-Ball remembered classes with Doyle Gilliam from Malawi who helped him become interested in the Old Testament. After telling his stories about fun, he said "It was the Bible classes that made the biggest impression on a lot of those young people. A lot of them became Christians."

Growing Opportunities Among the amaNdebele

Foy mentioned several African brethren who stood out in the early years of his work in Bulawayo. "Beginning in 1948–1950 brethren Fazo Shandavu, Madrai Ndlovu and Jeffrey Nyembezi worked hard to promote the growth of churches in the western part of Zimbabwe centering around Bulawayo. As they preached they taught and trained other men, especially the boys growing to manhood, who would become preachers of the gospel."[256]

Madrai Ndlovu

Madrai Ndlovu passed away from cerebral malaria in 1950 while helping Foy on a successful evangelistic trip. When Foy realized that his mind was being affected by his illness and after several attempts to get treatment for him in local towns, he took him to the hospital in Bulawayo where the malaria attacked his heart and he died.[257] Foy said that before his death, perhaps buoyed by the success of their work, Ndlovu said, "Bro. Short, we shall sweep away this country like a new floor, so that everyone you ask will say that he is a member of the church of Christ."[258]

Foy praised Madrai Ndlovu in a letter to his best friend, Bennie Lee Fudge.

> He was around 30 years of age and one of the finest native Christians I have ever known. He put the Kingdom of God first in his life in every way possible, and worked untiringly to see it spread. He frequently traveled 100 to 150 miles on preaching trips. He was held in high esteem and respect by his fellow natives, and was respected highly by the white people. He was very humble, and invariably courteous, even to the most backward naked native out in the bush. He was also very courageous. He was once threatened with a beating by a group of three or four native men. Although he was a small man he just laughed in their face and stood his ground, going on to explain what it was he wanted done.
>
> When we were in Northern Rhodesia in December he was with me on a trip out in the bush. We came to a river, and I started to wade across first to see how deep it was and whether our pack donkeys would be able to cross. Madrai insisted that I should not go alone, but that he was coming with me. I had a revolver strapped around my waist in readiness for any croc that might be around. Madrai of course had no weapon. But he crossed with me all the same. He said he wanted to be near to help in case I got into trouble.[259]

Foy remarked in a report in 2000, "Some years ago when visiting among the churches in Matabeleland if a preacher was asked who taught him,

Fazo Shandavu

the answer was almost always: 'Bro. Shandavu!' or 'Bro. Nyembezi!' depending on the area of Matabeleland where the question was asked."[260] The old pioneer preacher, John Sherriff, converted Shandavu's father, Daniel. Fazo Shandavu trained himself as a schoolteacher and supported himself in that way so he could preach the gospel. Foy said, "Wherever posted to teach school, he started a congregation. How many he started or helped to start, I do not know. But there are now many preachers who tell of how they were taught and encouraged by brother Fazo."[261] Shandavu passed away in the late 1980s.

Jeffrey Nyembezi and David Ndlovu were effective workers among the amaNdbele into the 1990s. Another successful evangelist was Teli Moyo who worked as a waiter when Jeffrey Nyembezi taught him the gospel. His grandson Bigboy Dube, who worked with the Shorts into the 2000s, told Ellen Baize about how his grandfather conducted Bible classes for the young Ndebele men and taught them about preaching.

In later years Foy used the examples of Fazo Shandavu and Jeffrey Nyembezi to illustrate that church supported schools were not necessary to train preachers. Evangelists like Shandavu and Nymebezi trained young men who usually had much more spiritual success than certificate bearing graduates of formal institutes. He said in a letter to an African brother,

There were two preachers who came to Matabeleland from the Nhowe Mission School of the Bible. But they brought only trouble where they preached. They started no new churches. They trained no new preachers. The churches were all happy when they left. Yet both of them had passed with high marks at Nhowe Mission and at

Mutare, and they came with letters praising them very highly.

There are those who have been sent to America to receive training in different schools of the Bible. You yourself know at least two of these men. They did not learn anything in the schools of the Bible which they attended that helped them to preach in a way that started new churches in Zimbabwe. All of them who have come back have tried to take over churches that were already started by the brethren who were taught in Zimbabwe by Zimbabwe preachers such as Fazo Shandavu, Geoffrey Nymebezi, Teli Moyo, David Ndlovu, Nesu Moyo, Mountbatten Brewer, Newman Gumbo and other such faithful brethren.

There are more than 100 churches in Matabeleland, where there were only a few in 1948. Who did this great work? It is the Zimbabwe preachers who have done it. Where did they receive their training? Where were they taught? None of them ever came from a School of the Bible. Then how could they do such a great work? They followed God's plan, just as the apostle Paul gave it to Timothy. Paul took young preachers with him as he preached, and he taught them what they should know and how they should work. Then he commanded them to teach others also.[262]

Jeffrey Nyembezi

Foy wrote the brethren in Ferris, Texas in December, 1951 about a rarity that he had just witnessed. A white couple, Mr. and Mrs. Frank Neville, allowed themselves to be taught by Jeffry Nyembezi. Nyembezi worked for Neville, who was in charge of a railroad work crew and soon began talking to him at length about the Bible. Mr. Neville was so impressed with Nyembezi's wisdom and Bible knowledge that after a few days he invited him into his home where he and his wife talked with him until two a.m. when they decided they would be baptized. Nyembezi then called Foy. Foy came as soon as possible and arranged for the baptism. Foy remarked, "It is an almost unprecedented thing in this country for a white man to allow a native to teach him anything about the Bible, or about anything much. I feel that the circumstances show a remarkable character in Bro. and Sis. Neville."[263]

Enoch Ncube, Others

While preaching in Bulawayo, Foy ran across a young man named Enoch Ncube who was a teacher in a school run by a mainstream Protestant church. He gave him a tract that contrasted Bible teaching about the work and worship of local churches with that of popular religious denominations. Ncube said that he took the tract and "studied it every day for two weeks so that he could prove what it said was wrong." Ellen Baize said,

> In two weeks he returned to Bulawayo and told dad that he must baptize him. He left teaching at the school and got a job working at a furniture factory, where he learned carpentry, which later helped him take care of his family. After he was baptized he used every opportunity to translate for Dad, Henry Ewing, C.H. Bankston and even the young men like Harold, Paddy and Harrison, because it gave him the opportunity to learn more about the Bible.[264]

Ncube would eventually become Foy's "right hand man" and build up churches in the area around Gwelo well into the twenty-first century.

Examples of Faith and Courage

Foy bristled at the idea that preaching to native brethren wasn't useful because of the claim that after their baptism, "they go right back to their heathen ways."[265] Though acknowledging that such was sometimes the case, he wrote emphatically "it doesn't always happen." To illustrate his point he talked of traveling through a rural area and by chance coming across a Ndeble Christian who had been baptized into Christ a year earlier in Bulawayo. The brother invited Foy to stay and preach in his village. Foy accepted and found that the Christian had been meeting every Sunday with his wife in his home. They invited neighbors to worship with them and as many as twenty attended on some Sundays.

They had no hymnbooks, so they just sang as best they could such parts of songs as they could remember. Neither of the men was able to preach, but they would read a portion of the Bible and make a few remarks. We preached there two nights before having to press on with our journey. We had no baptisms but good interest, having around 50 present each evening. Brother Jeffrey Nyembezi... has agreed to go to this area and spend a month preaching.

Foy had no use for those who felt that Africans were inferior. He wrote in a radio transcript,

Growing up, as I did, among the African people I learned to know and appreciate them. Many times white men condemned the native for his dullness and slowness in learning to operate some white man's machinery. But I've seen those same dull-witted Africans out in the heart of the bush follow the trail of an animal through country where I could not so much as see a mark on the ground.

I've seen the same dull-witted Africans take their spear and an axe and make a living for themselves out in the middle of the forest, where if those white men had been placed with nothing more than that same spear, they would have died of exposure within a week.

The natives have been criticized for lack of courage – but I know of instant after instance where native men have defended friends or their families against lion or leopard with nothing more than an axe in their hands.

Many have shown no less courage in the acceptance of and adherence to the gospel of Christ.

He then wrote of the courage of Mooka the leper who became a Christian but was then expelled from his village because of his conversion and subsequent efforts "to change their age-old superstitions and customs." He was forced to build his hut out in the forest, away from the village. After Mooka planted some corn so that he would have food, "in spite, the villagers allowed their cattle to trample and eat the young corn." A white official responsible for administration of the district saw Mooka's hut while on an infrequent visit to the village and ordered his constables to burn it down since it violated a law that natives must build huts in villages, not in isolated forests. Poor Mooka was forced to wander through the countryside with no place to call home. Foy said,

> But he would not renounce his Christian faith, neither would he compromise with the evil customs of the villagers. He continued to teach the truth of God's word, and eventually found a refuge in another village where the people were more kindly. Mooka the leper is preaching among his people to this very day. I have seen him with my own eyes.[266]

Foy mentioned an African named Edward in another radio transcript.

> The first time I saw Edward was when he came to a gospel meeting in a village dressed in a suit of long-handled underwear... One of the missionaries had received a parcel of clothing from friends in the U.S.A. and had handed out the garments where he thought they were needed. Among the articles given to Edward were these long-handled underwear. That kind of garment was strange to him and being practically new was ever so much better than his tattered clothes. So he wore it as a Sunday suit!
>
> Edward farmed for a living but the soil was so poor that he seldom made much of a crop. In fact he put so much time into preaching that he seldom gave his crops the attention they needed. So he couldn't afford to buy a bicycle for traveling from village to village. Instead he just walked. The day he came to the meeting in his new suit of underwear he had walked or trotted 17 miles in four hours in order to be present.
>
> Through a piece of country a hundred or more miles across Edward has walked and preached. No man will ever know just how

many people have been led to obey the commandments of Christ and thus given a hope for eternity by that humble, poverty stricken gospel preacher.[267]

Learning isiNdebele

As a part of his efforts to help the Ndebele brethren, Foy began taking night classes to learn their language, isiNdebele, his third African language. The language, which is close to the Zulu language of South Africa, has popping and clicking consonants that give it a very distinctive sound. When talking about the language in his home in White House, Tennessee, Foy demonstrated some of the consonants. He said, "They click with their front teeth (c's) and (x's) with tongue against the side of the mouth, then another with the tongue on the roof of the mouth (q's)." As happens when learning any foreign language, Foy made occasional gaffes when beginning to use it. Ellen laughed when recalling that the words for mealie meal (the staple food made from corn meal) and beer are very similar. When a sister asked him what he wanted at a meal he replied that he wanted beer. When all present stopped and looked at him quizzically, he realized that he had used the wrong word.

Foy's reports are full of little African proverbs and discussions of idiomatic expressions. For example in his monthly report, May 30, 1998, he said,

Almost every day I come across interesting details in the translating and concordance work. The African languages are rich in graphic expressions. The Ndebele word for conquer is "*nqoba*" with the "q" given the sound of a hard click made by sharply withdrawing the tongue from the back part of the roof of the mouth. The resulting sound is a good imitation of a club hitting a person's head.[268]

Foy lamented the fact that schools for Europeans in Rhodesia/Zimbabwe did not require the study of one of the two major local languages, Shona or isiNdebele.[269] Perhaps knowledge of the local language among Europeans would have promoted understanding between them and those of African descent. As it was, Foy estimated that perhaps only one in a hundred of those of European descent might have a little knowledge of African languages.

The Parable of the Frogs and the Fish Eagle

In the mid 1950s as the Ndebele congregations were enjoying a period of growth, an impressive and eloquent Methodist preacher named William Kwete was baptized into Christ. Kwete was also a successful farmer and businessman who was used to getting things done quickly.[270] However, it soon became apparent that he hadn't left all of his old concepts behind because he began to try to organize the congregations collectively with a central committee that could receive contributions from churches to support evangelists. He called for a general meeting of the preachers to discuss the plan with them. Foy decided to attend, fearing that because of his poise and eloquence, Kwete might be able to persuade a large number of African brethren to form the organization. The meeting began and the recently converted Methodist began to talk forcefully of the advantages of a central organization for the churches. When he finished there was a period of silence and Foy feared that he would have to speak. But then an African preacher named Major Mpofu stood up and after asking a few clarifying questions, quietly began to tell the following story that his mother told him as a child.

> The frogs in a pond decided that they weren't accomplishing much since they just sat around croaking all day and decided they needed someone to be their king. First they asked the stump at the edge of the pond to accept the position, but it just sat there without saying anything. They kept croaking and nothing was accomplished. Finally the frogs asked the fish eagle to be their king and he readily agreed but on the condition that they obey him without question. The frogs agreed and the fish eagle began to rule over them, sitting on the stump and looking over his new kingdom, the pond.
>
> The next day the fish eagle commanded a frog to come to him. The frog obeyed and the eagle ate him. The next day he called an-

other frog to him with the same result. Finally the eagle ate all the frogs until none were left in the pond!

After telling the story, Mpofu told the brother who was proposing the central organization, "What you are proposing is a fish eagle that will destroy the churches of Christ in this country." There was then a long silence, and then the preachers began talking quietly among themselves about the wisdom revealed in the parable. The plans for the central organization were shelved and Foy put away his notes, happy that he didn't have to say a word.

Foy mentioned on several occasions that the African mind is more like the oriental mind that characterized first century Palestine. Africans tend to respond better to illustrative parables and anecdotes than to the syllogisms of the West.

Sadly, Major Mpofu (his wife's name was Maina), whose wisdom helped stop an unhealthy project, fell permanently away from the Lord in the late 1980's after becoming entangled in politics and choosing the wrong side of the political battles.

Trip to Plumtree

Plumtree is a town on the western edge of Zimbabwe near the border with Botswana. A church of Christ was established there in the 1950s, but brethren soon heard that Pentecostalism had made inroads into the congregation. After Foy returned in 1956 from his trip to the States, he, Harold, Jeffrey Nyembezi, Paddy Kendall-Ball, several Ndebele brethren and a few from Queen's Park in Bulawayo traveled to Plumtree on a Saturday afternoon to see if they could rescue the group. Paddy Kendall-Ball has vivid memories of the visit. "

The first night we met with them in a schoolroom. There was one window and one door. We were in the front. There was not enough seating. So Harold and I sat facing the audience. We could see ev-

erything that was going on. Every time one of [our] men would try
to speak, someone would "get the Holy Spirit."[271]

Kendall-Ball remembered two things that the natives of Plumtree would do
when receiving what they thought was the Holy Spirit: (1) They would cry
out with a sound that sounded something like 'chichichichichi.'(2) Then
they would throw themselves against the backboard. He laughed when recalling Foy's dignified silence in the midst of such mindless absurdities.

> There was a crippled man who was sitting next to Foy… who
> started growling like a dog. Foy was being very stoic, very calm,
> sitting there with his legs crossed. Harold and I looked over there
> and thought it was very funny. Norman Flynn [a Christian from
> Queens Park who accompanied Foy and the others] could see the
> looks on our face so he reached over, touched us on the leg and said
> firmly, "Don't laugh!"

Then Paddy realized that Flynn was right and that it could be dangerous
to laugh. There "were about 75 people and there was no way out except
through them, and if you got them upset, you would be in trouble."

Jeffrey Nyembezi realized that his friend, Foster Moyo, was arriving late so
he went out to greet him. Nyembezi reported that there was a man crawling around the building growling like a lion, throwing "holy dust" into the
window, which in turn agitated those who were sitting in the audience.

Foy and his companions sat quietly for hours until about ten o'clock that
night when the natives of Plumtree tired of their "Holy Spirit possessions,"
Then he and his companions talked until about midnight when there were
questions that continued into the wee morning hours. Paddy Kendall-Ball
said, "Harold and I left at 4 a.m. to go to bed and they were still asking
questions. The other guys came in about 7 a.m."

Kendall-Ball continued his account,

> Sunday morning we were outside the village. It was like two opposing armies. All of the people were sitting together. We were sitting on seats. As soon as Foy got up to speak, the chief prophet got the spirit. Foy took him by the arm and physically dragged him into the village and told him to stay there. When he came back he said, "All who want to worship the Lord with us are welcome to stay. But if you don't want to worship with us, we'd like you to leave." Every one in the main group got up and left. There were six teachers from a nearby school. They stayed. [After services with the six teachers] we got up, shook the dust off our feet and left.

However, the story has a happy ending. Years later, Lamech Ncube, the nephew of the "chief prophet," was working in Bulawayo where he ran into Paddy Kendall-Ball. Paddy said, "He was helping us unload, saw a Bible and asked, 'Could I have one?'" Paddy gave him a Bible and later a Bible Correspondence course. The young man obeyed the gospel and brought his wife, Chiwa, from Plumtree for Sandra Kendall-Ball to teach. Chiwa became a Christian and began teaching her neighbors in Plumtree. A gospel preacher, Newman Gumbo and several others began going to Plumtree in 2004 and eventually a strong congregation existed, fifty years after Foy and his companions shook the dust off their feet and left. Paddy said in 2009 that the congregation had about 75 members in spite of the fact that many had to leave the country due to the economic crisis.

An Object Lesson at Nhowe Mission

Foy's son, Jim, remembered an object lesson that Foy used when asked to speak to Shona brethren at a lectureship at the Nhowe mission. Foy preached on premillennialism, a theory that had enjoyed popular support in the areas around the mission in the 1930s and 1940s. Foy wanted to show that physical Israel had rejected God to the point that the idea that he would again work through that secular nation again was ludicrous. He decided to copy Jeremiah's object lesson of smashing a clay jar to show that physical Israel was irreparably broken (Jeremiah 19). Jim said that when Foy smashed an African pot in front of the brethren, it made quite an impression.[272] "All the people said, 'Ahhh!'" It made quite an impact on Jim who remembered it vividly almost fifty years later.

Back to the States — 1955

Foy, Margaret and their three children left Rhodesia in December of 1954 to return to the States to visit supporting churches and work for eighteen months at the Eastside congregation in Athens, Alabama. An article in the *Gospel Guardian* appealed for help for their travel expenses and referenced their work at Queens Park.

> The Foy Short family plans to return to the States this summer for the first "furlough" since they went to Africa seven years ago.
>
> During the past year the young congregation of English-speaking Europeans (whites) in Bulawayo, Southern Rhodesia, where Brother Short labors, made a remarkable growth. Sixteen were baptized and seven members moved in from other places, more than doubling the membership of the congregation. There are now thirty-seven members, with an average attendance of more than forty at preaching services and a Sunday School enrollment of more than one hundred. The contribution of the group tripled during 1953.
>
> A $10,000 meeting house is nearing completion. The local congregation in Bulawayo bought the lot, have furnished the labor, and propose to seat and equip the building. American churches have paid for most of the materials for the building thus far...
>
> Railway and steamship fare (with necessary incidental expenses) for Brother Short and his family's return home will come to $2,500. We are hoping to secure both funds in the near future. Your cooperation will certainly be appreciated.[273]

After receiving the needed funds, the Shorts left Bulawayo and traveled to South Africa where they visited members of the church. After visiting Doonside on the southern coast of Natal, the Shorts took the twenty thousand-ton liner the *HMS Carnarvon Castle* of the Union Castle line for a two-week voyage to England. Before reaching the Atlantic, the ship stopped at various ports along the South African Coast. At East London, the Shorts met a young man named Ray Votaw and his family, who came to the port to meet them. They spent Saturday with the Votaws. Little did they know at the time that Votaw would become a very close friend and ally when confronting the promoters of institutionalism in the churches in the 1960s. The ship next stopped in Port Elizabeth on Sunday and the Shorts were able to attend services and spend a portion of the day with the John Hardin family. The *Carnarvon Castle* finally arrived in Cape Town for a five day stay in port. The Shorts were able to sleep on the ship and sightsee and visit during the day. Foy visited with two old childhood friends, George and Ottis Scott, who had been pioneer workers in South Africa. The Scotts would both pass away in the coming year. Finally, the *Carnarvon Castle* departed for the two-week voyage to Southampton, England.

The *HMS Canarvon Castle* had an illustrious history, having been converted to an armed merchant cruiser during World War 2 and winning a battle with a German raider, the *Thor*. After the war it was converted back to passenger service, primarily between London and Cape Town.[274] Margaret had pleasant memories of the two week cruise.

> These were great ships to travel on, with plenty of activities — deck games, and other organized things like chess tournaments, quiz shows, etc. There was a special hostess to organize activities for the children. We were on board during Christmas and New Year and on New Year's Eve there was a children's fancy dress contest. I got some crepe paper from the shop and made costumes for Ellen and Jim — Ellen as a fairy queen and Jim as a pixie. They won first prize in their age group.[275]

She added,

> I traveled from Southampton to Cape Town on their flagship, the

Windsor Castle in May of 1976 on its second last voyage. It was such a pity they had to be scrapped, but much, if not most, of their income was from the cargo they carried. Containers were coming in and it was impossible to convert those ships to hold containers. The *Carnarvon* had already been scrapped by then.

Foy and his family left South Africa in the middle of the hot African summer. However, they arrived in England in the middle of winter. After making port in Southhampton, they took the train to London, where they spent five days with the R.B. Scott family who had given his parents hospitality in the 1930s. Scott was a fixture in the congregation at Kentish Town in London and provided hospitality to evangelists from all over the world from the 1910s until his death in the 1980's. His daughter, Margaret took the family all over London. Margaret Short said, "We really saw a lot because she knew exactly where to go. I'll never forget that!" Margaret Scott eventually married Derek Daniell and together with him raised a large family that is still active in the Lord's work in southeastern England.

From London, the Shorts boarded the the fifty-five thousand ton French ship *Liberté* for their trip across the North Atlantic to New York. Margaret said, "It was by far the largest ship we were ever on. It came from Le Havre and didn't dock in England but anchored in the Solent — that stretch of water between the mainland and the Isle of Wight. We were taken from Southampton to the ship in boats … It was quite an experience!"[276] She added, "We stayed in the cabin with the kids most of the time but took part in some of the activities. I remember the food on that French ship, especially the cheese, crackers and olives. I was in seventh heaven."

When they arrived in New York they went on the deck but "almost froze" until the Statue of Liberty came into view. Foy said, "When she saw the Statue of Liberty she [Margaret] started crying." From New York, the Shorts took the train to Athens, Alabama where they were met by the Fudges and all of Margaret's family from Huntsville.

Foy, Margaret and the children spent twenty months in North Alabama from January of 1955 until August of 1956. Foy preached at the Eastside congregation in Athens and rented a house on Lee Street near the railway line. Bennie Lee and Sybil Fudge had a small house opposite theirs at the corner of Chandler Street and Washington Street that became vacant and the Shorts moved into it.

Ellen and Harold attended Athens Bible School in 1955 and 1956. The family occasionally traveled around the country presenting a report on their work in Southern Africa. Foy showed movies of Africa and during a scene of worship services conducted under a tree, his family would sing a hymn in isiNdebele, "*Wathanda izwe Kangaka.*"

Foy enjoyed the time he spent with his best friend and brother-in-law, Bennie Lee Fudge. Both concurrently came to a decision that would affect them the rest of their lives. The big issue among known churches of Christ in the middle 1950s was whether congregations could send contributions to brotherhood institutions and sponsoring churches. The more fundamental issue beyond the use of the church's treasury was whether God's church was a network of local congregations that should support colleges and other institutions of the network, or simply saved individuals that weren't an organization that could have such adjuncts.

Foy and Fudge had written each other earlier about the gathering storm over institutionalism, Foy defending the national "Church of Christ Missions" organization in Northern Rhodesia/Zambia in 1950 and 1951, while Fudge expressed strong doubts about it. In his letters to Fudge, Foy also expressed disagreement on several occasions with many writers in the *Gospel Guardian.*[277]

The two close friends drove to Franklin, Tennessee in March 1956 where Charles Holt and James W. Nichols conducted a debate on the issue. Nichols was one of the founders of the *Herald of Truth*, a national radio program sponsored by the Highland church in Abilene, Texas. Both Fudge and Foy had received funds from sponsoring churches. In the terminology of the 1950s and 1960s, sponsoring churches were those that took in funds from other congregations to pay for projects that their elders supervised. After hearing the two sides presented in the debate the two men rode quietly back towards Athens, immersed in their thoughts. Foy said that after driving for miles in silence, "almost simultaneously we looked at each other and said, 'that settles it.'" They both realized that back-to-basics service of the Master excluded church support of the machinery that was being pushed so aggressively. Their new convictions would cost them.

Fudge lost business for his bookstore and Foy lost support from a church in Kansas. Margaret recalled, "They wrote a letter after we returned to Rhodesia, asking for his views. Foy replied and we never heard from them again – support stopped without any notice."[278] However, the Eastside congregation in Athens took up what he lost and he was able to continue in his work.

While in the States, Foy and Margaret were able to convince the C.H. Bankston family from Decatur, Alabama, to return to Rhodesia with them. The Bankstons would be effective workers in Bulawayo for five years. Foy said that C.H. wasn't a public speaker but that he and Sarah were "good personal workers." Their son, Harrison, would marry Carol Roberts, one of the impressive teens that the Shorts converted in Queens Park. When the Bankstons returned from Rhodesia in 1961 he preached for a time, but eventually obtained a job with Lockheed in Marietta, Georgia. He and Sarah helped start the Powers Ferry Road congregation near Marietta.

The Shorts and Bankstons left for New York in the summer of 1956 to catch their ship to Africa. Foy bought a Plymouth station wagon and a Jeep and hauled a trailer behind the latter that was stuffed with items that would be useful to them back in Africa, especially a washing machine and dryer. The Bankstons shipped a station wagon for their use. However, when they arrived in New York during the height of tourist season they realized they would not be able to take the ship they had hoped to take with the Bankstons since it had a collision with another ship in the North Sea. They would have to wait two weeks for another ship! To fill up the two weeks, the Bankstons went to visit family members in Detroit. A member of the Manhattan church of Christ let Foy, Margaret and the kids spend the two weeks in an apartment he had "in the middle of the Latin quarter of the Bronx." Margaret said, "We had a very interesting time, especially weekends. We were able to keep our car until the night before we were to sail. We did a lot of driving around the area."

Finally the Shorts were able to sail for Southampton, England on a 9,000-ton ship of the Holland America line, the *Zuiderkruis*, arriving in Southampton on July 3. After spending several days in London, the Shorts and Bankstons sailed on a small ship across the English channel from Harwich to the Hook of Holland. They did a little sightseeing in Amsterdam and visited a small congregation in the area. The two families then separated temporarily to visit different European destinations. The Shorts spent five days with Margaret's brother who was in the Air Force in Wiesbaden, Germany. While there, they visited American brethren who were working with the congregation in Frankfort.

The Shorts and Bankstons then reunited in Amsterdam and departed for South Africa on the *Waterman*, of the Holland Africa line. They arrived in Cape Town and drove their station wagons and jeep to Bulawayo where the brethren greeted them enthusiastically. Harrison Bankston recalled that when arriving back in Africa, Foy expressed that he was overjoyed to be back where they made the good, crusty bread.[279] When hearing of Bankston's remarks, Margaret said, "We often went to the bakery to pick it up, where it was always fresh and often hot from the oven. The crust was delicious! In later years they did begin to slice bread but it was never as good as the unsliced loaves."[280]

Final Years of the First Stay in Bulawayo

When the Shorts returned to Bulawayo in August of 1956 they found the church at Queens Park consolidating its earlier numerical gains. Alan Hadfield had begun preaching full time and was working with the Ewings. Since the Shorts brought the Bankstons with them, from the latter part of 1956 and through 1957 there were a total of four families that could dedicate themselves completely to the work. There was a corresponding period of rapid numerical growth. Foy said, "By the end of 1957, there were about 120 in attendance at Queens Park. Twenty-one were baptized in a meeting in November 1957, in which I did the preaching and a number of members went from house to house inviting people."[281]

By late 1957, the evangelists in Bulawayo agreed that two families should move to other population centers in the country. The Hadfields moved to Salisbury, (later called Harare) and at first had services in the apartment of a couple who had moved there from Queens Park. Foy and Margaret decided to move to Gwelo (later called Gweru) a smaller city about one hundred miles Northeast of Bulawayo. Their exciting pioneering work in Bulawayo was ending. They would return in the late 1970s to a different set of opportunities and challenges. For the next twenty-one years, they would base their work in Gwelo.

Chapter 4

Gwelo

Gwelo, later called Gweru, had a population of 38,000 in 1961 and now is the third largest city in Zimbabwe. Its population in 2002 was 137,000.[282] Shona and isiNdebele are both spoken there.

The Shorts decided to move to Gwelo because the Pote family, baptized in Bulawayo, had moved there along with Olwen Bowen Craig. These brethren helped start the English work. Foy already had some contacts among those of African descent in the area through a paper his father published.

The Shorts carried much of their furniture and other goods to the train station in Bulawayo on borrowed pickup trucks where it was shipped up the line to Gwelo. They bought a house with five acres of land on Selukwe Road (now Shurugwi Road), three miles southeast of the center of Gwelo in late 1957 and rented it out a few months before they actually moved in.

Beginning the Work

The Shorts held the first service of the new congregation in the Pote's home. Then they conducted most services in their own house until the congregation was able to rent the Hellenic Hall of a local Greek association. After renting the Hellenic Hall, the brethren bought a house and removed a partition in it to form an adequate meeting place for a number of years. Finally, the brethren built their own building and moved into it on March 28, 1971.[283]

The new congregation invited John Maples to come up from Durban, South Africa to hold a meeting. The Bankstons came over from Bulawayo with a station wagon full of teenagers to help with the effort. Margaret said, "That week I had at least twenty for every meal." The meeting was a success with one family being baptized into Christ. They in turn invited their next-door neighbor, Jean Jackiw, who also became a Christian.

Margaret began holding women's Bible studies in various homes. At one point she conducted two sessions each week. She invited a Catholic woman, Dorthy Dams, who was teaching her music. Dorthy Dams "hit if off" with Jean Jackiw and was eventually converted. Foy reported in the new bulletin, "Our hearts were made to rejoice on the 9th of May when Mrs. Dorthy Dams was baptized into Christ."[284]

Dorothy Dams became very close to the Short family. Margaret said that she "was like a member of our family. She was like a second mother to me and I was like a daughter she had never had."[285] She taught violin and piano lessons to different members of the Short family during the years they spent in Gwelo. Foy wrote a tribute to Dorthy Dams, who died in 1978, in his April, 2001 report. He said that from the time of her conversion on, "her life was a living demonstration of what it means to love the Lord and to love His body, the church." As a music teacher she had a musician's approach to the Bible. She would say, "Play it like it is written. The composer had a reason for writing the music the way he did." So, the Lord's work began to grow in Gwelo just as it had in Bulawayo, though it never became as large.

Paddy Kendall-Ball says that Foy and others did a lot of door knocking during the first years in Gwelo. When Foy found contacts willing to study, he used a series of eight charts that he designed for teaching the lost. The first lesson showed why belief in the Bible is rational. Later lessons demonstrated how the Bible reveals the gospel and the appropriate response to it. The final lesson was about serving Christ after becoming a Christian. Foy had many exchanges with Jehovah's Witnesses both in Bulawayo and Gwelo, but especially in Gwelo. He studied their materials extensively and elaborated two study guides about their doctrine: "*Witness Versus the Bible*," and "*Witness Versus Witness*." The latter dealt with contradictions among the Witnesses. After the leading Witness in Gwelo began studying with Foy, the home office in Salisbury ordered him to stop because he had difficulty answering Foy's reasoning.[286]

Through his preaching years Foy developed a number of other study notes on religious errors and difficult texts. Margaret recalls in particular a study of Matthew 24. In his later life he prepared extensive notes on Revelation, taking the position that many of the prophesies of the book had their primary fulfillment in the destruction of Jerusalem. He preferred to use his own material in Bible classes, handing out notes that the members kept in loose leaf notebooks.

In 2011 Margaret received a letter from Adele Margerison in which she said that her husband, Mike, used Foy's old Bible class notes as a basis for the sermons he preaches in a congregation in England. Adele's family had a long relationship with the Shorts. John Sherriff and his wife had cared for her mother, Ella, and aunt, Rhoda, before sending them to Sinde mission with Will and Delia Short to help with their children. Eventually Adele and her husband, Mike, became very close to the Shorts through association both in Gwelo and later in Bulawayo. Mike and Adele's third son, Angus, was an accomplished musician. Margaret called him her "adopted son." Angus moved to England where he taught school before dying prematurely of lung cancer. Adele and Mike Margerison were among some of the many long-term friendships that the Shorts established in Gwelo.

Many of the contacts for the work in Gwelo came through the Short children and their friends at school. Therefore, just as in Bulawayo, the congregation began to fill up with teenagers. Ellen Baize said, "Mom and dad had Bible study almost every night of the week. On Fridays we still had games for young people as we'd done in Bulawayo." Doyle Gilliam who was working in Malawi visited the Short's home for a meeting in Gwelo. After observing the coming and going of the different brethren, he said that he never had been to a place so much like Grand Central Station.

Trip to Barotseland, 1958

Foy's father, W.N. (Will) Short, made contacts in an isolated British protectorate called Barotseland, a semi desert wilderness area which is the home of the Lozi people.[287] The territory is now a part of Western Zambia. Shortly after Foy moved to Gwelo, he and his father decided to visit the area, seeking the contacts in remote villages. The trip was reminiscent of Will's long treks into remote parts of Zambia in the 1920s and his son Foy's later trips into the Zambesi River escarpment. However, motorized vehicles available in the late 1950s made it possible to take family members into this remote region. The only roads in the area were sand tracks. Margaret wrote,

Only four-wheel-drive vehicles were allowed. They gave permission for us to take Daddy Short's small pickup since we had a jeep – American military surplus – which we had taken back to Rhodesia in 1956. The pickup did get stuck in the sand several times and had to be pulled out with the jeep. Once it got stuck in the middle of a wide dry riverbed of sand. When the jeep went back to pull it out, the jeep also got stuck and they both had to be pulled out with a block and tackle.[288]

The trip, taken during the three week Rhodesian school vacation in August and September of 1958, required extensive planning for food, diapers, bedding, gasoline and other supplies. Margaret said, "Most of our nights were spent camping in the open. Foy's parents took small stretchers and the rest of us spread our blankets on the ground."[289] She added,

We traveled along the northern route and crossed the Zambesi River… where Foy remembers it was just a series of small channels that we could drive over. We then traveled south along the west bank of the river. By the time we reached the southern crossing at Sesheke, it had been fed by tributaries and was very wide. One of my most vivid memories is of crossing this vast expanse of water on a very crude sort of ferry.[290]

The adventure made an impact on young Jim who was seven years old and Ellen who was nine. Jim re- membered the lions roaring in the evenings around the family's camp.[291] Margaret and Ellen both remembered an incident one night while camping on the banks of the Zambesi River. Margaret wrote, "Daddy Short and Foy had chosen a camp site well back

Crossing the Zambezi River

from the river's edge because of the danger of crocodiles." However, Ellen remembered that her brother Harold, who was thirteen years old and Uncle Bill, who was fifteen, wanted to show their teenage independence by camping a distance away from the others by a large tree. However to the boys' chagrin, Foy and his father wouldn't let them do it. According to their experienced eyes, their proposed campsite seemed too close to an access route to the river. Margaret said,

> I woke up in the middle of the night to see Foy and Daddy Short beside a large fire they had started. Daddy had woken to the roar of lions, and we stayed up until we were pretty sure they had passed. Well, sure enough, the next morning we found the lions' spoor be- tween the big tree and us! This took care of some of the disappoint- ment Harold and Bill had felt about not having their own camp. [292]

The boys learned to respect their elders' bush knowledge!

On the return route through the southern part of Barotseland the Shorts stopped at the village of Will Short's old friend and companion evangelist, Kambole Matapamatenga. Kambole had worked with Will extensively over thirty years earlier at Sinde Mission and on one occasion, when Will had an extreme attack of malaria, carried one end of his stretcher almost twenty miles to a hospital (see chapter one). Kambole gave Bill and Harold bows and arrows that he had made. They became treasured possessions in the Short family as mementos of their relationship with the pioneer African evangelist.

The Shorts spent one of the last nights in Barotseland in a double story house at a forestry station. During the night, Margaret heard footsteps on the stairs. She opened the door and looked out and no one was there! The next morning when they were leaving and thanking the forestry officials for their hospitality, one of them said, "We didn't want to worry you last night but thought you would be interested to know that this house is supposed to be haunted."

An interesting sequel to the story of the haunted house occurred twenty-two years later in 1980 when Foy and Margaret attended a convention of the Rotary Club in South Africa. There they stayed in the home of Bernard and Bridgette de Soussa, a high official in the South African Forestry Department. De Soussa told them that after graduating from the University of Cape Town he had worked in Baroteseland. The Shorts then told him of their trip to Barotseland and they realized that they spent the night in the same house he had lived in! When he realized this he asked them, "Did they tell you it was haunted? We often heard footsteps on the stairs!"[293]

The trip to Barotseland made an indelible impression on the Short family, not only because of the adventures, but also because of the time spent together as three generations of a godly family seeking to spread God's message in areas where it had scarcely been heard.

Trips to Namwianga Mission

Foy's parents, W.N. and Delia, worked at the Namwianga Mission in Zambia until 1961, when they moved to Bulawayo. Therefore during the

1950s until 1961 the family traveled at least once a year to the mission for visits with the children's grandparents, other family members and Christians there. One year the families from the mission made a special trip to nearby Victoria Falls for the Christmas holidays.

One August, Foy's brother Bill was in Gwelo. The Shorts decided to take him and a friend of Harold's with them to Namwianga. The trip would be almost four hundred miles over rough roads. The only family vehicle at the time was a Volkswagen Beetle and yet Foy decided that with some improvisation all eight travelers could fit with their clothes and Bill's camping gear. Ellen recalled, "The three guys, Harold, Bill and Harold's friend got in the back seat. Either Jim or I got in the little open well behind the back seat.

The other one would either sit on the guys' laps or in the space between the two front seats where the handbrake was located. Kay was a baby so she sat on Mom's lap." She added, "We had to go through Bulawayo and I remember Sarah Bankston coming out and saying, 'wow!' when seeing how loaded it was." When thinking of the crowded trip to Namwianga, Margaret remembered an occasion when Foy carried thirteen young people to camp in the Volkswagen.[294] Of course, there were no traffic laws at that time that limited the number of passengers, so trips in the overloaded Volkswagon were perfectly legal.

Family trips to Namwianga Mission were magical for little Ellen. She remembered getting up in the morning for Bible readings and prayer before breakfast and then being allowed to play in her grandfather's print shop with all its little cubbyholes where different type was kept. She helped her grandmother bake cookies and usually ate more dough during the preparation than cookies. Another memory was of sitting in the grove of mango trees with her cousins eating mangos until they were about to pop. What stood out most in her mind, however, was sitting around at night with her grandparents, aunt, uncle and cousins reading the Bible and singing, with the only light coming from the little flickering paraffin lamps. "Then," Ellen said, "we were allowed to take the paraffin lights up to our bedrooms." There the children talked and giggled until they finally fell asleep.[295]

Trip to the USA 1961–62

Foy, Margaret and the children made a four-month trip to the States in December of 1961. The plane trip made a big impression on Jim Short who was ten years old at the time. The family left Salisbury on a BOAC Comet 4 jetliner to London via Nairobi, Khartoum and Rome. After a day's lay-over in London, the family took a long flight on a turboprop across the Atlantic to New York. After landing at Idlewild airport in New York (now JFK airport) the airline put them on a helicopter that flew over Manhattan to Newark airport where they took a flight to Huntsville. Jim said, "It was about seven o'clock in the morning flying over Manhattan. It was quite a thrill for a ten year old from the boondocks of Zimbabwe."[296]

When the family arrived in Huntsville, they went to a house that Margaret's family had rented in Huntsville next to Margaret's sister Kay's house. Jim said, "That was our base of operation." Foy spent much of the four months in the Athens area and visiting congregations to speak to them about the work in Africa. He traveled over 18,000 miles through a number of states in seventeen weeks. Jim said, "When he added up all the talks, he averaged giving a talk for each day of the trip."[297]

A highlight of this trip was a family reunion in Athens, Alabama at the Bennie Lee Fudge house at the corner of Washington and Chandler Streets. Bennie Lee Fudge realized that since Foy and his family were in the States, almost the entire Short clan was in the country and could be brought to-gether for the first time under one roof. Bill Short was born only after Foy, Sybil and Beth left home to study at Abilene, so the family had never been together. The only missing pieces to a possible family reunion were Foy's parents, William Newton and Delia who had not visited the States since

1947. Sybil said that Bennie Lee "raised money and bought them an airplane ticket to come over."

Jim remembered that the families all piled into the Fudge's house and that everyone "got three or four hours of sleep at night."[298] Sybil said, "We had children all over the floor." There were 31 people in the house, including a young Filipino student who was living with the Fudges.[299] Sybil added, "The women spent time in the kitchen fixing the meals and tending to the little kids. The men were off in the other room talking their heads off. We got together and sang a lot."

Will (W.N.) and Delia Short, **seated**, with their children. **Standing L to R:** Bill, Margaret Ann, Beth, Sybil and Foy.

Ellen remembered a poignant talk that her uncle Bill Short gave at the end of the reunion to all the Shorts, Fudges, Ewings and Mansurs about the spiritual heritage that they had been handed by their parents and the need to thank God for it and serve him all the more diligently because of it. Then the family sang, "Blest be the Tie that Binds," said their farewells and departed back to their own places.[300] To paraphrase Gardner S. Hall Sr., families that give themselves to the Lord's service must often be separated in this world so that they can be together in the next.

At the end of their four-month stay in the States the Shorts flew from Huntsville to Atlanta and then to Idlewild airport. After flying to London, their return flight skipped Rome flying directly to Khartoum, then Nairobi and finally to Salisbury where they took a Central African Airlines flight to Bulawayo. On the trip Foy and Margaret bought a little cap gun for Jim at Heathrow airport in London that looked like a .38 caliber pistol. When they arrived in Khartoum, Ellen and Jim got permission to get off the plane while it was being refueled. Jim said, "My parents were happy for us to burn off some energy!" Since little Kay was asleep, Foy and Margaret decided they would stay on board. Jim left his cap pistol on the seat with his black, "fake leather" jacket over it. When the cleaning people came through the cabin, one of them picked up Jim's little jacket and saw the cap pistol. Foy and Margaret were watching from the other side of the plane and said that the cleaning man's eyes got huge when he saw the gun. He gently put the jacket back over the pistol and ran to get a supervisor, who came and then called an immigration official who carefully picked the gun up, saw what it was and started laughing. Jim said, "It was almost an international incident."[301] Though airline security wasn't nearly as tight in the early sixties as it became forty years later, the sight of the toy gun still caused a commotion!

Holiday/Meetings in South Africa

When Rhodesia was first settled by Europeans the government advised them to go to the coast once a year for health reasons since Rhodesia was considered to be in the tropics.[302] Though the climate turned out to be healthier than the early authorities expected it to be, Foy and Margaret found out when arriving in the country that many white Rhodesians still had the habit of going to South Africa or Mozambique for holiday. Foy decided that his family needed a break and built a caravan (camper trailer) from scratch that could be hauled behind the family's car, a Vauxhall Victor. The caravan made the trip more economical. It also made it easier to afford shorter breaks to visit Game Parks and other points of interest within the country. Margaret, who was an excellent seamstress, sewed the cushions and curtains for the caravan and also made a tent that was attached to its side. Kathryn said of the caravan and its furnishings, "People said it didn't look homemade."[303] The family set out in December 1964 for their holiday in a caravan park at Doonside just south of Durban, South Africa. Jim said, "It was the first family vacation that I could remember." Margaret said,

Caravanning was a big thing in Southern Africa and almost every town would have a caravan club and park. I was secretary of the Gwelo branch of the Rhodesian Caravan Club for some years. We met some very interesting people at the various parks. During the year, there would be meetings at various towns. … Both the Rhodesian and South African clubs printed small magazines monthly and the various dates and venues would be printed in those. Everyone … was surprised that Foy had built ours as it didn't look homemade.[304]

The joys of the vacation in South Africa and the fellowship with the Topes, Votaws and DeKlerks was tempered by the shunning the Shorts received from old friends in South Africa who were pushing institutionalism, including some who had lived for months with them in 1949 in Bulawayo. Foy thought that friendships should not be severed by the controversy over institutionalism, but instead that there should be a gentlemanly exchange of ideas that would eventually bring like minded followers of Christ to a better understanding of God's will. Though there were a few frustrating exchanges about the issue in Rhodesia, most of those who disagreed about it, at least in the southern part of the country, maintained cordial relationships with those of the other persuasion. Such would not be the case, however, in South Africa where conservatives like Gene Tope, Ray Votaw and Andy DeKlerk were rapidly shunned by the promoters who told their followers to have nothing to do with the "antis." When Foy and his family came to visit South Africa in December 1964 they realized that the spiritual quarantine had been extended to them. Foy's old friends who had stayed in his home in Bulawayo refused to shake his hand because he couldn't conscientiously go along with the church-supported machinery they were promoting. This breech of etiquette was very disturbing to gentlemanly Foy, whose shock about some of the unpleasant confrontations was still evident when he talked about it over forty years later. The emphasis on courtesy and gentility in Foy's upbringing, both at home and at his English boarding school, probably made him a bit naïve about the rough and tumble approach to controversy that characterized many of his American friends. To be fair, Foy would have been just as shocked by similarly aggressive styles of some in the United States who agreed with him that institutionalism was wrong. Jim recalled that as a young teen, it was strange to observe the coolness between those who had formerly been close friends. "It was clear to the kids that there were issues in the relationship that hadn't been there previously."[305]

In spite of the difficulties, Jim said that his parents didn't allow the rejection of their old friends to ruin their vacation. It probably wasn't a complete surprise to them since they had heard that the Topes and Votaws had already been ostracized because of their convictions and they themselves had already lost some support from American churches because of the issue.

The Shorts enjoyed their holiday so much in 1964 that they returned to South Africa in 1965 for a more adventurous jaunt. Foy went down early in his Volkswagen Beetle to preach in Krugersdorf with the Topes, Springs where the Votaws lived and Port Elizabeth where Andy DeKlerk worked. When Foy was in Springs, someone got sick while he was preaching. Ray Votaw then began to tell others that Foy "had them throwing up in the aisles."[306]

By the time Foy's meetings were over, school was out in Rhodesia and the family drove the Vauxhall and the caravan down to meet him for another holiday. Jim said, "We met up with him in Port Elizabeth where he was finishing his meeting. Then we traveled down the 'Garden Route' south of Port Elizabeth." However, they began to have problems with the car's gearbox (transmission). Foy took it to a garage in Port Elizabeth where mechanics were supposed to have fixed it. However, after driving further towards Cape Town the gearbox seized up completely. They had to have the car towed to the nearest town, George, where it was found that the mechanics in Port Elizabeth had forgotten to put a retaining bolt in place. Margaret said, "George was a beautiful little place a few miles from the sea with mountains behind it. With the Beetle, we were able to drive around the area while the Vauxhall was being worked on and met some nice folks. Caravanners were always very friendly."[307] She added, "We then stayed a few days at a lovely place called Wilderness, where we had great fun playing in the sea." In 1984 two grandsons, Jody Baize and Eliot Short, visited Foy and Margaret. When they drove Eliot back to Cape Town with Jody, they stopped again at Wilderness, allowing their grandsons to frolic in the ocean in the same place their parents had played nineteen years before.

Foy returned to Port Elizabeth to try to get the company that had neglected to put the retaining bolt in to pay at least for part of the repairs. They tried to excuse themselves but at least paid for half the cost of rebuilding the gearbox.[308] Harold traveled further west to Hermanus in the Volkswagon, where his girlfriend's family were holidaying in their cottage, but the rest of the family decided to return to Rhodesia.

There were no more family vacations to South Africa until 1968 when Kay and Jim accompanied their parents to Port Saint Johns, which is just below the South Coast of Natal. By this time Harold and Ellen had already left home. The Shorts traveled with the Nieuwoudt family, who had three sons. The oldest was a close friend of Jim's and the youngest was Kay's age. Mr. Neiuwoudt was Jim's rugby coach. Margaret said, "Port Saint Johns was a fascinating place on the Wild Coast."[309] She vividly remembered climbing one steep cliff with Foy.

> It didn't look too bad and we had loved climbing quite steep sides of some bare granite hills in the Matobo. Well, it turned out to be steeper than it looked and that climb was the most frightening experience of my life, thus my memory of cliffs! The Nieuwoudts were waiting in the car at the top and I think they were just about as relieved as we were when we got there.[310]

Foy continued to hold meetings in South Africa through the years and especially enjoyed the time he spent with Ray Votaw, Gene Tope and Paul

Williams. He reported in 1973 that a trip there had been "a real boost."[311] These close friends from South Africa also visited congregations where Foy worked in Rhodesia in the 1960s and 1970s. Ray Votaw remembered that when visiting Foy, "he forgot the keys to his house about five times. We had to break into his house!"[312] He said that he recommended on occasions that Foy be given the topic, "forgetting those things which are behind," because he was so good at forgetting! On another occasion Foy wanted Votaw to ride a horse that he had just bought, stating in effect that since Votaw was from Texas he should know something about horses. However, Votaw said, "He must have put a burr under the saddle because as soon as I got on the horse, he threw me off." Votaw said that Foy thought it was funny, but he didn't at the time.

Intensive Training of Young Preachers

While in Gwelo, Foy decided to spend a large portion of his time teaching young preachers in a regimented training program. His first students were his protégé from Bulawayo, Paddy Kendall-Ball, Melville Sheasby and "Foy's right hand man," Enoch

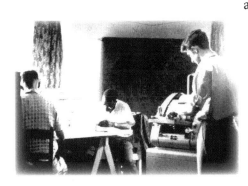

Melville Sheasby, Enoch Ncube, Paddy Kendall working in the office in Gwelo.

Ncube.[313] Kendall-Ball recalled, "We studied Greek, Hebrew, Old Testament, New Testament, denominational doctrines and speaking." The young men were expected to be in class from 8 a.m. until 1 p.m. each day and then afterwards study and fulfill their other obligations.

Paddy Kendall-Ball laughed when recalling the class on public speaking. Each participant in the class had to make a talk and then be critiqued, including Foy! Paddy and the other students decided to "really nail" Foy for what they called his "monotone." They told him, "It's dry! It's not interesting." Foy seemed to take their suggestions to heart and Kendall-Ball said,

"I would like to think that we taught Foy to preach properly." He acknowledged, however, that Foy gave as "good as he got" when the time came to critique others.

It was impossible to continue at the first semester's pace. Kendall-Ball said that besides their 8 a.m. to 1 p.m. class schedule, he and the others had to also teach a daily class at the local schools, study for their lessons and work with the church at Gwelo and with the African brethren in the rural areas. Therefore, the second semester they only met for classes once a week, but with more homework. Melville Sheasby studied that way for two years. Paddy studied for three and a half years with Foy. Several others, including Richard Lang, also studied with Foy during his early years at Gwelo.

Foy continued special study sessions with young men throughout his years in Gwelo, although on a smaller scale. He reported in May of 1973 that he had special classes with seven African preachers and praised their down-to-earth approach to the scriptures when compared to the tendency of some Americans to seek loopholes.[314]

Instrumental Music, Institutionalism

One of Foy's students in his intensive training in Gwelo was Wendall Freeman, the preacher at the local Christian church. Foy and the others received him into the program with open arms. Foy invited him to write an article defending instrumental music in worship in an English paper called *The Enquirer* that Foy published to provide a forum for giving both sides of controversial issues such as institutionalism. Foy always clearly stated his convictions, but felt it important to be loving and respectful in doing so, while giving those of "the other side" opportunities to present their case. After discussing the fact that God entrusted the gospel to man he said in the first issue,

> It is not the prerogative of any man or group of men to seek to build a wall about truth or followers of truth, to cut them off from contact with error. Rather it is man's responsibility to proclaim truth as

widely and vigourously as possible, following the Divine example of leaving it to the hearer to discern what is right and wrong. Jesus taught in this way, placing truth clearly, openly, alongside error, that the deceptions of error might be exposed by truth. … It is our purpose in publishing this magazine, *The Enquirer*, to provide an open forum for the investigation of Bible subjects, both controversial and non-controversial.[315]

Foy added, "Articles which, in the editor's judgment, contain sarcastic or disparaging expressions, if printed at all, will be edited to remove the objectionable features." He later promised, "We will endeavour to be completely impartial in our allocation of space …"[316]

However, Foy wasn't able to convince his brethren and even close family members to participate in exchanges about institutionalism in *The Enquirer*. His father, William Newton, whom he greatly loved, was sympathetic with the promoters of institutionalism as was his brother-in-law, Henry Ewing, with whom he had worked so closely and so effectively at Queens Park in Bulawayo in the 1950s. Ewing, in explaining his desire not to participate in exchanges told Foy, "It would be fine to have a paper if we all agreed."[317] Foy said, "We had to just use printed articles for the liberal viewpoint as there was no interest among more liberal brethren to participate."[318]

In 1962, brethren in Bulawayo asked Foy to come and speak at the dedication service of the new building for the Hillside congregation. However, fearing that he might mention institutionalism, they put in a few restrictions about what he could say. Foy wrote back and said that he just taught the scriptures, but that he wasn't going to preach anywhere where there were restrictions on what he would preach. The restrictions were lifted and Foy was able to conscientiously preach in the new building.

For many years Foy sent his father copies of *The Enquirer* to distribute among the brethren at Hillside where he was an elder. Later he found out that his father put the papers on the top shelf of the library and never distributed them to anyone. The Hillside church in Bulawayo, therefore, went for years without allowing any teaching one way or the other on the topic of institutionalism. The Queens Park congregation in Bulawayo taught against institutionalism while the Belleview congregation, started in the 1970s by J.C. Shewmaker, actively sympathized with it.

One day in the early 1960s Foy was having a lively discussion about institutionalism with his mother at the house in Gwelo. Both enjoyed the give and take, little noticing how uncomfortable Foy's father was with what was going on. Suddenly Foy's father said that it was time to leave, got up and took Delia out the door to the car and they drove away without any goodbyes. The abruptness of the departure shook up Foy and his family. Ellen recalls that her mother was crying.

After driving away, Delia began to talk to her husband to convince him to return to the house and explain why the discussion had upset him so much. A few minutes later they returned to the house in a much calmer frame of mind and Foy's father gave them an explanation of his actions. He told them that as a child he had heard family members constantly bickering over issues like instrumental music, Bible classes and the number of containers to be used in the Lord's Supper, to the point that he was very much averse to that kind of discussion. They upset him so much that he could not tolerate them.

Jim Short recalled that his grandfather had a brother who did not believe in Bible classes in the church nor the use of multiple containers in the Lord's Supper. Though this brother was quite prosperous during the depression, he sent no financial help to W.N. who was struggling to survive on remote outposts in Southern Africa. His brother considered him a "false teacher."

W.N. Short was also affected by the fierce attacks against his mentor, J.N. Armstrong, by Foy Wallace and others for not being aggressive enough in fighting premillennialism. Short felt that such attacks were totally unchristian and destructive. This combination of factors led the pioneer evangelist to avoid sharp disagreements with his brethren, though he did have exchanges with those of mainstream denominations.

The controversy about institutionalism was never as acrimonious in the southern part of Rhodesia as it was in South Africa and parts of the United States. Though firm in his convictions, Foy maintained friendly relationships with most of his brethren who disagreed with him about it. However, in Salisbury in the north, Americans from the Nhowe mission were more militant in marking those who opposed their teaching. They were able to take over the congregation in Salisbury in the early 1960s and made unflattering remarks about Foy to his son, Harold, Alan Hadfield and others. Alan Hadfield returned to Bulawayo to help start the congregation in Hillside. After the Americans left Salisbury, conservative brethren there started a new congregation in 1971 and invited Foy to come and preach for them whenever possible. Jim Short worked with the group from 1975 through 1981.

Opportunities in English in Neighboring Cities

The Shorts had opportunities to teach the Bible in English in neighboring towns. Doug Bauer was from a family converted by Foy's father, W.N. Short in Macheke. In speaking of Bauer, Margaret said, "One of his young brothers was living in Que Que about 40 miles from us. We went up once a week to study, they were baptized. Eventually Doug came and worked in Que Que." (The spelling was changed to Kwe Kwe when the country became Zimbabwe.) She added, "One family that we baptized in Gwelo and one that had been baptized in Bulawayo had moved to Masvingo (formerly Fort Victoria). They met in each other's homes. We went down there fairly often to help."

There were close ties between the brethren in Gwelo and those in Que Que. In 1972 Foy wrote in his bulletin, "We had 23 visitors from the Que Que congregation on Sunday night. What a boost it gave us to enjoy their fellowship during the evening service."[319] He wrote an encouraging report in 1972 about a meeting Paul Williams held in Que Que and Gwelo, where there was one baptism. He said, "Brother Williams did the church much good, giving us lessons that were sorely needed. Four days after the meeting there was a second baptism."[320]

Periodical in the Shona and isiNdebele Languages

As in Bulawayo, Foy and his companions would find many opportunities to teach those of the amaNdebele tribe in Gwelo. Since they were in the Midlands region which also had a border with Mashonaland, they would also have opportunities with the Shonas. Jim remembers that Sunday mornings were always dedicated to the English speaking work and then Foy would go in the afternoons out into the countryside and preach for brethren of African descent. Often he took Jim and other members of his family with him.

To supplement that work, Foy began to publish a monthly teaching paper in 1962, titled *Inquiniso* and *Zwakadi* (Truth)" in the isiNdebele and Shona languages. At first he used a mimeograph machine to print up the papers but eventually was able to buy a big Kodak camera to make plates and use an offset press. At first he printed almost 2000 copies of the paper in each language, using articles that dealt primarily with the first principles of the Bible. Later his circulation count approached 10,000. He dedicated much space in his papers to analyzing the false teachings of the religious sects and denominations.

Foy wrote in 1962,

> One way we are trying to teach the native Christians more is through the printing and distributing of literature. The Market St. congregation in Athens, Ala. is supplying us with the funds needed to buy supplies for this and to hire a native man to translate mate-

rial. Bro. Enoch Ncube is working with us in this and we are teaching him to type. Until he learns to type, Margaret and I are having to double up on our work and do the typing of stencils in the Sindebele language. During May and June, we have printed a total of about 3,500 items, and this will be increased as Bro. Ncube can take over some of the typing.[321]

Foy mailed the paper to individuals and congregations. He said,
It was amazing how those things spread. I got letters from 200-300 miles away from people who got them and wanted information about them. A number of congregations were started from them. Even today when I go to a few congregations people will bring out an old tattered paper and say, "These are the papers that got us started here."

The paper became especially important during the bush war that started in the late 1960s when it became more dangerous for Foy and others to go into the countryside to teach. Foy continued to publish the paper until 1984 by which time the bush war had ended and post-election political violence was beginning to wane. At that time he had so many appointments with churches that he didn't feel that he had the time to continue the printing.

With any publication there is usually the frustrating need to fight with balky machines. Though such aggravations didn't make it into official reports, they made it into private letters. Foy wrote Ellen in 1968,
I've had a lot of trouble with the printing press, mainly because I am (or was) so inexperienced in the use of it. For about three months I could hardly get anything printed. But now I've mastered the art of adjusting it and things are going smoothly, only I've been trying to catch up on three months of printing. … On Friday (21st) I finished the May papers. Tomorrow I plan to get started on June's

paper. If I can get that done in the next 7 to 10 days, then I'll be ready to start on the July paper before July is more than half gone.[322]

Progress Among African Churches

Paddy Kendall-Ball says that five names stand out in his mind when thinking of effective African workers among the amaNdebele in the 1960s: Jeffrey Nyembezi, Teli Moyo, Major Mpofu, Enoch Ncube and David Ndlovu. Newman Gumbo became prominent in the work later. He said that they "just worked and worked and taught and taught." All remained faithful to the Lord into the 1970s and 1980s except for Major Mpofu. When seeing Kendall-Ball's list, Foy and Margaret insisted on adding another preacher, Nesu Moyo, to the list of outstanding preachers stating, "He was one of our favorites."[323] Foy's reports in the 1970s also mention the work of James Machaya, a preacher he taught out of a Pentecostal denomination.

Of these effective evangelists, Kendall-Ball was especially close to Enoch Ncube who he says was like a father to him. Kendall-Ball said in 2008, "He's the only one that's still living. He's 78 and still going strong, He's very knowledgeable about the scriptures and a great teacher. He's fantastic!" Ellen Baize said of Ncube, "I don't know of any person in this world that I respect more than that man."[324]

Kendall-Ball talked of the growth of churches he knew in the rural areas around Gwelo/Gweru and their numbers in the early 2000's. He mentioned Cinderella (19.5 km SE of Gweru) with twenty-five or thirty members. Another congregation in the Ghoko Plains area, an area heavily populated by Seventh Day Adventists, had only seven members for many years until Newman Gumbo and other evangelists began giving special attention to the area, "sitting up all hours of the night" teaching contacts. There were two congregations on the other side (North) of Gweru with over one hundred members apiece.

Once Paddy and his wife Sandi gave a ride to a woman from the Ghoko Plains area to Gwelo who was a Seventh Day Adventist. Sandi encouraged her to attend services with them but the woman was very reluctant. However, she said something that encouraged the Kendall-Balls, "You have captured many of our people." Paddy thought, "Yes!" and then good-naturedly asked the woman, "Can we capture you?" However, she replied, "no."

Foy was constantly amazed at the ability of some of the African evangelists to explain Biblical principles in simple terms to the people. Once, when a Lutheran preacher asked about predestination, Teli Moyo responded that farmers should understand the principle well.

God predestined, made a law, that every seed would bring forth after its kind. If you want to raise mealies (corn), you must plant mealies. If you want to raise peanuts, you must plant peanuts. That's God's law for the field.

Brother Moyo then pointed out that God's spiritual law of pre-destination is similar to this. ... Paul teaches us in Galatians 6 that as a man sows, so he shall reap. If we plant righteousness, we will reap eternal life. This is God's law for the Spirit. In both cases, God predestined (made these laws) for sowing and reaping.

Foy said of the illustration, "I have never heard predestination explained more simply nor accurately."[325']

Ellen Baize said, "Bigboy Dube, tells me on nearly every trip how dad confronted problems. He went directly to the source and asked questions."[326] On one occasion a group of brethren were together and Foy asked one to repeat an accusation he had made against another. Since it was false, the man declined and the issue was laid to rest. On another occasion, a preacher was very upset because another preacher had "put a curse on him." Ellen said, "Dad talked with the man who had been cursed and asked him who was the greatest spirit — God or this 'spirit' who was suppose to curse him?"[327]

Foy summed up his feelings about work among African brethren in 1962.

It is a never-failing thrill to see the eagerness with which the African people respond to the gospel. They see so much in it that they instinctively feel that they need. But it is sad to see how discouraged they can get too. What we must endeavor to do is to provide them with more teaching, not on merely becoming a Christian, but that infinitely more difficult and longer process of living the Christian life.[328]

African Customs and Food

In an outline titled "Preaching the Gospel in Zimbabwe" that Foy elaborated in 1999 he pointed out cultural traditions in Southern Africa that sometimes puzzled Westerners.

- Innate courtesy
  1. Request permission to enter district, village, house, church assembly ...
  2. Respect of younger for the elderly (Western influence causing this to change)
  3. Women kneel or curtsey when serving men.
  4. Women sit in the floor, giving chairs to men.
  5. All when offering a gift with the right hand, place left hand on right hand wrist. Why? Some say it is so that it may be seen that nothing is in the left hand and that no weapon is concealed in the left hand.
- Non-confrontational attitude
- Disregard for queues [waiting lines]
- No thought for an individual's "space." They crowd upon each other in gatherings.
- When passing your house at night they will talk and sing loudly. This is to let you know they are passing. Only those with criminal intent will sneak past quietly!
- The place and role of women
  1. Much of work is done by women

2. American preachers can effectively preach on husband/wife relationship.

3. [Foy mentioned observing a preacher allow his friend's wife to carry his big suitcase as well as her own two big bundles.]

Foy concluded the outline by pointing out that differences not contrary to the Bible must be left alone, while cultural differences violating scriptural principles must be dealt with. Preachers from Zimbabwe were more capable of dealing with these problems and therefore their training was of supreme importance.

When giving a report on the work in Zimbabwe to brethren in the Bellaire congregation near Houston, Texas, Foy described other African customs in more detail.

When people are talking and you come upon them, you don't avoid going between them. [Going around them] would indicate some kind of an underhanded scheme, that you didn't want to face them or that you wanted to sneak around. They'll walk right between conversing people whereas you and I wouldn't dream of it.

Many walk fifteen miles, bring food and cook it. It's served to the men first by women who curtsy or get on their knees to hand the food to the men. An American woman and her husband went there to preach. She saw this and thought it wasn't … maintaining the dignity women should have. So, she began talking to the women and telling them they shouldn't do this. After a little bit, the women came to her and said, "We would like to ask you not to teach about this matter of kneeling any more. It is our custom. It is our way of showing our love and respect for our husbands."

Foy then said, "To her credit, she listened to their advice. There are some Americans that are too hard headed to listen to anything like that." Another American woman told Zimbabwean women in Kensington, a congregation in Bulawayo started by Newman Gumbo, that they only had to wear the covering when worshipping because of their custom, not because the Bible taught it. Lillian Gumbo spoke up and told her that Margaret Short had taught them about this from the Bible. To the woman's credit, she dropped the subject and never brought it up again.[329]

Foy gave an explanation to the brethren in Bellaire about mealie meal, the primary food in Zimbabwe. "Corn meal is the main food, cooked mushy with gravy or a stew or stewed vegetable to help the mush go down. It's cooked very thick and served on a plate. You take a handful of it, roll it up in your hands and then dip it in the gravy or put some of their relish with it. That's their way of eating. That's their staple diet."

Foy described the traditional way of building their huts, where small groups would sometimes crowd for a service, especially during his younger days.

They put poles in the ground and then plaster them over with mud. Sometimes they'll have a little window for air to flow through, but many times they won't. They'll have a wood fire in the center of the hut and there's no chimney. The smoke gets real heavy in there. There've been times when I've had to sit in one of those huts while an African preacher preached for an hour or two and my eyes started streaming. It was hard to breathe. They seemed to get along with it all right.

Foy discussed the fact that funerals were always a challenge to Christians because of superstitions that surrounded them.

The belief is that after death the spirit wanders about for a year, looking for a place to live. At the close of that year, the family has a feast and beats the grave, indicating that this is the place the departed spirit should come to live. The feast not only involves drinking the ceremonial beer, but eating that which is devoted to the memory of the spirit. The accession of the elder son as head of his late father's family, in particular, hinges on this. This entails a major part of the family property. An eldest son who refuses to participate in this ceremony cannot be his father's heir... Other children who refuse to participate lose their standing in the family circle and will usually be blamed for any tragedy or distress that comes upon the family.[330]

Jim Short recalled some events in his life that illustrated interesting aspects of African culture. One illustrated the African sense of humor.

They will laugh at situations that we would not. When people are in trouble or embarrassed they (including the person at the center of the situation) will simply laugh uproariously about it. I was teaching a class with about eight young men who wanted to become preachers. One of them asked me what kind of body we would receive at the resurrection. I referred to I Corinthians 15 and said that it would be glorified, eternal body. Well that wasn't sufficient and he wanted to know more. Exactly what kind of a body would that be? I again suggested that we did not know, but that it would be wonderful and eternal. Well, he continued to press the question. I finally just asked him to read aloud I Corinthians15:35-36 where Paul suggests that people may ask that question, but how foolish to do so. As he read it, he just cracked up, as did everyone else in the class. He thought it was a great answer and we went on with the class. I don't think I could have done that in the US, at least not with a lot of folks![331]

He also told a story about Newman Gumbo that illustrated the Africans' "indirect directness."

When I was there in 1993 after my Dad's heart surgery, I was driving with Newman Gumbo to one of the rural churches when he began a conversation that went along these lines.

"There is a lot of work to be done here in Zimbabwe." I of course agreed.

"Your father is getting older." Again, I agreed.

"Your father is damaging his health by trying to do all of the work." I again agreed.

"Your father needs someone to help him." Again I had to agree.

"Someone a little younger needs to come to help him." What could I do but agree?

"Someone your age."

Without actually saying it, he had in fact said that I should come to Zimbabwe to work with my Dad! Had there been a way for me to do that and be able to provide for my family, I would have done it.[332]

Trip to the USA in 1967

Foy took the family to the States in early 1967, primarily to visit Ellen and supporting churches. He traveled all over the country giving reports on the work in Rhodesia.

Margaret wrote Ellen while on the road to Arizona to visit the Gene Tope family. She said that after visiting the Topes they planned, "to get back to Abilene on Sunday night the 12th, after being in Pampa and Lubbock for two services, then on back to Irving on Monday the 13th."[333] After staying in Irving they planned to go to Pine Bluff, Arkansas and then on to Atlanta for a visit with the Bankstons and their return flight to Rhodesia. Margaret was happy to be writing on a portable typewriter that the (Dan) Clendennings had loaned them and felt quite satisfied to be working on her seventh letter of the day, even though the typewriter, "skips a bit and of course the bumps in the road make that worse."

Foy and Margaret returned to Rhodesia through London where they visited with their old friends, the R.B. Scotts and the church in Kentish Town. Margaret Scott Daniell once again took Kay and Margaret sightseeing, though Foy came down with a cold, partly because "the Kentish Town building was not properly heated."[334]

From London the Shorts flew to Lagos, Nigeria for a brief visit with Leslie Diestelkamp and Nigerian brethren. Foy was amazed at the hustle and bustle of Lagos. After talking about the poverty there, he wrote Ellen,

> The filth was perhaps even worse than the poverty. Concrete lined ditches on each side of the road, open to the air, to flies and to scavenging chickens, serve as sewage disposal systems, and carried a sluggishly moving mass of human waste. The stench is unbelievable. How the entire population escapes being wiped out by plague or typhoid fever I cannot imagine. And the noise is beyond belief too. Everybody talks, shouts, laughs at the top of their voices. Cars roar up and down, each with its hooter going full blast. Even the motor scooters buzz along adding their shrill beep-beeps to the surging cacophony of sound. And on top of that the RADIOS!! The Nigerian may have literally nothing else, but he will have a transistor radio. And large or small, it will be turned on full blast. You find yourself longing for just a short half hour of blessed quiet.[335]

After taking a Pan Am flight out of Lagos to Johannesburg, Foy expressed relief to be back in Southern Africa.

Social Life, Raising Teenagers

The middle and late 1960s in Gwelo were teenage years for the Short children. Their five acres provided space for gardening and livestock. Harold used the Jeep to plow and help with other farming chores. Margaret said, "We grew cabbage so I did a lot of sauerkraut and froze that." They also grew corn.

Jim remembered that his parents were active in the school's PTA and very supportive of them in all their school activities. He and Harold played cricket and rugby. Foy and Margaret attended all of their games. Foy wrote rather proudly to Ellen in June of 1968 that Jim was playing regularly for Chaplin High School's third rugby team and that Kay had made the "CJR hockey team" even though she was only in "standard 4" and had to compete against girls in the "standard 5."[336] In the same letter he reported that Jim, Harold and Alan went to Salisbury to see the British Lions rugby team play Rhodesia. However, he didn't go because he didn't think it would be a wise use of his money.

In 1969 Margaret wrote Ellen about a school play. "Jimmy played the part of the American Col. in '*Teahouse of the August Noon*' and did very well indeed. His American accent wasn't there all the time, but sounded very authentic when it did come through."[337]

Margaret appreciated the fact that school activities in Rhodesia followed a family-friendly predictable schedule.

> School was in session between eight and one, with one PT period. Everything closed for lunch between one and two, so we brought the kids home for lunch In the afternoons they went back for any other activities they were interested in — sports, including swimming, debating club, etc. There were no practices or games at night, but some things like debating competitions were sometimes held in the early evening. Other activities such as class parties took place on Friday nights. Any kind of matches against other schools were played on Saturdays. This meant we could keep regular schedules and have three meals together every day.

Ellen recalls that her parents, though personally strict in their teaching (for example, they didn't attend movies), allowed their children to make choices on attending school activities and parties, even those that included dancing. However, they made an exception when one of her friends in the congregation invited her to a birthday party where there would be dancing. Ellen said, "I did not plan to dance, having made the decision that it was not an activity in which I could participate as a Christian, but I wanted to go, especially since a boy I really liked would be there. Mom and dad told me that I couldn't go, as they felt my attendance would be taken as approval of dancing by them."[338]

To help their daughter feel better, Foy and Margaret suggested inviting the same friends to a party at their home. Ellen hated to tell her parents, "no," but was afraid of what all the "cute guys" would do when they came to her party and found out there would be no dancing. However, her dad pulled out an ice cream freezer and "all the guys had a blast taking turns cranking" it. Then Margaret pulled out the usual games she organized for Friday nights. Ellen said, "Afterwards these friends told me that they had had more fun than they had at parties with dancing."

According to Ellen, "Supper time was discussion time. We were allowed to make our points and never ridiculed."[339] She remembered that Jim often disagreed with her parents, but that they patiently asked questions that gradually led him to "seeing things their way. … Many times mother got up from the table and took down the encyclopedia to look up something we were discussing. We discussed sports, music, politics, religion — anything of interest."

Foy and Margaret in Gwelo in the early 1970s.

Foy and Margaret's daughter, Kathryn, recalled her father's skill with horses. Her maternal grandfather bought a horse for her so Foy bought one to be able to ride with her. She recalled in particular his skill with a horse named Shadow.

> Shadow had been very badly mistreated by a previous owner and would tremble violently whenever anyone came near him. Nobody could ride him. Dad rode him home the day he bought him! Within a few months Shadow didn't tremble anymore, and within a few years had progressed from only letting Dad ride him to letting some children down the road ride him.[340]

In thinking of her parents, Kathryn said, "They have been the most generous, loving (with an unconditional love) and God-fearing parents, who
taught by example. I have always said that they never had much materially,
but in other ways … they are extremely wealthy.[341]

The Shorts were active in musical circles in Gwelo. All of the children
learned to play musical instruments, with Harold, Ellen and Kay becoming
accomplished pianists. Harold learned to play the trombone for the cadet
band. Jim preferred the guitar to the piano and played the trumpet in the
cadet band, although the separation in the boys' age did not allow them to
play together. (The cadets were similar to the ROTC. The boys' activities
not only involved the band, but constant polishing of shoes and prepartion
of uniforms.) Ellen played the violin. Singing was, and still is an important
part of family life.[342] Ellen ended up majoring in music, and Harold is, and
has been for many years, a member of the London Chorale.[343] Both boys
were also excellent song leaders.

Margaret auditioned for the Gondoliers and was a member of the choir
for ten years, participating in various productions such as *The Pirates of
Penzance* and *The Mikado*. The group did a concert production of *The
Magic Flute*, Vivaldi's *Gloria* and Haydn's *Creation*. There were also numerous popular concerts and one year a night of opera, in which Margaret
sang the Flower Duet from *Madame Butterfly* with her voice teacher.[344] She
also sang with the Madrigal group.

Foy took violin lessons with Dorthy Dams. He said, "She is very critical
and adamant on getting the technique right – but of course that is as it
should be, and I'm thoroughly enjoying it."[345]

Foy played golf in Gwelo after being introduced to the game by Harold in
1964. He wrote his children, "My golf is improving steadily. Yesterday afternoon I played a round and had a score of 81… I'm expecting to be out
to 12 handicap any time now, as I've had two good rounds in succession."[346]

One of the members at the Gwelo club, a Mr. Beddingfield told a Mr. Smith in front of Foy, "You know, Foy is having a very marked and beneficial sobering influence on the Gwelo Golf Club. The men are taming their language down and their topics of conversation. The atmosphere is becoming more pleasant." Foy seemed somewhat unconvinced when remarking to Ellen, "I've never rebuked any of them for bad language. It will be interesting to see how far this influence extends."[347]

Foy and Margaret were active in various clubs and benevolent groups during the Gwelo years. Foy was chairman of the Cancer Society and both were active in the Caravan club, with Margaret serving as secretary. Later, they became members of the Rotary Club. Foy served as president in 1978.[348]

Early during his stay in Gwelo, Foy went to a game reserve to hunt for eland, a giant antelope. When he started to cross a clearing he heard a rustling sound on the side of the clearing and instinctively stepped back into the bushes next to the clearing and squatted down. Out into the clearing stepped a large Cape buffalo bull, considered by many to be the most dangerous animal in Africa. According to expert David Meisel, "Lone bulls are very nervous as they don't have the safety and security of numbers and are therefore very quick to charge at any sign of danger. A charging buffalo is difficult to stop and many hunters have fallen victim to them, even after shooting warning shots."[349]

The huge beast sniffed around, caught Foy's scent and started walking towards him. To Foy's horror, he realized he had soft nosed ammunition in his gun, which would be completely ineffective against the behemoth. He quickly loaded two hardnosed bullets into his weapon, but the buffalo heard the clicking sound of the reloading and stopped about twenty yards from Foy to try to determine where he was. One shot is often not enough to bring down a cape buffalo and Foy decided he had better try to get a shot off quickly, so that that if the animal charged after the first shot he would at least have one more hard nosed bullet to try to save himself. Foy, in a squatting position below the buffalo, aimed for the heart, fired and the enormous animal collapsed in a heap. It was a perfect shot, going through the heart and severing the spinal cord. Foy said modestly, "I was lucky."[350] Foy also loved to fish for bass around Bulawayo and Gwelo, often with Dennis Clark, but especially enjoyed traveling occasionally to the Zambezi River where even more challenging game fish awaited him. A large mounted tiger fish with razor sharp teeth that Foy caught on the Zambezi River decorated the wall at his home in White House, Tennessee until he moved into his daughter, Kay's basement.

Letters

After the older children left home, Foy and Margaret frequently wrote them, giving advice and reassurance. Sometimes the letters dealt with trivialities of life. Margaret wrote Ellen, "Be sure to buy your clothes at Sears as much as you possibly can so you can use practically all your other money for other things."[351] More often they dealt with important challenges their children were facing. They were always very personal, affectionate and full of little pearls of wisdom. Typical is what Foy wrote Ellen in 1967,

> We seem to stay awfully busy, but am old enough to know that life is so short that we'd better make time for the things we really want to do. So, am writing this even though there is a stack of slides to get ready for the show, and a stack of books for sermon preparation, all staring me in the face. I want you to know that you rate higher than all of them put together.[352]

In December, 1969 he wrote,

> You are in our hearts and minds at all times. How we wish we could do more for you – but perhaps it is better for you that we cannot. It never ceases to amaze me how our quiet, retiring, unsure little Ellen was able to leave home in her mid teens and cope with *life* the way you have done. Everyone speaks of how well you have coped and how mature you have shown yourself to be.[353]

Regarding Ellen's romantic ups and downs Foy advised her,

Just get as much emotional experience out of them as you can. Take the joy, the pain, the bewilderment, the anxiety, the beauty, the disappointment — learn from them all. They are the experiences of which life is made. Learn from them and you'll learn to evaluate situations properly, and be able to keep things in the proper perspective. ... Then one day you'll make the right choice for a life's mate. Just "make haste slowly" in these things. But there, I can't even write a letter without preaching.[354]

Sometimes the letters reveal that times were slightly lean financially. When advising Ellen to be as frugal as possible when she was short on money Foy admitted to her,

Mother and I have mostly had the same experiences throughout our married life. Things are a little easier now — although we still have a crisis now and again. Back in January we had to get an overdraft from the bank, which we are still paying back. For one thing two churches have dropped our support leaving me $75 per month short, and no one has taken that up yet.[355]

In other letters Foy wrote philosophically about their lives:

The other day Mother was talking about how many things she wanted to get done that she never seemed to get around to. And I have suggested that in our lives it must always necessarily be so. We have so many and so varied interests that our problem has never been in finding something to do, but rather in choosing which things to do first. Consequently many things have to come later, if time for them can be found at all. So I fully expect that when my time to die shall come, I will leave behind quite a list of things that I would have liked to have done had time sufficed. Which is just another way of saying that our lives are full. What I try to concentrate on is to do all that I can to see that they are filled with worthwhile things.[356]

Camp in Gwelo

Foy and Margaret started up a new camp for the young people in an area called Whitewaters Dam. They were able to run the camp there until 1968 when the bush war began to make it too dangerous to operate. Typically "fifty or sixty" young people would attend the camp and there were usually a number of baptisms.[357] Though the camp never became as large as the one in Bulawayo, Paddy Kendall-Ball felt that it accomplished much good. Jim remembered how much he enjoyed his father's Bible classes at the camp. Foy's father, W.N. (Will) wrote about Foy's camp at Gwelo as well as several others in Southern Africa, "The Lyons family, with helpers, with 28 children present, had such a camp near Lusaka, N. Rhodesia. H. F. Short and helpers had 30 children near Gwelo, while C H Bankston and others had 64 children out from Bulawayo, S. Rhodesia."[358]

Ellen recalled the primitive conditions at the camp. "Dad would take a 55-gallon drum, cut it in half and put it up on sticks. In the early morning you would go and get water and pour into that drum and wash. That was our bathing facility. The boys had their own drum in another area of the bush. Our toilet was a ditch with a grass enclosure around it. It was real camping."

Jim remembered having to dig the latrines every year before camp and then fill them in after camp. "Great fun!" he said with a bit of sarcastic humor. He also recalled that two young boys whose father was active in the Presbyterian Church attended camp. One year the boys' father said that his youngest son, David, returned from camp and asked him, "Do you think that Jesus knew as many scripture verses as Mr. Short?" Jim added with understatement, "Dad quoted scripture frequently!" Foy also encouraged the children at camp and his own children to memorize them.

Foy occasionally felt the need to reinforce the fact that though the camps did some spiritual good, the recreation and games in them took them out of the realm of church work. They, therefore, should not accept church contributions. Most of his weekly bulletin of April 13, 1972 was dedicated to analyzing this point.[359]

A Family Challenge

The middle and late 1960s were a challenging time for the Shorts because of growing differences with their older son Harold. He attended college in Salisbury and was confronted with the unbelieving professors and the political turmoil that characterized universities in that decade, not only in the United States, but also throughout the world. Harold was convinced that far-reaching changes were needed in Rhodesia while his parents were more concerned with "maintaining law and order."[360] This led to family disagreements.

While trying to cope with agnostic professors at college and differing opinions about social change with his parents, Harold also had to deal with brethren from the Nhowe mission who often expressed their displeasure with his father's refusal to go along with institutionalism. They told him he wasn't thinking for himself, but only believed what he did because of his father. That was exactly what he had been told many times at the university. The Americans from Nhowe mission also reminded him often that his grandfather didn't agree with them.[361]

According to his brother Jim, Harold also became discouraged when he observed the ungodly attitudes that surrounded the controversy about institutionalism in Southern Africa and the United States and the racism that characterized too many brethren in both places. [362] All of these challenges proved too much for young Harold. He stopped attending worship services, married and moved to England. How many others like him from the 1960s began to see primitivist Christianity as a source of petty squabbling instead of a fountain of love and peace in a shallow, materialistic world? Ellen felt that her parents often second-guessed themselves for Harold's abandonment of some of their convictions. She said, "They felt that they should have been more in contact with him during that critical time." Foy participated in a panel discussion on foreign evangelism at the Eastside congregation in Athens, Alabama in 1971. An unknowing and unthinking questioner asked Foy, "When you go overseas, what about your children? Isn't it possible that some of them could have problems?" There was a long uncomfortable pause, especially for those who knew of Foy's situation. His eyes watered, then he said slowly, "In any war, there will be casualties."[363] Perhaps thinking of Harold's spiritual challenges, Foy confided in a personal letter to Ellen in 1970 about his decision to raise his family on the spiritual frontier.

> Frontier life is a lonely life, full of hazards. But somebody must face them or no frontiers are conquered. Was I wrong to expose my family and my children to these hazards? And if there are casualties in the frontier battles, does that mean we should all have stayed where it is safe and avoided the casualties?… If the Lord will allow it and sees fit, I purpose to continue to battle on the frontiers of the gospel.[364]

Of course, "spiritual casualities" can occur anywhere as one elder in North Alabama reminded Foy and Margaret. Margaret recalls wondering out loud with him whether she and Foy should have returned to North Alabama "so our children could have attended Christian schools." The elder confided to them that the same type of thing had happened to his family even though they lived in Alabama. They had two sons. Both had attended the Bible school in Athens from the first grade to twelfth and then had gone to a college run by brethren. One continued to work among known churches of Christ. The other chose a different course in life.[365]

Foy and Margaret maintained a good relationship with Harold, who became highly proficient in computer publishing programs. As will be seen in the last chapter, he dedicated much time to help his father publish the Bible concordance in the isiNdebele language.

Bush War in the 1960s and 1970s

Political instability would affect Foy's work beginning on November 11, 1965 when Ian Smith and his allies declared independence from Great Britain so that they could continue a more gradual path toward majority rule, even as Britain and the nationalists demanded drastic changes. Shortly afterwards, Shona guerrilla forces trained in China and led by Robert Mugabe and Russian trained forces of the amaNdebele tribe led by Joshua Nkomo began attacks on the Smith regime and each other. Though Foy and other evangelists of European extraction endured inconvenience, especially in their travel, the ones who suffered the most were the Africans in the rural areas where competing groups of guerrillas rampaged.

Foy described some of the difficulties in the late 1960s and 1970s.

> During that period the violence also spread to the cities and along some of the main roads, so we had to open bags for inspection at every building we entered and could only travel on some of the main roads in a police convoy. We had to assemble at a point at the edge of a city and would travel with a police Land Rover at the head, another halfway back and a third one at the end. Sometimes the convoys were attacked but you were much safer than going it alone. Many missionaries were recalled during that period, including some of our own, mainly those in the more dangerous border areas.[366]

Because of the growing violence in the late 1960s and 1970s Foy and other evangelists were often unable to visit congregations in rural areas. Foy's paper had to do much of the teaching that he had done earlier in person.

Foy lamented the passing of the peaceful Rhodesia he had known as a young man, where he was often able to camp out in the wild with no concerns. In writing his children he described,

> … Camping out in or near Tribal Trust Lands, in the evenings especially, with the cattle lowing, children laughing, African voices call-

ing, talking, mostly at their uninhibited loudest, tentative throbbing
of drums breaking in now and then, as if testing themselves for the
evening's performance, and in the west the sun sinking in a bath
of blazing yet softening reds, blues, greens, golds and every shade
in between, and you could almost believe you were in the land of
make believe, so beautiful and peaceful and satisfying it could only
exist in your imagination. This is the Rhodesia I grew up in and so
did you children.

However, Foy realized that the peaceful, idyllic Rhodesia of his youth was
about to change forever.

But as all living things must change, grow old and give place to
the new, so, I am persuaded, must Rhodesia and her peoples also
change. Looking at the nations and peoples of the world around I
fear the changes will not all be for the best. With advocates of non-
violence bombing and machine gunning those who won't agree
with them, and the purgers of corruption merely making way for
their own brand of corruption, etc., I am forced more and more
back upon the only *living way,* the only answer to man's needs and
problems, the way of Christ.[367]

Even before 1965, there were signs of growing instability. In the early 1960s
one of Foy's heroes, Fazo Shandavu, had a frightening experience when
a group of revolutionaries knocked on his door asking him to show his
party membership card. He replied that he didn't believe that a Christian
should be a part of the party. The political thugs replied menacingly that
he had seven days to get a card and that if he didn't he would be killed.[368]
Shandavu's wife and children begged him to obtain a card, arguing that
it would not necessarily mean that he believed in violence, but he was
adamant, not wanting to appear to sympathize in any way with political
intimidation. The family knew that this was no idle threat, as others had
been assasinated by the political thugs. After the sixth day darkened into
night, the government banned the party, police arrested its leaders includ-

ing those who had threatened Shandavu and therefore they couldn't come to his house and carry out their threats.

As the bush war intensified, most African brethren continued to serve God at great personal risk. Though told on occasions by the guerrillas not to meet for worship, most did. Several died for their faith. A young man named Douglass Sibanda was bayoneted in front the congregation where he was preaching.[369]

Foy told of the persecution that his good friend Jeffrey Nyembezi had to suffer during this period.

> During the bush wars the terrorists sent word that there would be no church meetings because they looked upon the churches as a possible source of resistance to them… Jeffrey continued to meet with the brethren. Also, the guerrillas wanted them not to pay taxes to the government, but to them. Jeffrey said, "When you're the government, I'll pay taxes to you." For that reason and because he continued to preach, he was number three on the list of men they were going to assassinate.[370]

One day Nyembezi left his wife, Maina, at the house while he went out to visit a man whose father had passed away. While he was gone, a band of terrorists barged into his home and finding only Maina at home, asked her where her husband was. She knew that his life depended on her not telling them so she refused to divulge that information. They then began to beat her brutally to try to extract the information, but she refused to tell them anything. Finally, she was beaten so much that she slipped into merciful unconsciousness. When Nyembezi came home, he found his wife unconscious in the front yard. Foy said, "The nearest medical facilities were about twenty miles away and he had only a bicycle. He put his wife on the seat and started peddling there. He said that all the way he was praying that he wouldn't find any more terrorists."

Ellen Baize talked with Maina about this horrible experience when visiting her in October of 2010. Ellen said, "That was quite an experience listening to her tell the story. Wow! I've always thought she was a very good person, but now ... How many of us would have her courage and love to endure what she did for love of her husband and the gospel?"[371]

As the war was winding down, Foy was thrilled to find out about a congregation in the Matabo area of southern Matabeleland, a center of violent guerrilla activity that continued to meet faithfully throughout the perilous period. The main teacher in the congregation was Samuel Mpofu, who only had about a fourth grade education and had been a plodding student in some of Foy's extensive Bible classes in the 1950s and 1960s. However, Foy realized that he was the "kind that sticks, truly a soldier of the Lord who stood fast at his post regardless of hazards."[372] As news began to trickle out about how they survived the war, the story was told about their worship services being interrupted one Sunday by guerillas. The following conversation ensued:

GUERRILLAS: "What are you doing here?"

CHRISTIANS: "We are worshipping."

GUERILLAS: "Whom do you worship?"

CHRISTIANS: "We worship the one who cannot be seen?"

GUERRILLAS: "How can there be one who is unseen? We will shoot this one you speak of."

CHRISTIANS: "How can you say such a thing? The one we worship made all things. He made you and gave you the brains to make and use those guns. How can you shoot such a one?"

Foy said, "At this, the guerillas laughed and went away saying they did not think such people could harm them." However, he added, "not all such confrontations ended so easily."[373]

Foy wrote about two congregations in Matsholomotshe and Dadata who were left with only women during the bush war. "They sang, prayed, read the scriptures, and partook of the Lord's Supper. Perhaps one would give an exhortation. When peace finally came and I was able to visit them, they were quietly assembling as the Lord commanded. They offered no complaints, voiced no self pity."[374]

Foy often expressed to others that women often were the keys in maintaining many rural congregations during the bush war. He said, "During the … early 1970s there were times when women kept the work of the church going while the men were forced to leave the villages. Sometimes the women had to meet secretly, under cover of darkness. It was a dangerous business."[375] Though women in the amaNdebele and Shona tribes were by nature submissive, they often had an inner strength that surpassed that of their male counterparts. They were a primary factor in the strength of the kingdom in Zimbabwe.

Summary of Work in Gwelo/Gweru

Foy and Margaret felt that their English work in Gwelo was successful in the terms of the number of conversions to the Lord. However, Margaret felt that "it was a difficult place in many ways… It was a transient place where people would stay for a few years before being transferred to another place." She said, "the congregation would build up for a while to fifty or sixty members and then a lot of people would move away all at once." By the time Foy and Margaret left in 1979, there were a few families who held things together in the English speaking congregation. Commenting on the frequent departures of those baptized into Christ in Gwelo, Foy said, "It seems that most of them remained faithful wherever they went."[376] George Edy, though not a public speaker, was a very solid leader in the congregation in the years after the Shorts moved back to Bulawayo. Paddy Kendall-Ball reported in February of 2010 that George Edy accompanied him on a trip to Ghoko and that though he was in the "medium stages of Alzheimer's," he was still able to converse in Shona or isiNdebele and was highly respected by the African brethren.[377]

Foy confided to Ellen in 1969 that his reports from Gwelo were never spectacular:

> I've never been able to make breath-taking reports, the kind that
> make the whole brotherhood sit up and talk. But I don't worry
> about that and I'm certainly not complaining. Over the years it does
> seem that God has been able to use me, and I can truthfully say that
> wherever I've worked, the church has grown. It just seems to take
> me a long time to get the job done.[378]

What Foy didn't realize at the time was that much of the good he accomplished was done indirectly through those he trained. Though he perhaps didn't personally baptize large numbers of people, those he taught did. Among the amaNdbele in the area, many of his students such as his protégé, Enoch Ncube started a number of congregations that have continued to grow well into the twenty-first century. The African congregations, started by Ncube and others, have been Foy's longest living legacy in the area around Gweru.

Chapter 5

Back to Bulawayo

While in Gwelo, Foy always maintained ties with brethren in Bulawayo, especially at Queens Park, his old stomping grounds. In the late 1970s brethren at Queens Park became concerned about the influences of institutional brethren from Northeastern Rhodesia who wanted to have more control in Bulawayo. They asked Foy to come help them.

Foy was disinclined to move away from Gwelo, but felt that Queens Park needed him, so he and Margaret rented a small apartment in Bulawayo and for three years, 1976-1979, constantly traveled the hundred miles back and forth between the two cities. He went to Bulawayo on Wednesday afternoons to teach their midweek class and also preached there on Sunday mornings, returning to Gwelo for the evening service. Gwelo had their Bible study on Tuesday nights, so he was able to be with both congregations for their midweek studies.

Margaret said of their constant commuting, "By that time cars were a bit better. We brought a car from New York and then a little Citroen to ship down. We used the Citroen because it was very economical." On most Fridays Margaret would ride the bus to Bulawayo. Two young evangelists whom Foy trained, Donald Hadfield and Paul Fudge worked with the church in Gwelo, making Foy feel more comfortable about dedicating more time to Bulawayo. Foy studied three mornings a week with Hadfield and Fudge.

During this period, Foy and Margaret also made fairly regular trips to Salisbury to help Jim work with the Greendale congregation that Jim had started in 1976.[379] Foy, who was always close to his children, expressed on several occasions his joy at being able to work in the gospel with his son, Jim. Jim preached seven years in Zimbabwe, from February 1975 to January 1982. Since then, he has made seven trips back, the last one in 2006. He plans to return in 2012 and eventually move there with Carol when he can live off of his retirement income.[380]

Finally, Foy and Margaret decided to sell their house in Gwelo and move back permanently to Bulawayo. They began to transfer a few small things gradually from Gwelo, first to the small apartment they rented and then later to a small home they rented from their old friend, Leonard Bailey in Queens Park. Finally, a moving company transfered their furniture. After moving to Bulawayo, the Shorts continued returning a few days each month to the office where Foy's printing work was done. Enoch Ncube stayed on and worked in that office every day while continuing to work with African brethren in the area.

Foy and Margaret first bought a small two-bedroom house in the north end of Bulawayo. They lived in it from 1979 to 1981 and then bought another house on 6 Rockcliffe Road in Morningside near the meeting place of the congregation in Hillside. By then, many Zimbabweans of European descent were already beginning to leave the country and this helped Foy and Margaret buy the house at a bargain price. Margaret said, "It was in a better part of town where property values were higher and it was a much larger house with a large separate building with double garage doors, a carport with pit for working on cars, which Foy used a lot!" [381] The property also had another fairly large building with a work shop on one side and two rooms and half bath on the other. Margaret said,

> It also had a lovely established garden (word used there for yard and flowers) with lovely trees, shrubs, etc. That large double garage

had a large table with a train track for an electric train set, which hoisted up to the ceiling when not in use. Our grandsons had a ball with that when they visited and we bought more engines and cars for it almost every time we went to South Africa. We brought it over here with us and Jim's son is putting it up in a room in his house in California.[382]

As Foy was getting back into the work in Bulawayo he wrote to Dave and Ellen Baize that he and Margaret had not yet started to focus on evangelizing the lost, but rather were "concentrating on building up enthusiasm among the faithful ones and trying to restore those who have fallen away."[383] His reports mention several visiting preachers from other countries in the latter 1970s who helped encourage the brethren: Martin Broadwell, Marty Broadwell, Sewell Hall, Paul Williams, Ray Votaw, Jim Lovell, Gene Tope and Thernoor Cheddy.

Not only did Foy and Margaret feel that their presence was more needed in Bulawayo because of the work, but also because they would be closer to his elderly parents, William Newton (W.N.) and Delia. Foy's sister, Sybil, whose husband, Bennie Lee Fudge, died in the early 1970s came to Bulawayo in February of 1976 to help with her parents. His sister Beth also spent time there. Delia's mind was beginning to be affected by old age in the latter 1970s and she had a difficult time functioning. Foy's father became increasingly weak and unable to tend to his wife. Finally, Will Short, the old pioneer evangelist, passed away suddenly in June of 1980 leaving Delia whose dementia did not allow her to function. Sybil said, "She couldn't even swallow. She didn't know what to do with food in her mouth." When Delia was younger, her brother, George, suffered from dementia and was placed in Cordell Christian Home in Cordell, Oklahoma. She said at that time that if she were ever in that condition, she would want to be taken there as well. After her husband's death, her children granted her request. She left Africa for the last time in December of 1980 for Cordell and passed away there almost eighteen months later.[384]

W.N. (Will) and Delia Short in their final years.

Will and Delia always said they wanted to be buried in Africa. However, Delia's departure to pass her final days in Cordell, Oklahoma complicated that wish. The family decided then that cremation was the answer. Margaret said, "The funeral director said he would keep Daddy Short's ashes until hers were sent back. I took them back as part of my hand luggage on the next trip I made after she died and they were placed together in the Wall of Remembrance at the Garden of Rest in Bulawayo."[385]

Changes After Independence — 1980

Zimbabwe celebrated its complete independence from the United Kingdom on April 18, 1980 with a large ceremony in Rufaro stadium in Salisbury attended by Charles, Prince of Wales and a host of other political dignitaries. Musicians Bob Marley and Stevie Wonder performed new songs they had written for the occasion.[386]

According to Margaret, the situation during the first year after Zimbabwe's independence "wasn't too bad." The Shorts even started their camp again for one year in 1981. However, political instability began to rear its ugly head again with elements of Robert Mugabe's forces roaming the countryside to terrorize and kill. Mugabe, the elected president, formed what he called the Fifth Brigade, composed of revolutionaries from East Africa and North Korea. These insurgents went into rural areas terrorizing Africans who Mugabe feared might be potential political enemies, particularly Matabele who might sympathize with his political rival, Joshua Nkomo. When the ruthless Fifth Brigade was on the loose in Matabeleland in the 1980's, no one could go into the countryside. Foy said, "The stories that were coming out of the rural areas were horrible. Families would have sons and brothers taken off and beaten or more often simply disappear. It was a terrible time." Many bodies were thrown into old mine shafts that became mass graves.

Margaret said, "By '82 it wasn't safe to go camping. A year or two after that they burned the chapel and facilities down at the camp. It had to be men from the Shona tribe because the owner was so respected among the amaNdebele."

Two weeks after Foy visited his close friend Teli Moyo in Siwazi, political dissidents raided the town, with the Zimbabwean army hot on their heels. Some villagers were killed in the ensuing turmoil. A number of brethren were beaten, but thankfully none died. The dissidents demanded food, which was unlawful to give them, but Teli Moyo told Foy, "What could we do? They had guns!"[387]

Elements of Mugabe's army took their frustrations out on Europeans as well. A group of tourists from England stopped by the side of the road and were murdered. Though there were many rumors that the culprits were Mugabe's forces, no one was ever accused of the crime. Two of Foy and Margaret's grandchildren visited them in 1984. She and Foy took them to see Victoria Falls but had a flat tire on the way and had to stop by the side of the road. A European man stopped to help the Shorts

Foy and Margaret in the 1980s

and encouraged them to get on their way as soon as possible. Shortly before, some people had been murdered on the same stretch of road.

Foy began to limit his visits to brethren in rural areas again because of the raids in the country. He would rely on the word of his Ndebele brethren to determine whether it was safe to travel or not. On one occasion brethren in a certain area gave him the green light to visit them. However, after arriving with seven Ndebele brethren from Bulawayo, the locals told him that they had just received reports of terrorist forces in the area. It was late in the afternoon when he arrived and he and the others decided that it would be safer to spend the night in the danger zone than to drive back to Bulawayo at night, which would have been even riskier. Foy explained,

Usually on these trips, the Africans who went with me would accept invitations to sleep in the huts in the village. I would have my tent set up just outside the village. On this occasion when I set up my tent, the African brethren began to lay out their blankets around my tent. I asked them, "Why is this? Why aren't you sleeping with your friends?" They said, "Brother Short, there could be trouble tonight. If there is, we want to be around you."

Foy was very touched by the gesture of his brethren who took a risk by serving as bodyguards for him.

More Changes

The violence that followed independence and other signs of increasing destabilization in Zimbabwe caused more people to leave the country. The congregation at Queens Park needed to make some adjustments as the neighborhood around the building emptied of English speaking people of European descent and began to fill up with those of African ancestry who preferred services in their native language. The congregation invited Jeffrey Nyembezi to come and work in the isiNdebele language.

Finally, the English speaking Christians decided to begin worshipping in English at the Hillside congregation where Foy's father had been an elder, and turn the Queens Park building over to the Ndebele brethren. The Hillside church also had services in isiNdebele in the afternoon. Foy worked with both, while continuing to dedicate much of his time to rural churches. After Jim's departure in January 1982, he also went once a month to Harare (ex-Salisbury). In the past few years the congregation there has been meeting in homes.

Thankfully the tribal and political violence began to ease in the middle and late 1980's as Mugabe consolidated his control over the country. However, the stage had been set for the coming economic crisis and famine.

As the economy began to deteriorate, prices for food and goods began to escalate. Foy and Margaret began to make trips to South Africa for supplies. When returning they had to deal with customs agents at the border between the two countries, but these were often so overwhelmed at the number of people who were returning to the country that they didn't have time to hassle them much. Margaret said, "There were times when some would try to give you a hard time, especially the women. We would be in a long line. When my turn came and I saw that I would have to go to a woman, I would say to the person behind me, you go ahead, I'm not in a hurry."

Work in the Rural Areas

Foy and those he taught continued to work among the amaNdebele in rural areas in the 1980s and 1990s. Foy made frequent trips into the villages, taking dedicated African evangelists with him. When visiting Zimbabwe in 2010, Ellen Baize asked several of them about their experiences with her father. She wrote, "Bigboy Dube and Stanley Sithole told me how Dad used to pick them up and take them out to the villages, leaving two at each place while he went to furthest village. When he finished preaching, he'd come back and pick them up. Stanley and others from Bulawayo would meet him at Mike's Garage in downtown Bulawayo."[388] He picked up Bigboy Dube in Gwanda and others along the main roads to his final destination.

When Teli Moyo passed away in late 2002, Foy reminisced about the work of that spiritual giant. He told about meeting Moyo when the latter worked at a hotel on the primary road between Bulawayo and South Africa. Later Moyo worked in construction, while preaching and teaching in his spare time in the area around his home congregation in Saphila. That congregation grew to have about 100 members. He started a number of other congregations around Saphila.[389]

In his next report, Foy told about a letter he received from Teli Moyo informing him matter of factly about a new work that he was helping in Nyamime. When Foy began to think of the distances involved, he realized what a sacrifice Moyo was making to help the brethren, though his effort was not even hinted at in his letter. Foy wrote, "From Saphila to Nyamime is about 30 miles... which meant a 60 mile round trip every week by bicycle. It was heavy going over paths with deep sand. It would take from 3 to 4 hours of difficult cycling."[390] He continued, "We visiting preachers see all the results, but how many of us think of the hardships endured, the burning zeal motivating it all?" After mentioning the efforts of Teli Moyo he said, "In all the years I was privileged to work with Teli, he never indicated he thought he should be on American support."

Newman Gumbo was baptized when he was fourteen years old in the 1950s. He studied first with Jimmy Claassen and then worked and studied extensively with Foy during the 1980's and early 1990's. He was offered a lucrative job driving trucks in South Africa, but Foy and Margaret begged him to stay in Bulawayo. His continued presence was critical for their own efforts in drought relief since he was Foy's "right hand man" in the distribution of help to the needy congregations.

After talking with Foy and Margaret, Newman's wife, Lillian, told her husband that she had a request and did not want him to disappoint her and say no. Then she asked him to stay and preach in Bulawayo instead of taking the job in South Africa. Gumbo told her that if he did this, they would not have as much money to buy things for their family. She said that the Lord would provide. They stayed in Bulawayo and have been stalwarts in the Lord's work there. Ellen Baize said of Lillian, "She has worked hard at home all these years since, to help supplement his income, raising chickens, milk cows and crops. I have never seen her without a smile on her face."[391]

Foy reported in 1978, "Bro. Nyembezi reports 15 baptisms recently in the Gwanda area, 100 miles south of Bulawyo. There are about 20 congregations in that rather large area… Bro. Ngoro reports 5 baptisms in the Midlands area of Rhodesia. The Gwelo church is paying his expenses for a 10-day preaching trip in the Hartley-Selous area."[392]

Though many congregations survived the bush war, others did not. Foy gave a long list of places where churches were scattered in the war years: "Dendele, Machuchuda, Hartley, Serowe, Danangombe, Negwande, Dolo, Siwazi, Dadata, etc. etc."[393] Foy was determined to either visit these places personally or find others who could. He added ruefully, "If only there were another full time preacher here to help in answering all these calls." For a number of years Foy was the only known full time preacher in the country who understood the dangerous leavening influence of institutionalism. Several subsequent reports documented his efforts to travel to these towns and villages with varying results.

By 1983, drought and famine were becoming an increasing problem in rural areas. Foy's report of August 31, 1983 relates for the first time his efforts to take one hundred pound bags of mealie meal on his visits into rural areas.

Margaret commented on the drought situation, which would become increasingly severe in the coming years.

Matabeleland, being nearer the desert, was more prone to drought than the eastern part of the country. There was not as much grain grown there, but there were many cattle ranches. … There was always plenty of grain grown in the eastern districts and under the previous government, there was enough to keep a good reserve as well as export some. It was called the Bread Basket of Africa. After Mugabe took over the farms, it changed into a beggar nation, having to import much of its grain!

Some years, even before we left there was not enough in the country and though the government confiscated most of the grain that was given to them by the US and others, we usually managed to get some from the milling company to take out instead of cash as before. During the last years they have had to take the meal up from South Africa.

For a long time, they only expected a severe drought about every seven years, but then in the 80s they started coming more often and in fact, since then, there have been only a few good years.[394]

More information about drought relief will be placed in the last chapter.

In August 1984, the church in Dolo invited brethren from the area to a five-day Bible study session with Foy, Jeffrey Nyembezi and Enoch Ncube doing the teaching.[395] Over two hundred brethren attended, but the studies weren't given without incident. Foy said that about twenty minutes into his Friday evening sermon, thudding drumbeats began to drown him out.

To hear drumbeats in an African night is commonplace. I hadn't noticed them at first. Then as they gradually grew louder I still paid them no attention. But suddenly they were right outside the little meetinghouse and I had to notice them. I stopped and asked the men what was happening. About that time one who had stepped outside returned to tell us that a large number of local "maZoni" church had arrived. (I might add; arrived with a flourish!). The meetinghouse was already crammed full, so it was decided to move outside to continue the service. It was also felt wise for me to shift my lesson from the work of the church to the work of the Holy Spirit. So, all changes being duly effected, we settled down to nearly 2 hours of preaching, followed by 2½ hours of questions.[396]

Foy then explained that the "maZoni" were an offshoot of Pentecostalism, mixing traditional Pentecostal teaching about demon possession and miraculous power with African elements such as African style dancing and drumming. The brethren were obviously glad to receive their visit, in spite of their late and noisy arrival.

Besides Teli Moyo, Foy mentioned men like David Ndlovu, Newman Gumbo, Newhati Ndlovu, Obert Sibanda, Mountbatten Brewer, Joel Moyo and Enoch Ncube as being especially busy in the preaching of the gospel in Matabeleland the 1990's.[397]

Sister Dhlamini

Foy always expressed great admiration for the Christian women of Zimbabwe, who he believed often held many congregations together while men were either away working or sometimes showing less spiritual strength. One godly woman who he especially admired was sister Dhlamini who he felt represented hundreds of godly Matabele women. He wrote in May, 2002, "She was baptized by bro. Makhosi Ndlovu who started the church at Dolo about 1950 or 1951." After marriage she moved to the village of Mukhai, about 20 miles from Dolo, where she began talking with her neighbors about the gospel. When the time was right, she invited brother Ndlovu to her village where he baptized several and started a congregation. She was responsible for the establishment of the congregation and was a pillar in it throughout her life. Her son grew up and began to preach.

Foy continued,

> I met her near the end of her life, when she was blind and cru-
> elly afflicted with arthritis, her fingers so bent she could not hold
> anything, her legs and feet so crippled she had to be carried ev-
> erywhere. … But during the hour some African brethren and I
> spent singing and praying with her, she uttered not one word of
> complaint. She sang many songs by heart, and spoke with joy of the
> coming of the gospel to her village.[398]

When reminded of sister Dhlamini in 2011, Foy and Margaret recalled a
few more details about her. When hearing that Foy was in the area, she said
that she wanted to see the white man. When he went in to see her he realized that her bed was simply a couple of thin blankets on the floor. He also
remembered the particular song she asked them to sing, *"O nDodana ka-
Davida, ungihaukele, watcho njalo impupute Jesu edlulayo."* (Son of David,
have mercy on me said the blind person as Jesus was passing by.) The song
had several verses and she sang every word from memory with a surpris-
ingly strong voice.[399]

Crisis About Buildings in 1991

In 1991 Foy faced a stressful crisis that almost cost faithful brethren the use
of the buildings in Bulawayo that they had built and used for God's service
for many years. The strain of the battle may have contributed to the heart
attack he suffered as the problems were winding down. Margaret said that
the discouragement they felt in this predicament was the worst they suffered in all their years of working in Africa.

The problems could be attributed in part to the growing political destabilization in the country and the fact that the rule of law was gradually being
replaced with cronyism and party favoritism. Disputes were often resolved
not on the basis of judicial impartiality but rather on friendships or family
connections in the government.

The trouble began one Sunday morning at Queens Park when a young man who had the keys to the building was assaulted by a group of men who tried to take the keys away from him. Thankfully, enough brethren had already arrived for services to intervene and keep them from taking the keys. Foy knew nothing about what was going on, because at the time he taught a class in English at Hillside before coming to Queens Park for services in isiNdebele at 11 AM. By the time he arrived the brethren had called the police.

Margaret said that Edwin Moyo (not related to the evangelists, Teli Moyo nor Nesu Moyo) was one of the primary troublemakers. He had attended a college run by institutional brethren in the States, though Foy didn't blame the college for his actions. Jim Short opined that Michael Charles was the "real person behind it all."[400] Others including Austin Vimba and Gabriel Gazella helped in the plot. Charles had been a member of the church at Paddonhurst and had control of that building. He and the others, however, weren't content with controlling Paddonhurst. Foy said, "Their aim was to take over everything."

According to Foy, the men hoped to gain control of the buildings, especially Queens Park, which was the largest, and become the official representatives of the "Church of Christ" before the government. Then they would have power over the property and also control who could come in and out of the country in the church's name. Foy said that they were gloating over the fact that when they got control, that building would be large enough for all their combined gatherings![401] To complicate matters, Edwin Moyo had close friends in the police department and could count on their support to harass Foy and other faithful brethren who had worked so hard with the congregations through the years.

One tactic they used against Foy was to complain about the fact that he discouraged the support of native African preachers by American churches. Jim Short believed that the group tried "to use Dad's convictions about American support to accuse him of racism, in order to have the government deport him so that he could no longer oppose their plans and continue his teaching about the dangers of institutionalism and centralized control."[402]

Edwin Moyo's friends in the police department started harassing the leaders of the congregations at Queens Park and Bellevue, taking them into custody and holding them at the police headquarters with no real basis. One faithful brother who was forced to go to the police station for interrogation was Mountbatten Brewer whose wife was expecting their third child. Margaret took care of her and consoled her while her husband was in police custody. When the baby girl was born, she and her husband named her Margaret, much to Margaret's pleasure.

One ally that Foy and his brethren had in the crisis was an excellent lawyer of African descent, a Mr. Mahlangu of Lazarus & Sarif who knew how to handle the police. He told Foy, "If they come for you, be sure to phone your consulate in Harare before you go anywhere with them." Afterwards, they were helped by a white lawyer named David Coultard, later to become Minister of Education, Culture and Sport in the Government of National Unity in 2008.[403]

One of the plotters forged a letter that was supposed to have been written on Foy's typewriter and turned it over to the police. The police then came to Foy's house, rummaged through his office and his papers. The policemen were of the Shona tribe and as they searched his office, they conversed among themselves in the Shona language, with no idea that Foy understood everything they said! Finally, they asked him to drive his car to the police station with a policeman accompanying him. They followed behind in their own vehicle. Following his lawyer's advice, Foy insisted on calling the American consulate and his lawyer before leaving.

While driving to the station, Foy began to speak in Shona with the policeman riding with him. When he arrived, several other policemen started grilling him about why he discouraged American support of native preachers. Foy tried to explain his opinion with an illustration. He said, "If you have a child who is learning to walk, but you carry him all the time, he'll never learn to walk." As his inquisitors kept on quizzing him, Foy repeated the story several times till one of them said, "We don't want to hear that story again."

In between their questions the policemen at the station conversed among themselves in Shona. Foy noticed that the policeman who accompanied him to the station was trying to find a discreet way to motion to his companions to let them know that Foy could understand them, but couldn't get the message across without being blatant. Finally, to their shock, Foy spoke up in Shona, "Don't you know that I understand everything you're saying?" After an uncomfortable moment of silence, the policemen laughed, said they would sort everything out and told Foy he could leave. When reminded about the encounter in 2010, Foy laughed and said that he would always remember the startled look on the face of the policemen when he spoke to them in Shona.

The troublemakers tried to take their case to the governor of Matabeleland, hoping he would sympathize with their efforts to take control of the church buildings. The governor agreed to call Foy in. Foy asked for permission to bring some of his friends. The governor agreed and when Foy's friends filed in they completely filled the office. Only one, Dennis Clark, was white and another was a personal friend of the governor's. The governor looked at Foy and said, "Well Mr. Short, when you said that you were going to bring your friends with you, I thought you would have about a thousand white men and I see they're all black and one of them is my good friend." So, Michael Charles, Gabriel Gazella, Austin Vimba, Edwin Moyo and their allies weren't able to get the governor's help in their takeover attempt.

Towards the end of the crisis, the Shorts received another call from the police at a station near Bellevue requesting that they go to the police station.

When they entered they saw a group of their accusers who had in their possession a check that had been intended for them for drought relief, but sent by mistake to the Shorts. After Foy sent the check to them, they accused him of altering it because after the dollar amount the check writer had written "and no one hundreds" in the style of American check writing. Foy said matter-of-factly, "That's the way all American checks are written." The police were convinced, but Gabriel Gazella, a man they described as vicious, followed them back to their car pointing at them furiously. Margaret reported that later, when Foy was in the hospital in Johannesburg, Gazella prayed for his death at least once in a service at Bellevue. Ironically, Gazella died about a year later from stomach cancer![404]

The harassment and legal wrangling lasted two years until 1993. The final outcome was that Charles and his allies were able to gain control of the building at Bellevue and keep their control at Paddonhurst, but they were unsuccessful in gaining control of the ones in Queens Park and Hillside. However, the battle took a heavy emotional and physical toll on Foy.

Heart Attack

Towards the end of the crisis with the group headed by Michael Charles, Foy began to feel ill. His daughter, Ellen, said, "Of course Dad never says anything unless it's really bad. He was snappy. He had a headache." After a night of severe chest pains (Thursday) he knew he needed to see a doctor. After indecision by doctors on Friday about how to treat Foy and a painful Friday night, by Saturday night the doctors established that he had indeed suffered a heart attack and admitted him in the hospital. There he had a strong attack on Saturday night and was placed in intensive care.

Foy spent a month at the Mater Dei hospital in Bulawayo. Though doctors thought he was making progress, an American nurse told Margaret that he needed to go to Johannesburg where there were better facilities. Finally, the doctors agreed. His cardiologist said that he and his wife were going to Cape Town on vacation and therefore could accompany Foy on the plane to Johannesburg as was required by the airline since Foy was "a stretcher patient." However, when Foy arrived at Millpark Hospital in Johannesburg, he went into heart failure again and the doctors almost lost him. According to Ellen, "He said later that he had such difficulty breathing that he wanted to give up. He kept saying, 'I've got to see Margo one more time. One more time.' That may have pulled him through."

Though Foy was not as stable as doctors would have liked for the open-heart surgery, they decided that waiting for it any longer might cost him his life. They went ahead and operated on him, though Ellen hadn't arrived yet from the States. However, the Maydells and others were able to be with Margaret during the ordeal.

Margaret recalled,

> There was a small hotel on the hill just above the hospital which was very convenient for me. I kept telling the family I was okay, but was really happy to see Ellen on the Thursday! Harold was phoning me every day as was one of the three children over here. The late Jay Johnson from Birmingham also phoned me regularly. We had so much support.[405]

Foy made it through the surgery and began the long, slow recovery. After he was discharged from the hospital, Margaret and Ellen stayed with him in the garage apartment of their close friend, Ray Votaw. The Votaws loaned Ellen one of their cars, so she was able to run errands for her parents. Margaret recalled, "I had support from the church members in the area, especially the Maydells, Votaws, Hadfields and Fred Cluley, who had been baptized as a teenager in Bulawayo."[406]

Finally, Foy gained enough strength to return to Bulawayo. Dennis Clark drove his car to Johannesburg and then drove Foy and Margaret back to

Bulawayo. When Margaret visited the States in the summer of 1993, Jim came to help his father in Bulawayo and he gradually began to return to a teaching and preaching routine.

Foy later recalled with great appreciation the financial help he received from brethren in the States. He explained,

> Because of the troubled political situation in Zimbabwe we had been unable to get medical insurance… The expensive heart surgery had to be paid for. But when word was received in the USA, there was such a prompt and generous response that our needs were provided. Such has ever been God's care over us, provided through loving Christians. I think gratefully of many individuals and churches who helped us at that time.[407]

Margaret recalled, "Robert Hall got in touch with Kay straight away about raising money to pay for it and they kept me informed about what was in the bank, so I had enough every time I had to write another check for Les Maydell to deposit for me and bring me the rand."[408] Foy and Margaret always held a special place in their heart for Robert Hall because of his efforts to help them during this period of trial.

Ellen remarked that payment for the operation wasn't as difficult as it would have been in the States, "because the total cost of the hospitalization and open heart surgery in South Africa at that time was only $30,000, not the hundreds of thousands it would have cost in the US."[409]

In the mid 1990s, Foy begin to think of something that in the minds of others was unthinkable—leaving Zimbabwe. Paddy Kendall-Ball had said, "He'll be the one to close the door on the building."[410] Though Margaret in no way insisted on returning to the States and was quite happy to live the rest of her life in Zimbabwe and even be buried there, Jim felt that his father had her interests and his children's in making the decision to return. Jim said, "It was an expression of his love for his wife and family, and probably one of the hardest things he ever had to decide in his life!"[411] Foy also longed for time to be able to work on a Bible concordance in the isiNdebele language along with commentaries and other study aids. A return to the States would give him the time needed for those tedious projects. Ellen said, "It was this thought, that in some ways he could do more for the Zimbabwe work while living in the US, that made it possible for him to make the very difficult decision to return to live in the US."[412]

Though Margaret said that health wasn't the primary reason for the move, she's glad that it was made. She said, "In the intervening years the health service has deteriorated a lot. I'm glad we're here."

Final Farewell

When disciples heard that the Shorts were moving to the States, they began to make plans for an unforgettable send-off. A date was chosen and the news about a final farewell spread throughout Matabeleland. Brethren began to gather in Bulawayo from the countryside. Many camped around the church building at Queens Park bringing animals to prepare for the big feast on the final day. Ellen said, "We were inundated with pottery, embroidery and all kinds of gifts."

Before the final services several brethren took Jeffrey Nyembezi (who was in a wheelchair because of strokes) and Foy to an artist who did a special drawing of the two. Then they all went to the packed auditorium at Queens Park for singing, prayers and final messages. Jeffry Nyembezi, Newman Gumbo, Nesu Moyo, Mountbatten Brewer and Teli Moyo gave special lessons recalling Foy's time among them and asking for God's blessings for the future. Ellen said,

> All who spoke, both black and white, Frikkie Claassen and Dennis Clark, talked about dad insisting on book, chapter and verse. In fact some called him Mr. BCV. Several of the people told Dave and me that we must take good care of mother and dad or they would bring them back to Zimbabwe and take care of them.[413]

After all the hymns had been sung, prayers said, tears shed and a few days of final packing, there was nothing more to do than to go to the airport, watch Foy and Margaret board the plane and watch it take off. It is not difficult to imagine the nostalgia Foy must have felt as he watched the land he knew best disappearing into the haze. Though he would be back for visits, it would never be the same. An era had ended. God's work would continue among the amaNdebele without the permanent presence of one of its pioneers.

Chapter 6

Return to the States

Church Family in Nashville

Foy and Margaret returned to Nashville and settled into their new home in White House, about 20 miles north of Nashville. He wrote in October 1995, "Our personal effects have arrived. Now to erect shelves for all my books, then unpack and sort."[414]

They began to worship regularly with the Kemper Heights congregation. It formed when members from the old Joseph Avenue church in Nashville decided to leave the deteriorating neighborhood where their building was located to form the new congregation. Ellen and David Baize attended the congregation in the 1970s and when Foy and Margaret's daughter, Kathryn, visited her sister there, she met her future husband, Roger Lee Smith. So, it was natural for Foy and Margaret to worship at Kemper Heights with their daughter and son in law. Soon they became close to the brethren there and eventually Foy was made an elder in the congregation with Bill Jones, James Perry, Vernon Allen and Jim Young.

Publications Work

The dearth of Bible study aids in the isiNdebele language was constantly on Foy's mind when he worked with people of that tribe. A translation of the New Testament became available in the dialect only shortly after Foy began his work among the amaNdebele in 1947. The Old Testament translation appeared first in the early 1970s. Until that time, those who spoke isiNdebele had to do the best they could to examine the Old Testament scriptures in the Zulu language, which though related to isiNdebele, is not exactly the same.

Foy began to dream of a concordance in the isiNdebele language when he visited a small congregation in a rural part of Zimbabwe and an evangelist asked him where to find a passage of scripture. Foy said, "He had been reading his Bible for months trying to find this verse. He knew it was there. I took my concordance and found it right away." From that time, Foy determined that if he ever found the time, he needed to work up a Bible concordance in the isiNdebele language. When thinking of returning to the States he realized that there he would have the time for that tedious project as well as commentaries and other needed materials.

Foy and his helpers with the concordance.
L to R: Enoch Ncube, Mthando Maphosa, Foy, Mountbatten Brewer and Newman Gumbo.

All of Foy's supporting congregations except for one decided to continue to support him in his publication endeavors and after settling in, he began the monotonous work. From the beginning a number of complications accompanied the concordance project. First, he had to obtain permission from the Bible society. Then he began the long process of scanning every page of the Bible in the isiNdebele language. However, there were snags when the OCR program tried to turn the foreign words from the scanned material into readable text that Foy could use with a word program. The program was designed for English and European languages and balked at reproducing the African words in their original form. The fact that so many proper names in the language begin with lower cased prefixes, threw the program completely off, especially when encountering names from the Old Testament.

Foy's son, Harold, was head of the Computers for Teaching the Humanities Department of King's College in London. He was highly proficient in working with software programs for printing applications and was an invaluable aid to his father in this frustrating process, spending long hours on the project in spite of having just suffered a serious automobile accident. Foy's son Jim said,

> In a very real sense the concordance should be seen as the joint effort of Harold and my Dad with a little help here and there from others. Without either one it would simply not have happened. When my Dad first had the idea, he spoke to Harold about it. Harold was the one who had the technical expertise to know how it could be done… My Dad had the Bible knowledge and understanding of the Sindebele language and culture that was essential to the task (and I know of no-one else who had both of these attributes like he did)… For both Harold and my Dad it was a way to work together to the benefit of the Lord's work in Zimbabwe which was deeply meaningful to both of them… My Dad spoke to Harold about his dream of a concordance, and Harold was the one who made the plan to make it happen.[415]

After a whole year, the scanning project was finally completed and Foy began to sort out the different categories and words that would comprise the concordance. He wrote in May 2002,

> The mysteries of the concordance software program are being unraveled. I've made an experimental concordance for Joshua and Judges. They are too detailed, listing every word. On that basis a concordance of the entire Bible would have to be well over 1000 pages. It would be too bulky to be useful and too expensive to print. So now I must learn how to set parameters that will limit the choice of words to be included.[416]

Foy wanted his published material to be reviewed by brethren who spoke the language as natives so that they could make suggestions about phrasing and word choice. Sometimes he would send the material to Mountbatten Brewer and sometimes he would take it with him on his trips back to Zimbabwe to review with his brethren there. Foy spent most of his time during his 2006 trip to Zimbabwe putting the finishing touches on the concordance with four brethren who were well versed in the isiNdebele language: Newman Gumbo, Mountbatten Brewer, Enoch Ncube and Mthando Maphosa. Finally in late 2006, the concordance was finished and Foy began to distribute it to some, though the large scale printing was not completed until early 2011.

Foy told Ken Green that the concordance "of 378 pages contains 4,062 word stems with 18,800 references. An index of personal names includes 404 persons with 1,543 references. An index of place names has 202 places with 867 references."[417]

Though Harold and Foy did the lion's share of the work on the project, other family members made important contributions.

Foy also wrote commentaries for those who spoke the isiNdebele language. He completed some while in Zimbabwe and had more time to work on them when he arrived in the States in 1995. He has written commentaries on Matthew, Luke, Acts, Romans, 1 and 2 Corinthians, Galatians and Ezekiel. He wrote in April 2003 about his commentary on Galatians,

When we get to Zimbabwe I can get help to complete it. I plan to have 1,000 copies printed for use in the classes and for distribution among the churches. Adventism is very strong, and most denominations have no idea of the significance of the difference between the Old and New Testaments. ... I prepared and used a commentary on Romans last year. It was enthusiastically received.[418]

Foy wrote the commentaries in English and had them translated into isiNdebele in Bulawayo. The translators then sent all but the last two back to him for revision before their final publication.

Relief for Needy Saints

Persistent drought along with government mismanagement produced increasing hardship and famine in Zimbabwe. The crisis produced a mass exodus of Zimbabweans to neighboring countries, especially South Africa, while those who stayed scrambled to find anything to eat. With the collapse of the Zimbabwean economy and resulting hyperinflation came the inevitable dark humor. Foy said that one joke that made the rounds was about a man who came down a path with a wheelbarrow full of money. "He left it for just a minute and when he came back someone had left all the money in a heap and stolen the wheelbarrow." The jokes were necessary as a coping mechanism when facing the devastating effects of the famine. Foy quoted the BBC news in 2003, "Elderly people are starving to death, while children have died of poisoning after eating the wrong leaves as a substitute for food."[419]

Foy and Margaret worked to encourage American brethren to send relief to the needy saints beginning in 1982. While doing so, they were careful to avoid setting up anything like a church supported human agency to do the work, encouraging instead the use of messengers to carry the relief directly to the needy congregations. They focused on helping the needy around Bulawayo. Several men such as Newman Gumbo, Dennis Clark, Teli Moyo and Bigboy Dube were especially reliable as messengers to get the aid to needy brethren. The messengers protected their reputations by having each church have three signatories to sign a receipt for what was received and thus were able to account for all the relief that was sent through them.[420] Others from South Africa, especially Leslie Maydell and David Beckley worked to raise relief for brethren in the South where the drought was often even more severe. Eventually Maydell and Beckley took over most of the relief that Foy was undertaking. Others like Mike Divas worked diligently to find ways to alleviate the suffering of the brethren.

As could be expected when such a large need was being met, there were some mix-ups and disagreements among Americans about shipments, currency exchange and other nuts and bolts challenges of distributing relief. Foy wrote a number of letters in the year 2000 to try to clear up what he felt to be misunderstandings.

Margaret emphasized that government mismanagement exacerbated the food crisis caused by the recurring droughts, especially after 2000. In February of that year a referendum was held on a new constitution that would have given Mugabe sweeping powers. The people rejected the new constitution and Mugabe immediately started taking over the productive, primarily white-owned farms, which were mainly in the less drought-prone areas. In some cases, farmers were murdered. Mugabe claimed that this land would be distributed to the "peasants," since the "settlers" had supposedly stolen it from them. Those he called settlers were second and third generation Zimbabweans who had bought the land and had worked hard to develop it. The land was given to his cronies who knew nothing about farming. Therefore very little, if anything was produced on what used to be productive land and expensive farm machinery was left to rust away. The food shortage became even more severe. However, good brethren from a number of places supplied food to the brethren, who were therefore able to survive.[421]

Dealing With Problems Associated with Age

Foy had hip replacement surgery in 1997.[422] A year later he began to have some symptoms of more heart problems and Margaret insisted on taking him to the hospital where doctors determined to give him a second bypass operation. However, Foy recuperated well from it, and continued to work on his printing projects and make his annual trips to Zimbabwe.

A second scare occurred in 2004 when doctors discovered a cancerous polyp in Foy's colon. However, after an operation and treatment, Foy seemed to be cancer free. Though he had helped fill in preaching at Kemper Heights for Ken Green when he first came to Nashville, his health problems led to a reduction in that responsibility. In the latter 2000's Ken Green asked him if he thought he could fill in again. Foy told him he thought he could preach for twenty minutes. When Green heard that, he retracted the offer saying, "If you did that they would want to hire you!"[423]

Trips back to Zimbabwe

Foy returned every year to Zimbabwe from the time he left in 1995 until 2007 except for 2004 when he had an operation for colon cancer. For each trip he had his close friend, Newman Gumbo, work up a schedule to make the maximum use of his time. Usually he would visit three congregations in the countryside and spend the weekends in Bulawayo conducting organized Bible studies on various topics. An exception to this schedule was made in 2006 when as noted earlier, Foy spent all his time reviewing the isiNdebele Bible concordance project with his helpers.

Foy wrote in 1996,

Reports concerning the Lord's work in Zimbabwe continue to be encouraging. Margaret and I are looking forward to spending some time with the Christians there in August and September… The Embry Hills church in Atlanta has undertaken to pay for our return airfares amounting to $3498, for which we are grateful indeed. That takes care of the major travel expense.[424]

He wrote in 2003, "Embry Hills church, Atlanta, GA, has paid for the air tickets for our trip to Zimbabwe, assistance they have given every year beginning with 1996."[425]

Foy summed up his trip in 1999. From August 6 through September 5, he "preached for 21 churches, conducted 17 Bible classes and had 15 discussions with individuals. This required driving 2536 miles, much of it over very rough trails." Then after Margaret, David and Ellen Baize met him in Bulawayo on September 5, they traveled 2,881 more miles and visited 28 more congregations teaching a combined total of 76 Bible classes and sermons.[426]

Foy mentioned three things that impressed him after his trip to Zimbabwe in 2002: (1) the barren desolation caused by the drought, (2) the growth and vigor among the Christians and (3) the diligence of Paddy and Sandi Kendall-Ball and how gladly they were received among the brethren.[427] Foy said of the Kendall-Balls, "Seldom can more diligent, zealous and faithful Christians be found. They are truly 'giving themselves' to God's work. I felt constrained to warn them of the need to get adequate rest lest they ruin their health."[428]

He described some of the special studies conducted among the brethren in 2002.

> Our first series of Bible studies were held at a central point about 120 miles south of Bulawayo at a little center called Guyu. In true African fashion not all those attending arrived in time for the first day's classes, but there were eventually over 200 who studied with us. The women's classes were taught by Margaret, Linda Maydell, Sarah Calvert and Sandi Kendall-Ball. Les Maydell and I taught the men's classes. Most of the time Paddy was busy with brother Gumbo delivering corn meal to the churches in need,

Foy eating mealie meal with his brethren.

> Our aim was to have classes 8 hours a day for 4 days. Due to travel problems we didn't quite achieve the full 8 hours per day.[429]

The efforts of African brethren to attend such Bible study sessions always impressed Foy. He said, "Many of those people do not have the money for bus tickets on very undependable bus lines. They either have to walk or travel by donkey or ox cart ... I remember vividly a woman who had lost one of her legs yet walked (?) with crutches 12 miles to attend Bible classes at Nswazi church."[430]

Jim Short recalled receiving a similar lesson on one of his own visits,

> I remember a lesson in humility from my visit in 2006. I was feel-
> ing a little proud of myself for getting up at 5 am on a Saturday
> morning to get ready to leave at 6 am to drive 3 hours to teach for 5
> hours or so in West Nicholson. Then when I got there I met a group
> of about 7 people who had arisen at 2 am to walk for 7 hours to get
> to the meeting place![431]

Foy usually used translators when teaching in isiNdebele even though
he knew the language. Margaret said, "Translators have always been a
bit nervous translating for him because he knew what they were saying.
Sometimes he would stop and tell them, 'No, this word's better.'" Stanley
Sithole was one of the young translators who Foy would sometimes correct. He told Ellen Baize in 2010 that Foy's suggestions made him a better
translator and gave him a better understanding of the scriptures.[432] Stanley,
whose father is an elder at the Magwegwe congregation in Bulawayo, became an excellent translator according to Paddy Kendall-Ball. He helped
with the final revisions of the Bible concordance.

When not in rural areas, Foy stayed with Dennis and Ann Clark in
Bulawayo until Dennis Clark passed away. Then he stayed with the George
Edys who had bought their home in Bulawayo when they left in 1995. He
always worked closely with Mountbatten Brewer who had started a new
congregation in Bulawayo. In spite of economic crises and political instability, the Hillside (English) and Queens Park (isiNdebele) congregations
continued their work in Bulawayo along with five other congregations that
worshiped in the isiNdebele language.

Several American evangelists accompanied Foy on his travels including
Gerry Sandusky and Ken Green. Green said that he accompanied Foy
about five times.[433] As he observed Foy on his trips, Green was impressed
with Foy's "kind approach to teaching." He said, "He often taught by raising
questions just as the Lord did. He is an extremely liberal fellow in the sense

of being open minded and charitable and generous with those he has an issue with. He tries to get across his point of view softly. As a matter of fact, and he has shown a number of times ... that he is willing to change."[434]

Gerry Sandusky told in a sermon of an all night drive with Foy from Bulawayo to South Africa. When they started off, Foy began to settle into his seat and told Sandusky to drive the whole way while he slept. Somewhat perturbed, Sandusky said, "I don't know the roads to South Africa! You're going to have to stay awake and help me navigate."

Foy responded calmly, "Down here we have the Southern Cross constellation." He pointed out the formation of stars in the Southern sky to Sandusky and said, "When you come to an intersection, just take the road that goes towards the cross and that will get us to our destination." Sandusky made a spiritual application of Foy's words, to the effect that when we come to crossroads in our lives, we should always proceed in the direction of the cross.

Ken Green recalled an occasion when he was driving with Foy over a rough stretch of road near the border between Zimbabwe and South Africa. Their rental car had badly adjusted headlights and evidently appeared to oncoming drivers to be on high beam. They responded by turning on their high beams almost blinding Green, who was already having enough of a challenge by having to drive on the left side of the road. After a while Foy told Green, "Ken, I admire your driving and how you keep the car on the road with these bright lights shining in your eyes." Green responded, "Foy, when I can't see I just close my eyes and pray!" That story became a favorite of Foy's.

Though Foy was thrilled at the hundreds of people who attended the special Bible studies he conducted when visiting his homeland and at seeing new generations of children focusing upon the word, the general trend in Africa was to follow the moral decline of the West.

He said in an oral report,
Things are changing in
Africa all over. The influence
of Western Civilization, if
you can call it that … is taking root among them. It's
the bad habits that are taking place first and that are
most sought after. Where
you used to see courtesy and
politeness towards elders,
the young people are learning that that doesn't matter.[435]

Paddy Kendall-Ball

Foy mentioned in 2002 his appreciation for the concern many had for his safety when traveling. However, he reassured readers of his report that he was discreet about avoiding visits to problem areas. Then he reminded his readers about the dangers of parts of Nashville and the "high speed high-ways." He concluded, "Tell you what! We will pray for your safety in this country, while you pray for ours in Zimbabwe."[436]

Travel into Zimbabwe grew even more dangerous after Foy stopped travel-ing to the country. Warren Sholtz, a faithful Christian from South Africa was brutally attacked when traveling to the country to preach in March 2010 and was thankful to be released alive by his assailants.[437]

Visits to Zimbabwe by Other American Evangelists
During Foy's latter years in Africa and after his return to the States a num-ber of American evangelists began to travel into Zimbabwe. Foy felt that most of them encouraged the brethren and did good work. However, he strongly disagreed with a few who began to recommend Zimbabwean preachers for American salaries. Besides discouraging sacrifice among Zimbabwean brethren to help their own evangelists, Foy felt that American support "fosters an attitude of looking to people overseas rather than look-

ing to God … and breeds jealousy …"[438] He felt that Americans often don't understand other harmful effects caused by American dollars.

Americans have no way of understanding how little it takes, by our standards, to be rich by their standards. I have known some good preachers to become discouraged because they were not receiving outside support while others were. "I must not be a good preacher because I was not chosen to be supported," is the response I have heard before.[439]

On one occasion Foy remarked, "I don't understand how Americans, who love their independence so much, seem determined to create dependency among others."[440]

In 2006, Foy summed up his feelings about changing attitudes that accompanied American salaries. "There are over one hundred congregations in the SW part of Zimbabwe. This could not have been achieved without the hard work and faithful teaching of the African preachers, living and working within their own economy. I see this changing now and it concerns me deeply."[441]

David Beckley, whom Foy highly respected, wrote a detailed article about the harm caused by American support for those Zimbabwean preachers that were relatively untaught.[442] He lamented, "When an American preacher or elder or any Christian comes to preach or teach in Africa for short periods of time, wisdom dictates that he listen to those who have been working in Africa with African brethren for a number of years."[443] However, Foy's advice about American support for Zimbabwean preachers and that of other veterans of the African work like Ray Votaw, Gene Tope, Paul Williams and David Beckley was sometimes ignored. Beckley said, "Those of us who have to work with these men to help sort out the resultant problems, see the reality that visiting Americans only glance at and then seemingly dismiss or forget."

David Maxson visited a country where many native evangelists were heavily supported by American churches when he was in his early twenties. Then he visited Zimbabwe in August of 2010 with Joe Greer. He said that there was a tremendous difference between the evangelists in the two places. Conversations with preachers like Enoch Ncube, Newman Gumbo and others in Zimbabwe were deep and satisfying, dealing with spiritual needs and Biblical analysis, whereas preachers in the first country "fawned" over him, dropping hints for American dollars. He felt very uncomfortable with preachers in the first country who were seeking dollars, but was greatly encouraged by the maturity and depth of those in Zimbabwe.[444]

Foy received criticism from some who thought he was inconsistent in his position about American salaries for African evangelists because on one occasion he recommended temporary part time support for a respected Zimbabwean evangelist.[445] However, he and Margaret felt that the temporary nature of the recommended support at a critical time and the fact that it was an exception meant that it didn't violate Foy's generally held views. Foy was also courteously challenged by friends who respected his work but who felt that he shouldn't allow congregations to help him by sending money to a work fund.[446]

Time with Family

After returning to the States, Foy and Margaret enjoyed more time with their children and grandchildren. Margaret wrote about a trip to visit Ellen and Dave in Virginia in 1998 and seeing their new great-grandchild, Marissa Ellen. After Jim arrived from California, the whole crew traveled up Chesapeake Bay to Chincoteague Island and then to Washington D.C. She mentioned a shop in Hampton, Virginia that specialized in British merchandise where she was able to buy items that she enjoyed in Zimbabwe: "cream crackers, marie and lemon cream, lemon curd, marmite, Bovril, anchovette, Lyle's golden syrup, Dettol, etc." Her biggest find, however, was "a Morphy Richards automatic kettle made for American current."[447]

Foy reported on his 65th Anniversary celebration with Margaret in 2009. "One of the most enjoyable periods was when we celebrated our 65th wedding anniversary on the 23rd, and had all our children — from London, California, Virginia and Tennessee — with us for a few days. We had a great time just being together, and an enjoyable dinner at Catfish Inn in Springfield — a favorite place with all of us."[448]

Trips by David and Ellen Baize

Foy followed the travels of his son-in-law, David Baize, and daughter, Ellen, to Zimbabwe with particular interest. Ellen had visited Africa three times since moving away in the mid 1960s. Then in 1995 she took her husband, David, with her for the first time and stayed a few extra weeks after his departure, to help her parents with packing for their departure.

Before her parents left for the States, Ellen and her friend, Gail Hadfield du Chemin, traveled to the mission stations of Zambia to see the areas where her grandparents worked in the 1920s and again in the 1950s and early 1960s. Roy Merritt, son of pioneer preacher Dow Merritt, was in charge of the Namwianga Mission in 1995 and showed Ellen and Gail around. Ellen's initial impression was that the place "had shrunk. The mission wasn't as big as it used to be. It was like a time warp. You see things and they look familiar, but they're so little. Everything looked run down and different."

Ellen wondered what had happened to Alvin Hobby's telescope that she remembered from the 1950s. Roy Merritt told her that the ever-present termites got into the house and he had to pull it down. Other buildings were used for different purposes, including the dorm for the boys, and the Eureka school. She was glad that the church building that her grandfather, W.N. Short, built was still there. According to Roy Merritt, its longevity was due in great part to its granite foundation that Short learned to make from his association with the old pioneer, John Sherriff.

Since their trip in 1995, Ellen and Dave have traveled about once every two years to Zimbabwe, visiting brethren in various parts of the country. When in the cities, she and David have stayed with her friends such as Gail Hadfield du Chemin, George and Jenny Edy, her cousin Genie and Ed Duthie or George and Pauline O'Donnel. When in the country, she and David stayed in tents or drove back to nearest town to stay with friends or in a hotel.

In 2004, as was her custom she went through South Africa visiting the Leslie Maydells and her old college friends, Joanne Beckley and her husband, David, who were always a help to her. She said, "The Maydells have the car we use in Zimbabwe, and Joanne and David store our camping equipment; both print out our lessons for us and provide other assistance as needed, plus a place to stay as we travel through SA and transportation to and from Johannesburg airport."[449] She placed pictures of her trip in 2004 on her Facebook page. She did the same after a trip in 2010.

Foy felt that his son-in-law, David Baize, adapted quickly to preaching among the Africans, "He has quickly come to understand their limited knowledge of American idioms and illustrations, relating his lessons to their way of thinking and lifestyle."[450]

Conclusion

Foy's youngest brother Bill passed away in 2009. Foy wrote a heartfelt tribute about him in his monthly report.

We are grieving the death of my younger brother, Bill. He died suddenly last Friday from a heart attack. While they were checking his heart the aorta ruptured and he died soon after that. He had been a professor of languages at McMurry University in Abilene TX for many years. He had an outstanding record of service to the church, the university, the community and his many students. His children have been overwhelmed to find all the honors and awards he has received which he never displayed. His family always came first, before any of these groups he served so well. He taught his students so much more than languages.

Bill was only 66, 22 years younger than I, so we didn't grow up together. However, we watched him grow up with our children in the Rhodesias. He and Harold were only two years apart and had some great times together. He was more like a cousin to our children.[451]

In 2011 Foy and Margaret continue to work in the Lord's service in White House, Tennessee, though Foy is slowing down considerably because of his advancing age. He still spends a good portion of his days in the office working on various projects in the isiNdebele language. He wrote at the end of 2009, "I am getting near the end of Ezekiel. As I have said several times this has been the most difficult book that I have written a commentary for. I feel like a rest from that sometimes, so have begun some work on church history as well."[452] He wrote in February 2010,

Lately I have found it difficult to work as many hours as I would like and so have decided that when the present work is completed, I won't undertake any more. I enjoy working on the commentaries and will continue to do so, but at my own pace, without the pressure of feeling I must work to deadlines. I expect to finish the present work within the next couple of months and will let you know when it is completed, in case some of you feel you need to stop support at that time.[453]

A big adjustment for Foy and Margaret came in early 2010, when they moved from the house they had lived in for almost 15 years into a small apartment in their daughter Kay's basement. Ellen wrote,

Mom and dad have moved into the basement apartment at Kay's this last weekend, so now we are working on getting the last things sorted and sold/given away, etc. It is a hard time, especially for mom, to move from her own house into this tiny apartment. Dad seems too tired most of the time for it to really bother him. When I asked him about seeing all his books go, he said he felt more relief than sadness.[454]

After visiting a congregation in the Houston area in 2008, Sewell Hall told his son Gardner that he was able to visit Foy's old friend, Ray Votaw, who was in declining health. Votaw, like Foy, was one of Hall's heroes and had dedicated his life to establishing autonomous congregations in South Africa. He remarked that very few of the disciples in the Houston area seemed to realize what a spiritual giant they had among them or knew anything at all about Votaw's outstanding work in Africa. Such anonymity was understandable. Votaw's field of work was far from where he had to spend his last years in Southeastern Texas. A few more brethren in the Nashville area may have known of Foy Short's presence among them in his declining years, but most probably didn't. Neither he nor Votaw sought recognition. As their bodies wear out, however, their spirits can be refreshed by knowing that God has used them to change thousands of lives through the good news about Jesus Christ.

One evening during one of his later trips to Zimbabwe, Foy enjoyed a quiet conversation with his friend, David Ndlovu. Foy said of Ndlovu, "His name means elephant. He's not big but he did the work of an elephant… He was responsible for starting at least eight or ten churches around the area where he lived."[455] As they talked, Ndlovu said that he wished that he and Foy could cross the Jordan together at the end of their lives. Foy said, "I don't know of anyone I would rather cross Jordan with than you." In relating the story in 2006 Foy remarked, "However, he (Ndlovu) passed away about three years ago and so he's already crossed Jordan."

However, as Foy enters his 90s and his body battles the infirmities of old age, the time must certainly be approaching for him to cross the river. On the other side he will join so many that he has known in working for God's kingdom in America and Southern Africa. From his childhood there will be old pioneers like John Sherriff, Peter Masiya, Kambole Matapamatenga and George Scott. From his youth there will be Jack Rollings, Irven Lee and especially his closest friend, Bennie Lee Fudge. From his more mature years, Jeffry Nyembezi, David Ndlovu, Teli Moyo and others will be waiting for him.

Only God knows the future for Zimbabwe and other parts of Southern Africa, and whether there will be more political turmoil, famine and social upheaval or peace and recovery. Perhaps Christ will return and end history, as we know it. But whatever the future holds for earthly kingdoms, the faithful can give thanks for the thousands who have become a part of the kingdom which cannot be shaken and whose lives have been forever changed by the influence of this quiet, unassuming yet determined man named Foy Short.

Foy and Margaret in Tennessee.

A Brief History of Zimbabwe

To understand Foy Short's work it is helpful to know something about Zimbabwe, the place of his labor. The country is located in Southern Africa, just northeast of South Africa, east of Namibia and south of Zambia (originally Northern Rhodesia). Historically, it has had more ties with its neighbor to the south, South Africa, than with its other neighbors. Zimbabwe is not a land of jungles but is predominantly savanna (tropical grassland). The only true forests are the evergreen forests of the eastern border and the savanna woodland northwest of Bulawayo.[456]

Zimbabwe's modern history began when Bantu speaking peoples from the north populated most of the country by 1000 A.D. and developed an advanced civilization. They built a site called Great Zimbabwe whose stone ruins date from the 12th Century and can still be seen today. This settlement grew into the trading capital of the wealthiest and most powerful society in Southeastern Africa.[457] It was considered the birthplace of the Shona culture, which prevails in northern and eastern Zimbabwe today.

The Portuguese were the first Europeans to arrive in Zimbabwe in the 1500s. They encountered a weakening and fragmenting Shona presence.

In 1834 the amaNdebele, an offshoot of the Zulu nation of South Africa, assassinated the Shona leader of the Rozwi State and established a strong presence in the country, especially in the Southwest around their newly formed capital of Bulawayo. This would be the tribe with which Foy Short would work primarily in his later years. Short learned their language, isiN-debele, and found that he could use it to communicate with relative ease with his Zulu speaking brethren in South Africa,

The English began to exert their power in the late 1800s. Cecil Rhodes, a gold-seeker and explorer in South Africa, set up the British South Africa Company. He signed a treaty with the Ndebele king Lobengula, allowing him to mine for gold and diamonds. Rhodes planned to carve a "corridor of civilization" from the Southern Cape to Cairo.[458]

The first armed conflict between the English and Africans was in 1893 with the amaNdebele. Though much fewer in number, they were a warrior peo-ple descended from the Zulus, while the Shona were a pastoral, much more peaceful group. The English had been allowed by Lobengula to explore for gold in the Shona areas, and were horrified when amaNdebele raiders came and killed their Shona neighbors and workers. After defeating the amaNde-bele in 1893 the English took control of all of Rhodesia.[459]

In 1896 came what was known by whites as "The Native Rebellion" and by blacks as the first Chimurenga (War of Independence). Both amaNdebele and Shona people fought the whites and there were atrocities committed by both sides. According to the Embassy of Zimbabwe, "The uprising was suppressed by the use of unparalleled brutality and torture of the prisoners of war and civilians."[460]

The country was called Rhodesia in 1905 and became a British Colony in 1923. After a brief and unsuccessful effort to combine Southern Rhodesia, Northern Rhodesia and Nysaland in a federation in 1953, the latter two countries eventually broke away and became Zambia and Malawi.

During the period of European control, native Africans were kept from owning the best lands and holding positions of power. Many were illiter-ate or barely literate, but missionaries worked hard to change that, teaching them to read the Bible. White Europeans often resented such efforts. Eldred Echols, a companion of Foy Short's who preached extensively in Southern Africa in the latter half of the twentieth century, wrote,

> Some of the white settlers were very prejudiced against the educational work done by missionary groups, fearing the political awareness that would inevitably follow the ability to read newspapers and periodicals. Consequently, they were inclined to blame the missionaries when a black employee behaved irresponsibly or dishonestly, sniffing: "After all, he was a mission boy."[461]

By 1963 Great Britain began to press for more drastic changes and many Rhodesians of European ancestry resented it. Subsequently, Ian Smith led a move for independence from Great Britain that was declared on November 11, 1965. He and his minority government were able to survive until 1976 when the withdrawal of South African support signaled the beginning of the end for white European rule.[462] During this time Shona guerrilla forces trained in China and led by Robert Mugabe and Russian trained Ndebele forces led by Joshua Nkomo fought the Smith regime and each other. Africans who recognized the need for change, but not through the differing Marxists ideologies offered by the guerrillas, suffered greatly during this bush war. It also greatly affected Foy Short.[463]

Finally the Smith government conceded interim power to a moderate African leader, elections were held and Robert Mugabe was the landslide victor. The country's name was changed to Zimbabwe. Mugabe's rule in Zimbabwe along with a series of droughts has ruined Zimbabwe's economy and brought on famine and hardship. "Once heralded as a champion of the anticolonial movement, Mugabe is now viewed by much of the international community as an authoritarian ruler responsible for egregious human rights abuses and for running the economy of his country into the ground."[464]

Margaret Short recalled hearing many amaNdebele and even some Shona express longing for the stability they enjoyed under the British and even the Ian Smith government. She recalled,

A large crowd gathered outside a department store when they heard that Ian Smith was there. His security people urged him to leave by the back door. He replied that no way would he go out that way but he would go out the way he had come in. When he appeared, there was loud cheering![465]

The precipitous fall of the economy in Zimbabwe and the repressive instability of Mugabe's government led to the flight of most inhabitants of European ancestry and many of African descent from the country. Paddy Kendall-Ball said that it was estimated in 2008 that three million people had left the country because of the political and economic problems. One million Zimbabweans lived in South Africa.[466]

Christianity in Zimbabwe

The Portuguese Jesuit Gonzalo da Silveira initiated the first European religious contact with the Shona in 1561. Further efforts followed in the 1600s, but no permanent Catholic presence resulted until 1879. Since then, there has been substantial growth.[467] The first Protestant missionary to Zimbabwe was Robert Moffat who opened a London Missionary Society (LMS) station at Inyati in 1859.[468] The British Methodists and the United Methodists (USA) arrived in 1890. The former has a large white constituency while the latter is mostly African. The Salvation Army, which entered in 1891, has the largest single Protestant community, is predominately Shona and is rapidly increasing in size.[469]

Foy admired the early missionaries to Southern Africa though he did not agree with their doctrine. He wrote in the 1950s, "A Catholic Missionary was the first to be martyred for his faith. He was skinned alive and left to die in agony... The order of the civilizing process was: First and always first, the missionary, then the trader, then the empire builder who brought with him the colonists and settlers."[470]

The admirable sacrifices of early missionaries from mainstream denominations sometimes made Foy's teaching efforts difficult. He wrote,

One old man said to me, "Teacher Short, It is clear from your words and the words of the Bible that my church is wrong. But those first missionaries saw the wickedness and wretchedness of my people and came to us more than 60 years ago. By their coming they did not gain any wealth, but many of them lost their lives. They loved me and my people. They gave themselves to help us. It cannot be right for us now to turn against them. Why did not your missionaries of the church of Christ come to us before today."

Brethren, what answer would you have given that man?[471]

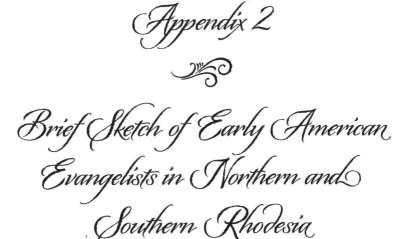

Appendix 2

Brief Sketch of Early American Evangelists in Northern and Southern Rhodesia

Dow and Alice Merritt—Merritt, like Will and Delia Short, studied at Cordell Christian College. After two years there, he joined the Navy in 1913 and became a medic.[472] He married Alice, from Odessa, Texas, after leaving the Navy. He moved to Africa in July of 1926 and spent most of the rest of his life there. After Alice tragically died of cancer, he married Helen Pearl Scott, George and Ottis Scott's daughter, on May 14, 1942.[473] Foy's sister, Sybil, said of the Merritts, "We loved them dearly." Dow's son, Roy, was in charge of the Namwianga mission through the 1990s and when Foy's daughter, Ellen, visited Zambia in 1995 he gave her a tour of the grounds that she had known as a child. Another son, Sterling, lived close to Ellen in Virginia Beach, Virginia and maintains contact with her.

George and Ottis Scott—The Scotts were highly respected Christians on the West Coast in the early 1900s. W.N. Short's paper, *Glimpses of Africa*, carried a biographical sketch of Scott and his wife written by Leonard Gray.[474] According to Gray, Scott was born in Kansas, December 19, 1874 and moved with his parents in 1884 to the State of Washington. His father passed away when he was 14 years old and young George had to struggle to survive working in logging camps, fruit camps and among fishermen. Ottis' grandfather attended Alexander Campbell's Bethany College. She married George's brother, Roy D., who tragically passed away in 1909.

After becoming a Christian at 16 years of age, George preached "to Indians in Alaska, Japanese in California and anyone who would listen."[475] He married Ottis in 1914 and began to work with her to teach others on the West Coast, making their living through various pursuits. The online history of the Pacific Christian Academy quotes a description of the school given by Ottis Scott who was the only full time teacher when that school began in 1918.[476]

Eldred Echols wrote,

> George Scott was in his mid-fifties when the pull of Africa became a fire in his bones that could not be quenched. He had been engaged in salmon fishing in Alaska, but his boat blew up and he was seriously burned. As he lay recuperating in a hospital, he had time to reflect on the priorities in his life, and then and there resolved to give up fishing for salmon and became a fisher of men. He wired his wife and daughter, who were living on the American west coast, to pack up and get ready to leave for Africa.[477]

The Scotts, who arrived in Africa in 1927, took care of a number of orphans throughout their lives. They believed in partaking the Lord's Supper with only one container, [478] but worked with those who believed in individual cups by partaking of one cup with each other when the communion tray was passed around. The Scotts worked in Africa for thirty years and only returned once to America after leaving it.[479]

Perhaps Scott was Foy's favorite among the early evangelists who worked with his father in Africa. He fondly recalled a visit with the Scotts in Cape Town in 1954 just before George's death in January of 1955. Ottis Scott died in December of the same year.[480]

Dewitt and Dolly Garrett—The S.D. Garretts worked first with the Shorts in Wuyu Wuyu before moving to Salisbury in the early 1930s. There are many references in the *Word and Work* to contact between the Garretts and the Shorts in the mid 1930s. Their children were close in age. Sybil said of the couple, "He didn't relate to kids very well. His wife was wonderful with us and she was a role model to me."

Foy said that there were problems in later years with Dewitt Garrett because he promoted his premillennial ideas. However, on one occasion in 1948 Foy appreciated Garrett's spirited defense of acapella singing in worship at the Colenbrander congregation in Bulawayo. He wrote Bennie Lee Fudge, "Bro. Garrett ... proved to be a first line stalwart throughout this meeting in his stand for New Testament practices."[481]

Leslie (W.L.) and Addie Brown—The Leslie Brown family arrived in Africa when the Shorts were in America in 1930. Eldred Echols described Leslie as "harsh and peremptory" in his treatment of the native blacks.[482] Foy and Sybil confirmed that he had a headstrong personality, though Foy said he was a "genius at organizing and getting things done."[483] Foy had a much higher personal regard for Brown's son, Robert.[484]

A.B. (Alva) Reese—Reese was born in 1888 in Carthage, Missouri, and married Margaret Langford in 1918.[485] He was encouraged by O.W. Gardner, J.L. Armstrong, L.O. Sanderson and Don Carlos Janes to move to Africa. His sister was Ottis Scott. After arriving in Africa in 1929, the Reeses worked for three years at Sinde Mission with the Scotts, then stayed five more years after the Scotts left. They never received more than $25 a month during the first years of their stay in Africa, but Reese, who was a capable woodworker, supplemented the family income by raising their food and making furniture and wagons. Their son Boyd traveled to Nigeria in 1950 with Eldred Echols and they became the first Americans to contact the churches there that had been established by C.A.O. Essien.

The Reeses returned to the States after twenty-five years in Zambia. Margaret and A.B passed away in 1972 and 1974 respectively in Arkansas.[486]

Alvin and Georgia Hobby—Alvin was from Ostella, Tennessee near Lewisburg. He studied at David Lipscomb and Harding College.[487] He met Georgia at Harding and Dow Merritt convinced them to go to Africa. They reached Africa in 1938 and worked primarily at Namwianga Mission until returning to the States in 1982.[488]

Myrtle Rowe—She was a forty two year old widow when she first arrived at Namwianga mission "at 3:00 PM Saturday, September 10, 1938."[489] She lived in Northern Rhodesia/Zambia for almost twenty years, working primarily at Namwianga Mission. Margaret Short loved Myrtle Rowe. Margaret recalling how she took her "under her wing" when she arrived at Namwianga in 1947.

Orville Brittell—Orville's parents, especially his resolute mother, Augusta, were very interested in mission work and encouraged him to go to Africa in the 1940s along with his wife, whose name was also Augusta. Orville, whom Foy and Margaret respected and loved, worked with them at Namwianga Mission in the later 1940s and accompanied Foy on his second preaching expedition into the Zambezi River Escarpment. He was mechanically inclined and rigged up an old truck to run on steam so that it could carry the evangelists' supplies into the previously unexplored area. He gave Foy and Margaret their first motorized transportation, a heavily modified motorcycle that they used when they first moved to Bulawayo.

After Orville went to Africa, his parents who were originally from Missouri but also lived in California, sold everything they had and moved there, working particularly with orphans in the area around Sinde mission near Livingstone. When, Orville's mother, Augusta, passed away in the 1960s, most of the family, including Orville, returned to the States. His sister Elaine stayed at Sinde mission until she was murdered in the 1970s. Six thousand people attended her funeral. After returning from Africa, Orville lived in Southeastern Pennsylvania, working some at Northeastern Christian College while it was in operation. He passed away in 2007.[490]

J.C. and Joyce Copeland Shewmaker – J.C. (Jimmy) was from Paragould, Arkansas and studied at David Lipscomb College where he heard John Sherriff talk about the work in Southern Africa.[491] He met Joyce when leading singing at her home congregation. They both became educators in Arkansas until Dow Merritt and A.B. Reese convinced them to go to Southern Africa in the late 1930s. They arrived too late to be much of an influence on Foy, but were highly respected for their work in Northern Rhodesia before moving later to Bulawayo in late 1967.[492] They returned to the States permanently in 1977, living in Searcy, Arkansas where J.C. died in 1985 and Joyce in 1987.[493]

Endnotes

Notes on Introduction

[1] Sewell Hall "A Lifetime Investment in Africa," *Christianity Magazine*, Vol. 2, No. 3, March, 1985, p. 31 [95].

[2] Foy Short interview 2/21/08.

[3] Ellen Baize, "Mom and Dad's Memories," unpublished paper sent to the author, April 2010.

[4] "National Profiles Republic of Zimbabwe" http://www.worldconvention.org/country. php?c=ZW, April 24, 2008.

[5] Baize, "Mom and Dad's Memories."

[6] Foy Short interview, 2/21/08.

[7] Ellen Baize, "Mom and Dad's Memories."

[8] Ellen Baize, email to the author, August 1, 2010.

[9] Foy Short, Oral Report on Work in Southern Africa, Bellaire church of Christ, Bellaire, Texas, July 30, 2006. <bellairecofc.com/audio/by/artist/foy_short>.

[10] Ellen Baize, "Mom and Dad's Memories."

[11] Stanley E. Granberg "Africa, Missions In" *Encyclopedia of the Stone-Campbell Movement,"* (Grand Rapids, Michigan: William B. Eerdmans Publishing Company, 2004) p. 7.

[12] Granberg, p. 7.

[13] Eldred Echols, *"Beyond the Rivers of Cush"* (Winona, Mississippi, J.C. Choate Publications, 2000) pp. 3–4.

[14] Michael W. Casey, "Todd, Sir Garfield (1908–2002) and Lady Grace (1911–2001)" *Encyclopedia of the Stone-Campbell Movement,"* (Grand Rapids, Michigan: William B. Eerdmans Publishing Company, 2004) p. 7.

[15] "Namwianga Mission" <http://angolateam.org/links.html>, April 25, 2008.

[16] David and Linda Gregerson "Namwianga Mission <http://dlgregersen.blogspot. com/2005/06/namwianga-mission.html>, April 25, 2008.

[17] "Nhowe Mission" <http://www.oaklandcoc.org/nhowe.html> April, 25, 2008.

[18] "Zimbabwe" <http://www.eastpointchurchofchrist.org/missions/missions.html> April 28, 2008.

[19] Dow Merritt, *"The Dew Breakers"* (Nashville, Tennessee, World Vision Publishing Company, 1973), p. 16.

[20] Dow Merritt.

[21] Ellen Baize interview with the author.

[22] "Matabele People," http://en.wikipedia.org/wiki/Ndebele_people_(Zimbabwe), /April 25, 2008.

[23] "Northern Ndebele language" http://en.wikipedia.org/wiki/Northern_Ndebele_language, April 25, 2008.

[24] "Zimbabwe People" http://www.tanzaniaodyssey.com/www.africanet.com/africanet/country/zimbabwe/people.htm, April 25, 2008.

[25] "Shona people" http://en.wikipedia.org/wiki/Shona_people April 25, 2008.

[26] http://www.mun.ca/rels/restmov/digital/ww/WW.HTM, December 2, 2010.

[27] Don Carlos Janes "Missionary Notes" *Word and Work*, Vol. 11, No. 11, November, 1920, p. 336.

²⁸ Zelma Wood Lawyer, *I Married A Missionary* (Abilene, Texas, Abilene Christian College Press, 1943) p. 197-202.

²⁹ Dow Merritt, p. 66-71.

³⁰ Earl Kimbrough, *"The Warrior from Rock Creek, Life Times and Thoughts of F.B. Srygley 1859-1940"* (Louisville, Kentucky, Religious Supply Center, 2008), p. 384.

³¹ Foy E. Wallace, "The Last Will and Testament of Don Carlos Janes" *The Bible Banner,* Vol. 6, No. 8, p. 3-5.

³² Bobby Ross Junior, *The Christian Chronicle* February, 2007, http://www.christianchronicle.org/article611~Are_we_growing%3F_Population_outpaces_church, April 28, 2008.

³³ "Our Heritage" http://www.singingoaks.org/history.aspx, April 28, 2008.

³⁴ Acts 20:28; 2 Timothy 2:19, etc.

³⁵ Georgia Hobby, *Give Us This Bread,* (Winona, Mississippi, J.C. Choate publications, 2002) p. 203.

³⁶ Roland Allen, *Missionary Methods St. Paul's or Ours* (Grand Rapids, MI, Wm. E. Eerdmans Publishing Co. 1962, Ninth Printing, July 1977).

³⁷ Robertson McQuilkin, "Stop Sending Money, Breaking the cycle of missions dependency" *Christianity Today,* March 1, 1999, p. 57.

Notes on Chapter 1

³⁸ Don Carlos Janes "Missionary Notes" *Word and Work,* Vol. 13, No. 6, June, 1920, p. 180.

³⁹ Ellen Baize, telephone interview with the author, April 18, 2008.

⁴⁰ Ellen Baize wrote the author, According to a history of Milton Township, written for the Jefferson County Historical Society sometime after 1908, the Manville Church started in a somewhat anomalous fashion, having two preachers, Joseph Hankins and Elder Leavitt. These men were not one in doctrine, resulting in two factions, standing respectively for open and closed communion. At the same time Jesse Vawter came occasionally to preach. "Then, one member, Jacob Short, became convinced of the ideas of Alexander Campbell, invited Beverly Vawter of the Christian or Disciples Church, to come and preach and the doctrines he presented proved so acceptable that the original Baptist Congregation became the Manville Christian Church, which name it sitll represents."

⁴¹ Baize interview.

⁴² Michael W. Casey, "Cordell Christian College" *Encyclopedia of the Stone-Campbell Movement,"* (Grand Rapids, Michigan: William B. Eerdmans Publishing Company, 2004) p. 242.

⁴³ Sybil Dewhirst interview.

⁴⁴ Casey.

⁴⁵ Baize interview.

⁴⁶ Baize interview.

⁴⁷ Baize interview.

⁴⁸ Baize interview.

⁴⁹ Elizabeth Reese, http://www.ancientfaces.com/research/story/409576, April 1, 2010.

⁵⁰ W.N. Short, "Times are Changing" Glimpses of Africa, Vol. 9, No. 2, September 1955, page 5.

⁵¹ W.N. Short, Diary entry, January 1, 1922, William Newton Short Diary, Florida College Library, Temple Terrace, Florida.

⁵² Short diary, 1922, p. 10.

[53] Joyce Copeland Shewmaker, quoted by Charles Royce Webb, *Putting out the Fleeece: The J.C. and Joyce Shewmaker Story* (Winona, Mississippi, J.C. Choate publications, 2002) p. 41.

[54] W.N. Short, Diary entry, March 27, 1923, William Newton Short Diary, Florida College Library, Temple Terrace, Florida.

[55] Shewmaker, p. 41.

[56] Short, Diary entry March 30, 1923.

[57] Short interview.

[58] Eldred Echols *Wings of the Morning* (Fort Worth, TX, Wings Press, 1989), p. 53.

[59] *Word and Work*, Vol. 16, No. 11, November 1923, P. 343.

[60] Sybil Dewhirst interview.

[61] Sybil Dewhirst interview.

[62] W.N. Short, diary entry.

[63] Sybil Dewhirst interview.

[64] Dewhirst interview.

[65] Elizabeth Reese, "The Reese Family" http://www.ancientfaces.com/research/story/409576 April 1, 2010.

[66] Foy Short, interview.

[67] Foy Short, undated radio transcript.

[68] Charles Quinch, unpublished biography found among the Short's papers, p. 22.

[69] Margaret Short, quoting Adele Margerison, note to the author, March 31, 2011.

[70] *Word and Work*, Vol. 18, No. 1, January1925.

[71] Will Short Diary 3/6/23.

[72] *Word and Work*, Vol. 18, No. 12, December 1925.

[73] *Word and Work*, Vol. 19, No. 7, July 1926.

[74] Zelma Wood Lawyer, "I Married a Missionary," (Abilene, Texas, Abilene Christian College Press, 1943).

[75] Don Carlos Janes "Missionary Notes" *Word and Work*, Vol. 21, No. 1, January, 1928.

[76] Don Carlos Janes "Missionary Notes" *Word and Work*, Vol. 21, No. 2, February, 1928.

[77] Will Short, diary entry 1/13/28.

[78] Sybil Dewhirst, excerpt from personal memoirs, sent to the author, June, 2010.

[79] W.N. Short "From Makuni Mission" *Word and Work*, Vol. 21, No. 5, May, 1928, p. 152.

[80] Short, "From Makuni Mission."

[81] Will Short, Diary entry 1/19/28.

[82] Z.C. Thompson, L.W. Babcock, John B. Mathes (elders Harper, Kansas) — "Brother Short's return to America" *Word and Work*, Vol. 21, No. 7, July, 1928.

[83] Merritt, p. 107.

[84] Merritt, p. 107.

[85] Don Carlos Janes "Missionary Notes" *Word and Work*, Vol. 22, No. 4, April 1929.

[86] *Word and Work*, Vol. 21, No. 12, December 1928.

[87] *Word and Work*, Vol. 21, No. 12, December 1928.

[88] *Word and Work*, Vol. 23, No. 5, May, 1930.

[89] Don Carlos Janes "Missionary Notes" *Word and Work*, Vol. 23, No. 7, July 1930.

[90] W.N. Short, "Macheke Mission" *Word and Work* Vol. 32, No. 8, August 1938.

[91] W. L. Brown *Word and Work*, Vol. 24, No. 1, January, 1931.

[92] Short, Foy, "Brief History of our work..." Unpublished manuscript, October, 15, 2009.

[93] *Word and Work*, Vol. 27, No. 3, March, 1934.

[94] *Word and Work*, Vol. 27, No. 5, May, 1934.

[95] W.N. Short, "Huyuyu Mission" *Word and Work*, Vol. 26, No. 5, May, 1933.

[96] Sybil Dewhirst, Poem, "My Big Brother, Name of Foy."

[97] Sybil Dewhirst, excerpt from personal memoirs, sent to the author, March 22, 2010.

[98] Foy Short, Report July 22, 1996.

[99] Sybil Dewhirst, excerpt from personal memoirs, sent to the author, June, 2010.

[100] Sybil Dewhirst, excerpt from personal memoirs, sent to the author, March 22, 2010.

[101] Ellen Baize, note to the author August 1, 2010.

[102] "Rugby Notes," *Prince Edward School Magazine*, Vol. 1, No. 6, November, 1938.

[103] A.J. Somerville, "Testimonial in Favor of Foy Short," Recommendation letter, Nov. 17, 1938.

[104] W.N. Short, "Notes," *Rays of Light*, Vol. 18, No. 4, September 1960, p. 17.

[105] Ellen Baize, "Mom and Dad's Memories." Unpublished document sent to the author, April 2010.

[106] W.N. Short, "Macheke" *Word and Work*, Vol. 32, No. 8, August 1938, p. 180.

[107] Kathryn Smith, conversation with the author, August 30, 2010.

[108] Paddy Kendall-Ball, Interview with the author, September, 2008.

[109] Sybil Dewhirst, memoirs.

[110] Jim Short, email to the author August 1, 2010.

[111] Don Carlos Janes "Missionary Notes" *Word and Work*, Vol. 35, No. 1, January 1941,

[112] Eldred Echols, *Wings of the Morning*, p. 72.

[113] Sybil Dewhirst excerpt from personal memoirs, sent to the author, March 22, 2010.

[114] Sybil Dewhirst, interview 11/12/09.

[115] W.N. Short, "Macheke" *Word and Work*, Vol. 34, No. 3, March 1940, p. 72.

[116] Sybil Short, "Macheke" *Word and Work*, Vol. 34, No. 8, August 1940, p. 170.

[117] W.N. Short, "Macheke" *Word and Work*, Vol. 34, No. 12, December 1940, p. 180.

Notes on Chapter 2

[118] Thomas Hartle "African letter" *Word and Work*, Vol. 35, No. 2, February 1941, p. 39.

[119] Ship's Passenger list from Ellen Short.

[120] Foy Short, interview with the author 2008.

[121] Short interview.

[122] "Allied Ships hit by U-boats, The City of New York," http://www.uboat.net/allies/merchants/1479.html, October 17, 2008.

[123] L.C. Sears, *The Biography of John Nelson Armstrong, For Freedom*, (Austin, Texas, Sweet Publishing Company, 1969) p. 301.

[124] Sears, p. 302.

[125] Sears, p. 302.

[126] Douglass A. Foster, "Abilene Christian College" " *Encyclopedia of the Stone-Campbell Movement*," (Grand Rapids, Michigan: William B. Eerdmans Publishing Company, 2004) p. 1.

[127] Sybil Dewhirt interview.

[128] Ellen Baize interview.

[129] Edward Fudge, *The Sound of His Voice*, (Orange, California, New Leaf Books, 1995, 2002) p. 37.

[130] History, http://www.athensbibleschool.org/about_abs/history/.

[131] Fudge, pp. 38–39.
[132] Bennie Lee Fudge, letter to Foy Short, June 3, 1948.
[133] Baize interview.
[134] Hicks and Valentine, p. 17.
[135] Richard Hughes, Reviving the Ancient Faith, pp. 121–127.
[136] Chris Cotten, email to the author.
[137] Sybil Dewhirst, interview.
[138] Margaret Short, interview with the author.
[139] Society News, The Abilene Reporter-News, May 10, 1943, p. 5.
[140] "Brother and Sister will Participate in Double Wedding Ceremony on Friday." The Alabama Courier, May 30, 1946, p. illegible.
[141] D.H. Moyers, letter to Foy Short, August 17, 1950.
[142] Howard L. Schug and Don H. Morris editors, The Harvest Field, Abilene Texas, Abilene Christian College Press, 1942.
[143] "ACC Honors Ranking Grads," The Abilene Reporter-News, June 1, 1943, p. 10.
[144] Foy Short, letter to Mr. and Mrs. R. Dugger, February 10, 2004.
[145] "Church Notes," The Limestone Democrat, July 1, 1943, p. 5.
[146] "History" http://www.athensbibleschool.org/about_abs/history/, November 3, 2008.
[147] Foy Short Interview.
[148] Ken Green, "Foy Short: Evangelistic Life in Rhodesia," Biblical Insights, March, 2006, p. 14.
[149] Bennie Lee Fudge, letter to Foy Short, January 5, 1948.
[150] Baize interview.
[151] Baize interview.
[152] Ken Green, "Foy Short: Evangelistic Life in Rhodesia," p. 14.
[153] J.V. Copeland and Ancil Jenkins, Charles Holder Pioneer Preacher in the Sequatchie Valley, Hester Publications, Henderson, TN, 2010, p. 119.
[154] Margaret Short, email to the author January 7, 2011.
[155] Baize interview.
[156] Margaret Short, email January 7, 2011.
[157] Margaret Short, interview.
[158] Baize interview.
[159] Baize interview.
[160] Foy Short, report July 22, 1996.
[161] Kathryn Smith, email to the author, September 12, 2010.
[162] Foy Short, report for the month of August, 1946.
[163] The Alabama Courier, May 8 1947, Classified.

Notes on Chapter 3

[164] Margaret Short, note to the author, 12/11/2010. She remembered the name of the plane. Information about the plane was found at <http://www.logbookmag.com/databases/articles.asp?ID=94&CatID=47>.
[165] Margaret Short note, 12/11/2010
[166] "Some memories" Undated letter from Margaret Short sent to Verna Hadfield reflecting on her relationship with Alan and Verna Hadfield. Copy sent to the author,
[167] Foy Short, financial report to Ferris, Texas church of Christ, July 1947.

[168] Foy Short, letter to D.H. Moyers, June 16, 1947.

[169] "Namwianga Mission" http://angolateam.org/links.html, April 25, 2008.

[170] Margaret Short, email to the author, January 31, 2011.

[171] Ellen Baize, "Mom and Dad's Memories." Unpublished document sent to the author, April 2010.

[172] Margaret Short, email to the author, January 8, 2010.

[173] Bessie Hardin Chenault, *Give Me This Mountain*, (Winona, Mississippi, J.C. Choate publications, 1986) p. 57.

[174] Margaret Short, email to the author, January 31, 2011.

[175] Foy Short, letter to D.H. Moyers, August 25, 1947.

[176] Foy Short, letter to W.N., Delia and Billy Short, October 17, 1947.

[177] Foy Short, letter to W.N., Delia and Billy Short.

[178] Foy Short letter.

[179] Eldred Echols, *Wings of the Morning*, p. 73.

[180] Eldred Echols, *Wings of the Morning*, p. 74.

[181] Foy Short, letter to Bennie Lee Fudge, January 24, 1949.

[182] J.C. Reed, Foy Short and Eldred Echols, "Christ Comes to Pukuma's Village", *Gospel Advocate*, January 1, 1948, p. 20.

[183] Charles Royce Webb, *Putting out the Fleece: The J.C. and Joyce Shewmaker Story* (Winona, Mississippi, J.C. Choate publications, 2002) p. 143.

[184] J.C. Reed, article in *Gospel Advocate*.

[185] J.C. Reed article.

[186] Foy Short, interview.

[187] Foy Short, letter to D.H. Moyers, January 15, 1948.

[188] Foy Short, "Elusive Mulola" seven-page typewritten manuscript, 1949.

[189] http://www.maplandia.com/zambia/central/mumbwa/mulola/, August 5, 2010.

[190] Echols, p. 85.

[191] Pukuma, Zambia Page, <http://www.fallingrain.com/world/ZA/5/Pukuma.html> 12/10/08.

[192] Foy Short, letter to D.H. Moyers, January 15, 1948.

[193] Foy Short, letter to Bennie Lee Fudge, November 24, 1947.

[194] Harrison Bankston, phone conversation with the author, October 30, 2010.

[195] Reuel Lemmons, "African Radio Work to be Continued", *Gospel Advocate*, February 10, 1949.

[196] Foy Short, "Brief History of our Work …"

[197] Foy Short, letter to Reuel Lemmons, August 8, 1948.

[198] Foy Short, letter the the elders of the church of Christ in Ferris, Texas, January 5, 1951.

[199] Foy Short, letter to Reuel Lemmons, September 6, 1948.

[200] Reuel Lemmons, letter to Foy Short, July 29, 1948.

[201] Foy Short, letter to Reuel Lemmons, September 6, 1948.

[202] Foy Short, letter to Bennie Lee Fudge, November 6, 1947.

[203] J.C. Reed, letter to Bennie Lee Fudge, July 10, 1949.

[204] Reed letter.

[205] Foy Short, letter to Bennie Lee Fudge, August 9, 1949.

[206] Foy Short, letter to Bennie Lee Fudge, October 26, 1949.

[207] Bennie Lee Fudge, letter to Foy Short, August 19, 1949.

[208] Bennie Lee Fudge, letter to Foy Short, November 5, 1949.

[209] J. C. Reed, "Premillennial Infiltration In Africa," *Gospel Guardian*, Vol. 3, No. 9, page 2, June 28, 1951.

[210] Bennie Lee Fudge, letter to Foy Short, October 24, 1947.

[211] Charles M. Campbell, "That Tract," *Bible Banner*, Vol. 8, No. 1, p. 33b, June 1945.

[212] Foy Short, letter to B.L. Fudge, October 20, 1947.

[213] Foy Short, "Brief History of our Work ..." Unpublished manuscript.

[214] Ellen Short, note to the author, August 1, 2010.

[215] D.H. Moyers, letter to Foy Short, January 9, 1949.

[216] Margaret Short, email to the author, January 31, 2011.

[217] Foy Short, "Brief History of our Work..."

[218] Margaret Short, note to the author, January 25, 2011.

[219] Margaret Short, note to the author, February 3, 2011.

[220] Margaret Short, note February 3, 2011.

[221] Ellen Baize, "Mom and Dad notes," unpublished paper sent to the author, April 2010.

[222] Margaret Short, email to the author, February 2, 2011.

[223] Margaret Short, email to the author, January 11, 2011.

[224] Foy Short, circular letter to homes in Queens Park, Bulwayo, March 10, 1949.

[225] Foy Short, letter to D.H. Moyers, August 23, 1949.

[226] Ellen Baize, email to the author, November 16, 2010.

[227] Foy Short, report to the church in Ferris, Texas, October 4, 1949.

[228] Foy Short, "A Sad Trip," undated report/article from early 1950.

[229] Margaret Short, email to the author, January 12, 2010.

[230] Margaret Short, interview.

[231] Foy Short, letter to D.H. Moyers, May 11, 1948.

[232] Foy Short, letter to D.H. Moyers, August 4, 1948.

[233] Foy Short, letter to D.H. Moyers, May 11, 1948.

[234] Foy Short, "Brief History of our Work ..."

[235] Margaret Short, note to the author, January 25 2011.

[236] Foy Short, letter to Bennie Lee Fudge, February 17, 1950.

[237] Margaret Short, interview.

[238] Margaret Short, interview.

[239] Margaret Short, email to the author, January 11, 2011.

[240] Bessie Hardin Chenault, p. 63.

[241] Margaret Short, email to the author, January 11, 2011.

[242] Margaret Short, email to the author, January 28, 2011.

[243] Foy Short, Brief Summary.

[244] Foy Short, letter to the elders of the church in Ferris, Texas, April 9, 1953.

[245] Kathryn Smith, email to the author, September 12, 2010.

[246] Ellen Baize, interview.

[247] Margaret Short, email to the author, January 28, 2011.

[248] Paddy Kendall-Ball interview.

[249] Melville Sheasby, "Earliest Memories of Queens Park", http://meldsheasby.wordpress.com/2009/12/26/earliest-memories-of-queens-park-church-of-christ/ February 4, 2010.

[250] Jim Short, email to the author, August 4, 2010.

[251] Foy Short, letter to D.H. Moyers, August 12, 1949.

252 Margaret Short, email to the author, February 10, 2011.

253 Foy Short, letter the elders of the church of Christ at Ferris, Texas, December 15, 1950.

254 Ellen Baize, note to the author, August 1, 2010.

255 Melville Sheasby, "In Tents Experience" http://meldsheasby.wordpress.com/2009/12/08/in-tents-experience/, February 24, 2010.

256 Foy Short, Report for November, December 5, 2002.

257 Foy Short, Report, January 30, 2001.

258 Foy Short, "A Sad Trip," undated report/article from early 1950.

259 Foy Short, letter to Bennie Lee Fudge, February 14, 1950.

260 Foy Short, Report, February 28, 2000.

261 Foy Short, Report, December 30, 1999.

262 Foy Short, letter to Mr. Oliver Thomas Maseko, February 1, 2000.

263 Foy Short, letter to the elders of the church in Ferris, Texas, December 15, 1951.

264 Ellen Baize, email to the author, November 16, 2010.

265 Foy Short, letter to the elders of the church in Ferris, Texas, March 31, 1951.

266 Foy Short, undated radio transcript, probably from the late 1950s.

267 Foy Short, undated radio transcript.

268 Foy Short, Report, May 30, 1998.

269 Foy Short, conversation with the author, August 30, 2010.

270 Margaret Short, email to the author, February 15, 2011.

271 Paddy Kendall-Ball interview.

272 Jim Short, interview with the author 10/23/09.

273 "News", *Gospel Guardian*, Vol. 5, No. 43, p. 14.

274 http://www.allatsea.co.za/unioncastle/carnarvon.htm, 2/10/2010.

275 Margaret Short, email to the author, February 15, 2011.

276 Margaret Short, email to the author, February 15, 2011.

277 Foy Short, letters to Bennie Lee Fudge, August 2, 1950; January 5, 1951.

278 Margaret Short, email to the author, February 15, 2011.

279 Harrison Bankston, phone interview with the author, October 20, 2010.

280 Margaret Short, email to the author, February 21, 2011.

281 Foy Short, *A Brief History ...*

Notes on Chapter 4

282 http://travel.mapsofworld.com/zimbabwe/tourist-destinations-in-zimbabwe/gweru.html, 11/02.2009.

283 Margaret Short, email, Februry 27, 2011.

284 Foy Short, Weekly Bulletin, Church of Christ, 1 Princess St., Gwelo, May 28, 1963.

285 Margaret Short, email, February27, 2011.

286 Margaret Short, email, February 27, 2011.

287 "Welcome to Barotseland.com" <http://www.barotseland.com/index.htm> October 24, 2009.

288 Margaret Short "A trip to Barotseland" unpublished paper, p. 1 December 2009.

289 Margaret Short, p. 2.

290 Margaret Short, p. 2.

291 Jim Short interview.

292 Margaret Short, p. 3.

[293] Margaret Short, p. 4.

[294] Margaret Short, conversation with the author, September 30, 2010.

[295] Ellen Baize interview October, 2009.

[296] Jim Short interview.

[297] Jim Short interview.

[298] Jim Short interview.

[299] Sybil Short Fudge Dewhirst, interview 11/12/09.

[300] Ellen Baize interview.

[301] Jim Short interview.

[302] Margaret Short, email to the author, March 1, 2011.

[303] Kathryn Smith, email to the author, September 23, 2010.

[304] Margaret Short, email to the author, March 1, 2011.

[305] Jim Short interview.

[306] Jim Short interview.

[307] Margaret Short, email, March 1, 2011.

[308] Jim Short interview.

[309] Margaret Short, note March 1, 2011.

[310] Margaret Short, email to the author, March 3, 2011.

[311] Foy Short, report June 10, 1973.

[312] Ray Votaw, Interview with the author, April 1, 2010.

[313] Paddy Kendall-Ball interview.

[314] Foy Short, letter to Jim Short, September 10, 1973.

[315] Foy Short, "Our Purpose and Policy ..." *The Enquirer*, Vol. 1, No. 1, May 1963, p. 2.

[316] Foy Short, "A Reiteration of Policy" *The Enquirer*, Vol. 1, No. 2, June 1963, p.5.

[317] Margaret Short, interview.

[318] Foy Short, *A Brief History* ...

[319] Gwelo church bulletin, November 30, 1972.

[320] Foy Short, report, January 31, 1972.

[321] *Truth Magazine* VII: 2, pp. 23–24, November 1962.

[322] Foy Short, letter to Ellen Short, June 23, 1968.

[323] Margaret Short, email to the author, March 10, 2011.

[324] Baize interview.

[325] Ken Green, "Foy Short: Evangelistic Life in Rhodesia" *Biblical Insights*, March, 2006, p. 15.

[326] Ellen Baize, email to the author, November 16, 2010.

[327] Baize email, November 16, 2010.

[328] *Truth Magazine* VII: 2, pp. 23–24, November 1962.

[329] Baize email, November 16, 2010.

[330] Ken Green, "Foy Short: Evangelistic Life in Rhodesia."

[331] Jim Short, email to the author, August 5, 2010.

[332] Jim Short email.

[333] Margaret Short, letter to Ellen Short, February 8, 1967.

[334] Foy Short, letter to Ellen Short, May 19, 1967.

[335] Foy Short, letter to Ellen Short, May 18, 1967.

[336] Foy Short, letter to Ellen Short, June 23, 1968.

[337] Margaret Short, letter to Ellen Short, April 2, 1969.

338 Ellen Baize, email to the author 2008.

339 Ellen Baize, email to the author, 2008.

340 Kathyn Smith, email to the author, September 23, 2010.

341 Kathryn Smith, email to the author, September 12, 2010.

342 Ellen Baize, note to the author, August 1, 2010.

343 Ellen Baize, note to the author, August 1, 2010.

344 Margaret Short, email to the author, July 31, 2010.

345 Foy Short, letter to Ellen Short, October 11, 1967.

346 Foy Short, letter to "Harold, Gwyneth, Ellen and Jimmy," March 19, 1970.

347 Foy Short, letter to Ellen Short, April 15, 1969.

348 Ellen Baize, note to the author, August 1, 2010.

349 David Meisel, "Cape Buffalo Facts," <http://www.articlesbase.com/environment-articles/cape-buffalo-facts-543051.html> April 12, 2010.

350 Foy Short, conversation with the author, April 11, 2010.

351 Foy Short, letter to Ellen Short, April, 2, 1968.

352 Foy Short, letter to Ellen Short, August 24, 1967.

353 Foy Short, letter to Ellen Short, December 3, 1969.

354 Foy Short, letter to Ellen Short, October 11, 1967.

355 Foy Short, letter to Ellen Short, June 23, 1968.

356 Foy Short, letter to Ellen Short, July 11, 1968.

357 Jim Short interview.

358 W.N. Short, "Notes," *Rays of Light*, Vol. 4, No. 18, September, 1960, p. 15.

359 Foy Short, "The Use of Church Money," Gwelo church bulletin, April 13, 1972.

360 Baize interview.

361 Margaret Short, email to the author, March 10, 2011.

362 Jim Short, note to author, August 5, 2010.

363 Observed by the author as a 16 year old.

364 Foy Short, letter to Ellen Short, April 23, 1970.

365 Margaret Short, note to the author, March 8, 2011.

366 Foy Short, Brief Summary.

367 Foy Short, letter to children, April 29, 1974.

368 Foy Short, Report, December 30, 1999.

369 Foy Short, Oral Report on Work in Southern Africa, Bellaire church of Christ, Bellaire, Texas, July 30, 2006. <www.bellairecofc.com/audio/by/artist/foy_short>.

370 Foy Short, Oral Report on Work in Southern Africa.

371 Ellen Baize, Email to the author, November 16, 2010.

372 Foy Short, Report, June 21, 1980.

373 Foy Short, Report, June 21, 1980.

374 Foy Short, Report, February 29, 2000.

375 Ken Green, "Foy Short: Evangelistic Life in Rhodesia."

376 Foy Short, Brief Summary.

377 Paddy Kendall-Ball, Report, February 27, 2010.

378 Foy Short, letter to Ellen Short, April 15, 1969.

Notes on Chapter 5

[379] Jim Short, note to the author, August 1, 2010.

[380] Jim short, email to the author, August 5, 2010.

[381] Margaret Short, email to the author, March 20, 2011.

[382] Margaret Short, email, March 20, 2011.

[383] Foy Short, letter to Dave and Ellen Baize, March 26, 1977.

[384] Sybil Dewhirst, interview 11/12/09.

[385] Margaret Short, email to the author, March 20, 2011.

[386] http://www.pri.org/theworld/?q=node/16947, Nov. 11, 2009.

[387] Foy Short, Report, May 26, 1983.

[388] Ellen Baize, email to the author November 16, 2010.

[389] Foy Short, Report for December 2002, December 31, 2002.

[390] Foy Short, Report for January, 2003, February 3, 2003.

[391] Ellen Baize, email to the author, November 16, 2010.

[392] Foy Short, report, June 7, 1978.

[393] Foy Short, report, July 22, 1981.

[394] Margaret Short, email to the author, April 6, 2011.

[395] Foy Short, report, September 4, 1984.

[396] Foy Short, report, September 4, 1984.

[397] Foy Short, Report, January 30, 2001.

[398] Foy Short, Report for the month of May, 2002, June 30, 2002.

[399] Margaret Short, email to the author, March 20, 2011.

[400] Jim Short, note to the author, August 1, 2010.

[401] Margaret Short, email to the author, April 5, 2011.

[402] Jim Short, note to the author, August 1, 2010.

[403] Ellen Baize, note to the author, August 1, 2010.

[404] Margaret Short, email to the author, April 4, 2011.

[405] Margaret Short, email, Aporil 4, 2011.

[406] Margaret Short, email, Aporil 4, 2011.

[407] Foy Short, report November 8, 2001.

[408] Margaret Short, email to the author, April 4, 2011.

[409] Ellen Baize, note to the author, August 1, 2010.

[410] Ellen Baize interview.

[411] Jim Short, note to the author, August 1, 2010.

[412] Ellen Short, note to the author, August 1, 2010.

[413] Ellen Short, note.

Notes on Chapter 6

[414] Foy Short, Report, October 27, 1995.

[415] Jim Short, email to the author, August 5, 2010.

[416] Foy Short, Report for the month of May, 2002, May 31, 2002.

[417] Ken Green, "Concordance to the Sindabele Bible," <http://www.facebook.com/notes/
ken-green/concordance-to-the-the-ndebele-bible/10150104985647517>, March 17, 2011.

[418] Foy Short, Report, April 30, 2003.

[419] Foy Short, "News Reports re Zimbabwe Drought" Undated report from 2002.

[420] Foy Short, "How the Funds are Handled." Undated report from 2002.

[421] Margaret Short, email to the author, May 5, 2011.

[422] Foy Short, Report, October 25, 1997.

[423] Ken Green, interview with the author, 10/21/2009.

[424] Foy Short, report May 31, 1996.

[425] Foy Short, Report, April 30, 2003.

[426] Foy Short, Report, October 29, 1999.

[427] Foy Short, Report for November, December 5, 2002.

[428] Foy Short, Report, November 5, 2002.

[429] Foy Short, Report for November, December 5, 2002.

[430] Foy Short, Report for the month of July 2002, July 30, 2002.

[431] Jim Short, note to the author, August 1, 2010.

[432] Ellen Baize, email to the author, November 16, 2010.

[433] Ken Green interview.

[434] Ken Green interview.

[435] Foy Short, Oral Report on Work in Southern Africa.

[436] Foy Short, Report for August 1-21, August 21, 2002.

[437] Joanne Beckley, circular email "Asking for prayers" March 19, 2010.

[438] Ken Green, "Foy Short: Evangelistic Life in Rhodesia" *Biblical Insights,* March, 2006, p. 15.

[439] Ken Green, "Foy Short: Evangelistic Life in Rhodesia" p. 15.

[440] Foy Short, conversation with the author, April 10, 2010.

[441] Ken Green article.

[442] David Beckley, "Concerning the Whole Picture of American Supported World Evangelism With Specific Reference to Zimbabwe," http://knowyourbible.co.za/Articles/AmericanSupportedWorldEvangelism/tabid/301/Default.aspx, March 27, 2010.

[443] Beckley article.

[444] David Maxson, conversation with the author, August 5, 2010.

[445] Ken Green interview.

[446] Bob Buchanon, conversation with the author, February 2009.

[447] Margaret Short, Circular letter for family and friends, March 19, 1999.

[448] Foy Short, December 2009 report.

[449] Ellean Baize, note to the author, August 1, 2010.

[450] Foy Short, October 1999 report.

[451] Foy Short, October 2009 report.

[452] Foy Short, October 2009 report.

[453] Foy Short, February 2010 report.

[454] Ellen Baize, email to the author, February 9, 2010.

[455] Foy Short, Oral Report on Work in Southern Africa, Bellaire church of Christ, Bellaire, Texas, July 30, 2006. bellairecofc.com/audio/by/artist/foy_short.

Notes on Appendix 1

[456] Zimbabwe, Britannica online, http://history1900s.about.com/gi/dynamic/offsite.htm?site=http://www.britannica.com/bcom/eb/article/7/0%2C5716%2C117947%2B1%2B109721%2C00.html, October 13, 2008.

[457] "A Brief History" http://www.telegraph.co.uk/news/main.jhtml?xml=/news/campaigns/zimbabwe/zimtime.xml April 24, 2008.

[458] David J. Cope, "Exhibiting at World's Fair" <http://www.jimcrowhistory.org/resources/lessonplans/hs_lp_worldfair_ex.htm,?> May 4, 2010.

[459] Ellen Baize, note to Gardner Hall.

[460] "History of Zimbabwe" http://www.zimembassy.se/history.html, April 24, 2008

[461] Eldred Echols *Wings of the Morning* (Wings Press, Fort Worth, Texas, 1989) p. 91.

[462] "Zimbabwe" http://www.infoplease.com/ipa/A0108169.html, April 24, 2008.

[463] Short, Foy, "A Brief History of Our Work in Southern Rhodesia…and Zimbabwe." Unpublished manuscript prepared for Bob Buchanon's lectureship at Florida College, February, 2008.

[464] "Zimbabwe" http://www.infoplease.com/ipa/A0108169.html, April 24, 2008.

[465] Margaret Short, note to the author, March 8, 2011.

[466] Paddy Kendall-Ball, interview with the author 2008.

[467] "History of Christianity" http://www.sim.org/country.asp?fun=1&CID=52, April 24, 2008.

[468] "History of Christianity."

[469] "History of Christianity."

[470] Foy Short, "The Cause of Christ in Africa" undated article found in his files.

[471] Foy Short, "The Cause of Christ in Africa."

Notes on Appendix 2

[472] Merritt, p. 6.

[473] Merritt, p. 195.

[474] Leonard Gray, "George M. Scott – Christian" *Glimpses of Africa*, Vol. 9, No. 2, September 1955, p. 2.

[475] Leonard Gray.

[476] Stephen Davis, <http://www.pacificchristianacademy.org/pcnsp1993_historya.html>, February 17, 2010.

[477] Eldred Echols, *"Beyond the Rivers of Cush"* p. 3.

[478] Echols, p. 2.

[479] Merritt, p. 234.

[480] Merritt, p. 234.

[481] Foy Short, letter to Bennie Lee Fudge.

[482] Echols, *Wings of the Morning*, p. 49.

[483] Foy Short, letter to Bennie Lee Fudge, August 22, 1948.

[484] Foy Short, letter to Bennie Lee Fudge, August 22, 1948.

[485] Elizabeth Reese, http://www.ancientfaces.com/research/story/409576, April 1, 2010.

[486] Elizabeth Reese.

[487] Georgia Hobby, *They Called Him Muluti*, (Winona, Mississippi, J.C. Choate publications, 2002) p. 6, 7.

[488] Hobby, p. 145.

[489] Myrtle Rowe, *Silhouettes of Life* (Winona, Mississippi, J.C. Choate publications, 2002) p. 86.

[490] Allen Brittell, grandson of Orville Brittell, phone conversation with the author, May 2009.

491 Charles Royce Webb, *Putting out the Fleeece: The J.C. and Joyce Shewmaker Story* (Winona, Mississippi, J.C. Choate publications, 2002) p. 13.
492 Webb, p. 251.
493 Webb, p. 263, 264.

Vivaldi, Antonio 151
Volkswagen 43, 127, 132
Votaw, Ray 115, 131, 132, 133, 134, 166,
180, 195, 200, 225

W

Wallace, Foy E. 9, 138, 213
Washington D.C 196
Washington, state of 207
Waterman 119
Watts, Jackie 92
Watts, Robert 92, 101
West Nicholson, Zimbabwe 192
White House, Tennessee 98, 109, 153, 184,
199
Whitewaters dam 155
Wiesbaden, Germany 119
Wilderness, South Africa 133
Williams, George 55
Williams, Paul 133, 139, 166, 195
Wings of the Morning 215, 217, 220
Wonder, Stevie 167
Word and Work Magazine 7, 8, 14, 20, 28,
29, 30, 38, 39, 44, 75, 76, 208, 213,
214, 215, 216, 217, 218
Wuyu Wuyu 3, 7, 29, 30, 32, 34, 35, 38, 47,
208

Y

Young, Jim 184

Z

Zambesi River 67, 124, 125
Zambesi River Valley 68, 70, 71, 153, 210
Zambia (Northern Rhodesia) 2, 5, 6, 7, 18,
67, 70, 74, 83, 101, 117, 124, 126,
197, 202, 203, 207, 209, 210, 221
Zuiderkruis 119
Zulu people, language 109, 184, 202, 203